RELIGION IN AMERICAN CULTURE

Religion

in American Culture

UNITY AND DIVERSITY IN A MIDWESTERN COUNTY

W. Widick Schroeder and *Victor Obenhaus*

The Free Press of Glencoe
Collier-Macmillan Limited, London

For information, address:
The Free Press of Glencoe
A Division of The Macmillan Company
The Crowell-Collier Publishing Company
60 Fifth Avenue, New York, N. Y. 10011

DESIGNED BY SIDNEY SOLOMON

Library of Congress Catalog Card Number: 64-16966
Collier-Macmillan Canada, Ltd., Toronto, Ontario

To Samuel C. Kincheloe

PIONEER EXPONENT OF THE USE OF SOCIAL SCIENTIFIC METHODS
IN THE STUDY OF RELIGION

PREFACE

THE FOCUS of this book is on the manifestation of religious life in a Midwestern county. Although the authors have employed survey research methods commonly used in the social studies, their general way of looking at the world is informed by presuppositions which find their roots in the Christian heritage. Consequently, the presentation of data and the interpretation given to them will differ in part from the pattern commonly employed by social scientists.

Although a more detailed consideration of the problem involved will be found in the body of this book, two preliminary observations should be made here. First, both normative and descriptive materials are included in the text. Because of the authors' conviction that fact and value are inextricably interrelated, it is not possible for them to present materials that exclude normative dimensions. At the same time, the authors are anxious to make the research data available to proponents of a variety of perspectives. Hence, they have tried to present most of the material at a low level of abstraction, attempting to distinguish descriptive and normative considerations wherever possible in spite of the fact that ultimately the dividing line between them is arbitrary. By "normative" the authors mean ideal rather than customary.

Second, the authors look upon human action as a complex of strands of influence from the causal past mediated by God and of the free response of the individual to these influences. This assumption of multi-causality, contextualism, and novelty of response suggests the rejection of analyses which attempt to discern "causal variables." The study attempts to evaluate the differential impact of various religious traditions and various manifest churches on their adherents not by tracing necessary causal relationships in a reductionist manner, but rather, by examining unity and diversity in the context of crucial structural components and institutional relationships.

The first factor noted differentiates the authors from social scientists in the Weberian tradition who make neo-Kantian distinctions between fact and value. The second factor explicitly dissociates the authors from the tradition of Pareto and Durkheim, which finds contemporary expression in the formulation of workers like W. Lloyd Warner and Louis Wirth and is implicit in much of the fashionable statistical analysis and manipulation of this period. Although very appreciative of much of the empirical data gathered by workers in this latter tradition, and in spite of a different understanding of the nature of reality entertained by the authors and by Weber and the fact-value differences noted above, the authors generally find the tradition of Weber (and some contemporary field theory) more useful. While on the one hand persons in either of these traditions may raise certain kinds of issues about the treatment of empirical data in this study, on the other hand theologians and philosophers who affirm a transcendental understanding of the nature of reality may object to the refusal of the authors to interpret systematically the data from this transcendental perspective.

The efforts to focus the analysis undertaken in this book around certain significant structural components and generally to deal with the data at a relatively low level of abstraction reflect our effort to minimize the differences among these various approaches to social study, even though, for different reasons, such an effort inevitably is not completely satisfactory to proponents of any of the major traditions. Those who would look toward a unity of parts may be dissatisfied with the extent of our discriminations; those who would affirm an autonomy of parts may be dissatisfied with our refusal to make even finer discriminations. As a consequence of this deliberate limitation, the study is primarily exploratory and descriptive rather than analytic or normative. The authors point this out here in the hope that critics will consider the work in the light of its own internal presuppositions.

The empirical materials presented in this book were collected in three summers of interviewing in three communities and two open country townships in the midwest. The assistance of the following persons is gratefully acknowledged: Jackson Campbell, Mrs. Charles England, Mr. and Mrs. Richard Rautio, Mr. and Mrs. Ronald Hutchinson, and Howard Russell, all of whom conducted interviews in the county where field work was undertaken; Charles England, an interviewer for two summers and field supervisor during the last summer of field work; Constance Obenhaus, who assisted with the coding; Mrs. Gisele Mendel, who analyzed the Thematic Apperception Test records; Mrs. Frances Ritsch, who served as secretary for the entire project; and for their helpful counsel in various stages of the research program Samuel Kincheloe and members of several research seminars in the Ethics and Society field of the Federated Theological Faculty of the University of Chicago and of the Chicago Theological Seminary.

Major financial support for the study came from the New World Foundation. The Sears-Roebuck Foundation, the Board of Home Missions of the Congregational Christian Churches, the Federated Theological Faculty of the University of Chicago, the Chicago Theological Seminary, and the Princeton, Illinois, Ministerial Association contributed substantial amounts, while smaller sums were received from the Presbyterian Board of National Missions and the Farm Foundation. To all of them we extend our appreciation.

W. Widick Schroeder
Victor Obenhaus

May, 1964

CONTENTS

LIST OF TABLES

Figures in tables are in per cent.

RELIGION IN AMERICAN CULTURE

1. THE SCOPE OF THE STUDY

THE STUDY reported in this volume is concerned primarily with the interplay between, on the one hand, institutional patterns, organizational structures, and intellectual or cognitive forms and, on the other, the religious beliefs, attitudes, and participation of the people in an area considered to be typical of the Midwestern Corn Belt farming region. It explores the theological, political, and social attitudes and studies the participation of people in the various churches in the communities studied.

The primary attention of this study has been directed toward interchurch differentials and interarea differentials in theological, political, and social attitudes of the interviewees studied. The investigation has been further concerned with assessing the influence of the various religious traditions on the personality development of their adherents. Hence, data have been examined which relate the basic personality structure of the interviewees to denominational affiliation. Significant differences would suggest that the different religious traditions have contributed to the molding of personality, whereas negative findings would suggest that the general American ethos has been dominant.

Both authors of this study come out of what is later described as the transforming wing of Calvinistic Protestantism. Though now residing in a metropolitan center, each of them has known farm or small town living. This background has contributed to their interest in the state of religious life in rural areas, wherein kaleidoscopic changes are now occurring. It is the authors' assumption that the phenomena reported throughout the study are not only characteristic of rural life, but that the changes transpiring in the small towns and rural areas of America are symptomatic of those to be observed in most parts of the the nation.

In 1958, the National Council of Churches, acting on behalf of and in cooperation with the major Protestant denominations of the United States, celebrated the 50th anniversary of the town and country movement. This fact proclaimed far more than a mere anniversary. It served as a reminder of a seminal and revolutionary movement. It was in 1908 that groups concerned about the troubled "country church" coalesced under the guidance of both ecclesiastical and political leaders. Out-migration of population from the country to the city had already begun. The Golden Age of Agriculture, when farm income bore a very favorable relation to prices paid by farmers, was fast coming to an end. The frontier had already closed, and with it closed the opportunities for land-hungry immigrants from all parts of Europe. People were beginning to realize that agriculture was increasingly becoming a business rather than being merely a way of 'life. The indefensible spawning of churches on the frontier to assure denominational advantage was proving as economically wasteful as it was ecclesiastically contradictory, denying the common locus of the Church among the churches.[1]

To attribute these changes to any single force or combination of forces is, of course, impossible. They are the products of innumerable factors, many of which could be subsumed under the general category of technology. A major change ultimately came over the way of life of almost everyone engaged in agriculture and of those living in towns and cities who depend on this part of our economy. Were we to try to enumerate all the forces responsible for this revolution, time would fail us and we would deviate from our primary purpose: to portray such differential beliefs, personality characteristics and participation patterns as may characterize those church members who have been affected by these changes in the past half-century.

One important factor aiding and stimulating the ever-accelerating change, however, must be mentioned. Perhaps more

---

1. Mark Rich has documented much of this history in *The Rural Church Movement* (Juniper-Knoll Press, 1957).

than any other single factor, the United States Department of Agriculture has been responsible for the revolution in methods of agriculture and the resultant psychological and philosophical reorganization.[2]

Some may feel that all this is but another way of describing urbanization, since rationalism and bureaucracy are intimately identified with urbanism in the western world. The authors recognize that the homogenization of culture draws most heavily upon the city and that both the instruments and content of communication are freighted with urban influence. Our concern is not to weigh the relative importance of contributing sources but rather to acknowledge that influences are and have been at work to modify the frame of mind and the concomitant actions of people and institutions in town and country.

Among theological seminary students and faculty it is common knowledge that a wide gap exists between the theological emphases of the seminary and the actual ongoing life of the churches. Possibly this gap is wider where the teaching of the seminary includes sociological analysis and a disposition to relate such disciplines as Biblical studies, history, and theology to the contemporary situation. The responsibility for this hiatus belongs, we believe, both with the seminaries and with the churches. The seminaries have given too little attention to the processes of teaching and communication, while constituents in the churches have looked suspiciously upon anything which obligated them to change. Equally, if not more, responsible for this gap is the fact that only recently has there been emerging in some communions an appreciation of a total Gospel which stands in judgment of the individualism of an earlier church emphasis. This appreciation comes as a threat and offers potential disruption to established patterns of social and personal life. In a world with so little that seems fixed and stable, it is understandable that people should want their churches to provide what they have been led to assume was stability.

Familiarity with church life at the local, denominational, and

2. Two volumes are of especial significance in portraying the development of agriculture in America: *The 1940 Yearbook of Agriculture* (United States Government Printing Office, 1940); and Edmund de S. Brunner, *The Growth of a Science* (Harper, 1957).

inter-denominational levels convinced the authors that emphases
being made at the interdenominational and national denominational levels were in large measure unheeded locally. Furthermore, it was apparent that no denomination revealed a constituency disposed to appropriate the fruits of Biblical and
theological scholarship. In fact, evidence pointed to staunch
resistance.[3] Was it because the church in the minds of its adherents serves a purpose other than that of discerning and ap-
propriating the Christian message? The Christian faith is
obviously competing with forces at least powerful enough to
dilute its imperatives for the realm of interpersonal relations.
Possibly, too, it is in conflict with those forces which anesthetize
individuals against comprehending the role of the Christian faith
both in the political and the economic order. It may be too
simple a conclusion to suggest that preoccupation with economic
life had produced these results. Nevertheless, the evidence was
strong that members of the churches were somewhat less than
eager to be informed and ordered by the faith they professed.

Having participated in the preparation of various instruments
for strengthening local church life and having engaged in programs designed to increase awareness by local congregations
of the relevance of the Christian message for self and community, the authors came to realize that the condition of insensitivity
to the implications of that message was widespread; and it was
not confined to one geographic area or to one or even to a few
denominations. Yet almost every religious organization was producing literature designed to heighten sensitivity to the relation
between spiritual values and the common life. Editors of religious publications, denominational officials, and communication experts wrestled with this problem. Theologians, psychologists of religion, and cultural anthropologists, of their own initiative or at the behest of others, made it their concern. Some
placed the blame on "secularization"—a term of many meanings
—others on a distortion of the Biblical message itself, and still
others on preoccupation with institutional life and the use of
institutions to enhance personal and group pride.

---

3. In one major denomination a national program designed to explore
the relevance of the Christian faith to the contemporary human situation
enlisted study groups in less than one-half of one per cent of the churches.

Diagnosticians of this situation are numerous and therapists abound. Much of the diagnosis and proposed therapy may be quite accurate, but it was the authors' conviction that detailed empirical data on the problem were lacking. Also, it was felt that much more must be known about the levels of religious comprehension and the influence of alternative ecclesiastical structures and cognitive forms on their adherents before remedial programs are considered. This conviction is not meant to imply that all such data can be acquired by survey research methods. Intimate association with the existential situation coupled with normative understanding may enable astute and sensitive observers to evaluate major social and cultural movements, although it does not permit reliable differential comparisons between groups in a society. Hence, accurate data are of benefit to the perspicacious observer and for all who may seek dependable resources in their constructive work. Thus it was with the hope that all individuals interested in the contemporary religious scene would benefit from an empirical study of some phases of religious life in an area qualifying as typical of a major region in the United States that this investigation was undertaken.

Residence in the Midwest, initial familiarity with some of its regional patterns, accessibility to a viable unit for study, and an advantage deriving from association with its people and churches suggested Corn County as an area suitable for study. The county is in the heart of a rich farming region and is economically in the top quintile of counties in the country as measured by income per family. This datum is important because it suggests that the level of professional religious leadership available in this county is probably equal to that found in almost any town and country setting in the United States. In addition to these qualifications, there is the close resemblance between Corn County and three other counties designated by the United States Department of Agriculture as typical of the Corn Belt.[4]

The Corn Belt is defined to include 469 counties which, in the evolution of United States agriculture, have been found most

4. Henry County, Indiana; Hamilton County, Iowa; Seward County, Nebraska.

suitable for the production of corn. Other parts of the country are well suited to raising corn, but no area presents so favorable a combination of factors for its cultivation and marketing, soil, rainfall, length of growing season, and proximity to numerous large population centers requiring the food products dependent on this one type of grain. The location of the great livestock terminals of Chicago, St. Paul, St. Louis, Omaha, Indianapolis, and many smaller ones scattered throughout the area attests to dependence upon this animal nutrient. Nor is it merely coincidental that the largest farm machinery companies have their headquarters and principal plants in the same area.

A British observer stationed in the Midwest during World War II made what for him was a surprising discovery: the heartland of the world was the Mississippi Valley, the Corn Belt of America.[5] Here, he felt, was the nerve center of the United States, and its culture both reflected and determined that of much of the rest of the nation. As an indication of the commercialization of agriculture, he found in almost every farmhouse faithful listeners to the grain and livestock market reports made hourly over certain radio stations. The mechanizing of agriculture is matched by commercial interest and preoccupation with the business phases of farming.

In the small towns and cities of the Midwest, not everyone, obviously, is as preoccupied with farming and its problems as are those residing on the farms themselves. Nevertheless, where merchants and professional people are dependent on the conditions of agriculture and where the livelihood of workers who provide services for farm people are inseparably tied to its economy, it is inevitable that the mentality and ideological framework of both town and open country should be affected by whatever affects agriculture.

Since World War II, however, a new phenomenon, or at least a sharp acceleration of an old one, can be observed. Need on the part of the small community for a more adequate tax base to support schools and services combined with a decision on the part of manufacturers to decentralize, reduce taxes, and attain more stability in labor supply (and possibly less expen-

---

5. Graham Hutton in *Midwest at Noon* (University of Chicago Press, 1946).

sive labor) have brought new industries to small towns. "Moon-lighting" (holding more than one job) is easily practiced by many farmers whose responsibility for land tillage or stock feeding does not require all their working hours. Electric lights on the tractor makes work in the fields possible regardless of time of day. Employees of the new plants are likely to be persons who have as strong an interest in the welfare of agriculture as in industry. Institutions once heavily influenced by agrarian-minded members now include constituents who, if not members of labor unions, are at least more sensitive to the problems of labor. It is this new complex—the presence of farmers and people dependent on farms with an increasingly market-oriented ideol-ogy and the skilled industrial workers in the proliferation of factories—that has inevitably affected the ideational framework of the residents of Corn County, the Corn Belt, and much of the rest of once rural America.

Corn County

So close is our generation to the opening of a continent that there are persons still living in Corn County who can remember some of the pioneers who came to the prairie from an over-crowded and industrializing New England. In the western fringes of the Corn Belt, there are a few pioneers still living who were themselves carried to this new land in covered wag-ons; this condition would, of course, be more true and hardly even exceptional for the Great Plains area. Not all of the mi-grants to the Corn Belt came from New England. In fact, some areas of the Corn Belt were predominantly settled by new-comers from other countries, who in many instances displaced earlier settlers. In this competition between nationality groups lies a story about varying educational objectives, land owner-ship values, and social institutions, a story of ethnic exclusive-ness and its gradual diminution. This study reflects the conse-quences of these factors. Because Corn County has been the scene for the manifestation of all of them, paralleling the experi-ence in many other counties of the United States, as a representative area it lends itself especially well to a study of individual beliefs and their relation to group life.

The Blackhawk War of 1831 accomplished two things of regional and national significance. It resolved the question of occupancy for the prairie by forcing the Indians to move further westward and to cease harassing white settlers, and it gave Abraham Lincoln a military record to support his subsequent political advance. Not all Indians complied willingly with these new arrangements, but the massacres ceased. By 1830, Corn County was sufficiently safe to attract a large-scale movement from New England. The decade from 1830 to 1840 saw all available land claimed, and it is understandable that almost all these communities bear names of towns, counties, or rivers in New England. The exceptions are those that adopted Indian names or the names of pioneers.

The use of names transplanted from places of earlier residence are symbolic of other transplanted characteristics. The New Englanders naturally brought with them a pattern of life closely resembling what they had known earlier (this practice is, of course, common for immigrants the world over). To the prairie the pioneers brought their passion for education; democracy in local government; Calvinism in religion expressed through Baptist, Congregational, and Episcopal churches; and a fondness for towns constructed around a village green to which churches and schools were adjacent.

Of importance for subsequent events was the process of land acquisition which established ownership and has since influenced the class and status structure of Corn County for more than a century.[6] The concept of land ownership has attraction for reasons other than economic return. Though America may be predominantly urban and industrial, there is a nostalgia for the farm, from which came so large a percentage of present-day urban residents. The farm symbolizes independence of judgment, teamwork in the family, and closeness to the good earth. All of these values may be seen in the desire of persons transplanted from farm to city to retain ownership of farmland if possible; moreover, land ownership as a hedge against inflation should not be underestimated. The increase of rural as well as

---

6. W. Lloyd Warner and Associates in *Democracy in Jonesville* (Harper, 1949) have described this process for another Corn Belt county in a most interesting fashion.

urban land values, despite the decline of agriculture's relative position in the total economy, has increased the incentive toward ownership. Accessibility of bank credit to landowners is another factor, for land is regarded as reliable security in good farming areas.

But these migrants were only reflecting people's almost universal and timeless desire for living space and for a livelihood. In those pioneers were compounded family values, a sense of the sanctity of soil, initiative and independence, a glorification of labor, and the conviction or assumption that there was certain correlation between labor and personal gain.

It would be difficult to construct a situation better designed to illustrate Max Weber's thesis about the relationship between the Protestant ethic and the development of capitalism. Here were all of the elements traditionally ascribed to Calvinism. The virtues of industry, frugality, and piety—all subsumed under a sense of national destiny, which itself had been frequently identified with Israelitish people moving into the Promised Land—were vigorously upheld. In this context the fact that the Old Testament played so large a part in the sermons and Sunday school materials can be readily understood.[7] Individual and national worth were basic themes, and judgment for sloth and Sabbath breaking by an omnipresent God, who rewarded integrity and punished duplicity, was very real. The God of judgment of the Old Testament was a vivid reality, and the Sermon on the Mount, with its perfectionist admonition, became a norm among many.

People in such a homogeneous culture, underguided by a strong Biblical base, would not have understood later requests to abandon Bible reading or prayers in the public school classroom. There was no marked variation in the theological emphases between the three major Protestant denominations—Baptist, Congregational, and Episcopal. This sharing of almost identical theologies is of special significance in the light of the subsequent fracturing of ideological uniformity with the arrival

---

7. Edward McNall Burns in *The American Idea of Mission* (Rutgers University Press, 1957) has drawn together numerous references to pioneer America's identification with the Old Testament seekers and occupants of the Promised Land.

and influence of other nationality groups and of the still more recent cognitive polarization or synthesis around another axis suggested by this study.

The Calvinistically-oriented Yankee pioneers established churches simultaneously with the founding of the towns and trading centers. When they designated themselves as "The First Church in _____," it was not an act of arrogance. Nevertheless, their monopoly was soon broken. The Methodists and Disciples, denominations with skill for ministering to the frontier mind, quickly established Sunday schools that shortly became full-fledged churches.[8]

The last religious group of Anglo-American origin that should be noted is the Presbyterian. It was not among the earliest to establish churches in Corn County but came to prominence later. A mutual national arrangement between the Congregationalists and the Presbyterians, known as the Plan of Union, had been designed to limit unhealthy competition on the frontier. Subsequently, a division, a result largely of differences on the slavery issue, arose between the two groups. In the county seat of Corn County, this division was manifested by the fact that the Presbyterian church was established by a group that split from the Congregational church in a protest against what it felt was too heavy a preoccupation with the antislavery movement.[9]

Up to this point, it will be noted, the newcomers to Corn County were what have been designated as "old-line British-American" in their church or religious affiliation. The potato famine of Ireland in 1848 and the upheavals in Germany of the same year started major movements of other nationality groups to the United States, which subsequently changed the homogeneity of many areas and communities. Ultimately, 40 million immigrants were absorbed into the life of the country. Though

---

8. Parenthetically, it should be recorded that the Disciples, with their congregational autonomy and loose central administration, have not survived as well as the Methodists, who were hierarchically structured. Further, they have not made the kind of adjustment to a particular type of evangelical religious interest characteristic of the Baptist contingent.

9. The Presbyterians had substantial membership in the South and had sought to keep the denomination united. Ultimately, the conflict of 1861-1865 made that impossible.

Corn County may not have received as heavy a concentration of any one particular nationality group as did some other areas, it did receive sufficient representation from many sections of Europe to provide pronounced variations in ethnic practices and ecclesiastical emphases. Irish came to build railroads, and some remained to become farmers and merchants. Swedes, the largest immigrant group, distributed themselves widely on the prairie and are still to be found extensively in farming, commerce, and the professions. Germans, representing both Lutherans and Mennonites, predominantly became farmers. Italians, Poles, and Lithuanians settled in and around a mining town, designated in the study as East Town, and in an industrial community in the county. The mines ceased operation shortly after World War I, but these immigrants or their descendants remained to work in the industrial city adjacent to Corn County, and even now many of them continue to live in East Town. In the county itself, there is one small community whose entire existence centers around a single industry. Its people are predominantly Italians. At the opposite end of the county, a small cluster of Belgians, who had been drawn to the area because of a strip coal mining operation, still resides.

By 1870, the first year in which the decennial census listed the foreign born by country of birth for each United States county, there were approximately 2,000 persons of German birth in a total county population of about 31,000. Correspondingly, there were some 1,200 Swedish-born inhabitants and some 1,300 Irish-born inhabitants in Corn County. By 1900, the proportion of persons of German and Irish birth had declined, while the population of Swedish origin had increased; it has remained substantially larger than the percentage of most other nationality groups until the present period. The heavy flow of Italian immigrants began in the last decade of the nineteenth century. As indicated earlier, the Italians moved almost exclusively into the industrial towns located in one corner of Corn County which was adjacent to a larger industrial complex in another county.

Throughout this study, we are partly concerned with the religious ideologies of these immigrants and of their descendants. Therefore, we now turn to a brief characterization of the type of religious institutions that these migrants brought with them and to a consideration of subsequent social and economic developments.

Scattered throughout Corn County are six German Lutheran churches, one Evangelical and Reformed church, and two Mennonite churches. Two of the Lutheran churches and one of the Mennonite churches are in areas of the county included in the study, although some of the constituents of the other churches were also included in the sample because of residence where the interviewing was conducted. As was true for many denominations composed of immigrants, the services in the churches of these German immigrants were originally conducted in their native tongue. The comment of one loyal churchwoman who deplored the shift to English-speaking services probably sums up the feeling of many who had left their native country: "If it's not in German, it's not Christian."

Many members of the churches of German background are still farmers. Among the Mennonites, another differentiating factor, which until only recently had caused additional exclusiveness, was their strong commitment to the practice of nonviolence. The cohesiveness provided by this commitment, although still substantial, is probably less today than it was a generation ago. Similarly, the prohibition against affiliation with those of other religious traditions, based on the Biblical injunction against being yoked with unbelievers, created a separation which gave these descendants of the Left Wing of the Reformation the designation "Come-outers." For many years a unique style of dress and certain other customs reinforced their consciousness of difference. Today, however, because of intermarriage, a common educational system, united economic activities, and community concern, interaction with other groups is more frequent and their style of life is less distinctive.

The population of Swedish origin of Corn County is similarly divided into two major denominational segments, the Augustana Lutheran church and the Mission Covenant church. The former reflects the constituency of what, in their native land, was the official church, and the latter reflects the independent or "free" church. By 1900 there were approximately 1,200 Swedish immigrants in Corn County. From that date forward the Swedish contingent and its descendants outnumbered immigrants from any other foreign country, with the possible exception of Italy.[10] Membership lists of all the "old-line British-American churches" are today heavily dotted with Swedish names, attesting to the mobility of this group and to the homogenization process characteristic of America. It should be added that political and economic power in substantial measure is to be found today among the membership of the churches of Swedish origin in Corn County. Further, the extent of land ownership of people of both Swedish and German origin reveals that individuals who came to the United States with only the assets of willingness to work and good intelligence have acquired many of the symbols of attainment prized in their adopted country.

In 1848 the potato famine in Ireland brought the first great wave of Irish to the United States, and by 1870 there were already approximately 1,300 Irish in Corn County. The two transcontinental railroads crossing the county, as well as the construction of a canal connecting the Mississippi River and the state's principal river, employed great numbers of Irish. The completion of these projects was simultaneous with the arrival of the Golden Age of Agriculture, thereby releasing a substantial supply of cheap labor for agriculture. In Corn County, the "hired hand," familiar to farm life prior to the 1930's, was most frequently either of Irish or Swedish origin. For reasons that have in part already been explored, the Swedes remained to rent and then to buy land.[11] The Irish, for the most part, have not distinguished themselves as farmers; rather, they have become dispensers of commercial, political, and personal services. Perhaps because the Swedish immigration to this rural area continued longer, there are ten times more first-generation Swedes now in Corn County than Irish, although in 1870 their numbers were about the same. The later Irish immigrants have obviously found the cities more receptive to their special skills.

The presence of seventeen Roman Catholic churches in Corn County can be attributed only in part to the continued presence of Irish immigrants and their descendants. Another important contributing factor was the arrival of immigrants from Italy, Po-

---

10. The Italians, however, remained concentrated in a single area as noted above.

11. Gerhard Lenski, *The Religious Factor* (Doubleday, 1961).

land, and Lithuania. Almost all of them had arrived since 1890; and in the case of the Lithuanians and Poles, most had arrived by World War I. As indicated above, they are concentrated in one area of the county and predominantly in the community designated hereafter as East Town. In East Town, the Italians are identified with the largest Roman Catholic church, whereas the Irish origin church is next in size with approximately half the membership of the predominantly Italian Catholic church. Two other ethnic churches, almost equal in size, are the Lithuanian and Polish churches, each considerably smaller than the Irish church. The constituencies of these four churches give East Town a 57 per cent Catholic population as compared with 13 per cent Protestant. These comparative figures are significant for the findings reported below. In the county seat (Maizeville), because of the development of new industry, the Roman Catholic population has increased so much that a new and larger sanctuary was recently constructed. In this community, however, the figures for East Town are more than reversed, being 70 per cent Protestant and 9 per cent Roman Catholic, again a significant point for the findings reported below.

Following the Italians, another wave of newcomers arrived in Corn County. They possessed little of the high visibility or colorful distinguishing characteristics of the foreign born. They were as indigenous as the family of Abraham Lincoln, for they were part of the same population movement. Even before the state of which Corn County is a political unit became a full-fledged state, these people had been moving into its borders. They were Anglo-Saxon Protestants in background, their ancestors having come to Corn County through the Cumberland Gap into Tennessee and Kentucky. Finding the hills and "hollers" inadequate to yield a livelihood for its consistently growing families, the excess population pressed steadily westward and northward. By World War I Corn County had already received many of these landless people from states south of the Corn Belt. As hired hands, they replaced the Irish, who were beginning to leave the land. One marked difference with the Irish was that these newest of the newcomers had been farmers, as had been their forefathers before them. They were not always as diligent as the Scandinavian newcomers, for, possibly as a result of the combination of diet, climate, and isolation, they had become accustomed to a slower pace. They did not seek education—especially as a means of mobility—as zealously as did some of the other groups. But they were willing to work; and in a period when farm workers were in demand, they found ready employment.

A prominent attribute of these newcomers who came from south of the Ohio River was a type of religious expression characteristic of the frontier. Inspiration and enthusiasm were criterions of authenticity. The education and instruction of the clergy were less important than was their ability to "move" hearers with threats of condemnation and promises of reward. The denominations they had known in their previous residence were likely to be either Methodist or Baptist. On arrival in the Corn Belt, apparently many discovered that the sophistication of those denominations was without appeal for them, and they often chose to identify with Pentecostal groups. A large enough number became affiliated with Baptist church groups to give, by sheer force of numbers, the existing Baptist churches a substantially different type of emphasis. Whereas all of the Baptist churches were originally of the New England variety and were composed of the pioneers who came out with the earlier Yankee migration, under the impact of this later migration their educational and economic level bowed somewhat. Although they still retain affiliation with the more liberal American Baptist Convention, they now resemble more nearly the churches of the Southern Baptist Convention in the type of religious emphasis, in social outlook, and in what is expected of their ministerial leadership.

Communities and Areas Studied

Within Corn County, four areas were selected for intensive study. The first of these areas, the county seat town, called Maizeville, is a community of about 6,000 people. It is the dominant service center community in the area and is the retirement mecca for farmers around it. It has one weekly newspaper which describes itself as "The Nation's Largest Country Weekly." As one would expect, it is devoted largely to reports of local activities. A daily newspaper published in a community of about 20,000 located 20 miles from Maizeville provides evening reading for a segment of Maizeville's population, while the *Chicago Tribune* is the dominant morning newspaper. Maizeville is the most prosperous of the communities studied and is dominantly Protestant. A major transcontinental railroad and two major transcontinental U.S. highways pass through the city.

The second community studied was a small service center of about 1,000, here called Serviceville. It is located within easy driving distance of Maizeville and is dominated by that town. It gives evidence of a declining, or at least a stable, population. Very small shops and stores catering to the needs of farmers and local townspeople comprise the town's business.[12] The predominance of old and deteriorating homes is very noticeable. The village is dominantly Protestant. The only concrete road in the community leads to the county seat town of Maizeville.

In sharp contrast to Maizeville is the third town which was studied. East Town, as it is here named, is an industrial town of about 5,000 people. It is adjacent to two larger towns in an adjoining county which together form an industrial complex of about 30,000 people. The town was founded when coal mining was the dominant industry in the area. Coal mining has declined drastically and almost all the descendants of the miners are industrial workers. It is the only area studied which is dominantly Catholic. As such, it provides further contrast with Maizeville. It is serviced by one major transcontinental highway and by one major transcontinental railroad.

The last intensively-examined area is an open-country farming area. It consists of two townships located near Serviceville. Serviceville is the only village in either of the townships studied.

Maizeville has the largest number of religious institutions, with fourteen. Included among them are the Catholic church and the following active Protestant churches: Baptist, Christian, Congregational, Christian Science, Jehovah's Witnesses, Augustana Lutheran, United Lutheran, Methodist, Presbyterian, United Pentecostal, and Wesleyan Methodist. At the time of the study,

---

12. For a detailed analysis of some dimensions of a town the size of Serviceville, see Arthur J. Vidich and Joseph Bensman, *Small Town in Mass Society* (Princeton University Press, 1958).

the German Lutheran church was nearly defunct, and efforts were being made to organize an Episcopal church.

In Serviceville, there were six churches, including the Catholic church and the following Protestant churches: Baptist, Episcopal, Methodist, Mennonite, and Pentecostal.

In East Town, there were four Catholic churches, one Syrian Orthodox church, one practically defunct Jewish synagogue, and one Protestant church which was Congregational. The four Catholic churches, as described earlier, were all nationality parishes, and local people would often refer to them by the name of the dominant ethnic group: Irish, Italian, Polish, or Lithuanian. Of the four, the Irish church had the greatest proportion of people of mixed ethnic backgrounds. It was also the only Catholic church that had a parochial school, which gave it considerable prestige among Catholics in the community.

The two country churches in the open country area were also examined in this study. One was Mennonite and the other was Congregational.

Selected demographic data are presented in Tables 1 to 4. Data are presented for the four areas examined intensely and for two other communities for which some participation data are detailed in Chapter 2.

Also included are comparable demographic data for similar areas in the United States. The areas studied in Corn County do not differ markedly from corresponding units in the United States.

Table 1. Population Changes for 1940-1950, 1950-1960 and 1940-1960 for
          Corn County, Maizeville, East Town, Coal Village, Serviceville, Elm
          Center, Rural-Farm Population of Three Selected Townships, and
          Approximate 1960 Population in Per Cent

Area	Per Cent Change 1940-1950	Per Cent Change 1950-1960	Per Cent Change 1940-1960	Approximate 1960 Population
Corn County	0	0	0	37,600
Maizeville	10	8	20	6,300
East Town	− 2	9	7	5,400
Coal Village	5	8	14	1,100
Serviceville	5	− 1	3	1,000
Elm Center	23	−11	10	200
Rural-farm population of three townships*	− 5	5	0	2,100

* Includes a township contiguous with Maizeville. The other two townships contiguous with Serviceville display a declining trend in common with national rural-farm population trends.

Table 2.   Sex Ratio in 1960 for Corn County, Maizeville, East Town, Coal Village,
           Serviceville, Elm Center, Rural Population of Three Townships, and
           Selected Other Areas

Area	Sex Ratio
Corn County	96
Maizeville	85
East Town	98
Coal Village	91
Serviceville	85
Elm Center	90
Rural population of three townships	99
Places of 2,500—10,000 outside urbanized areas in the United States	94
Places of 1,000—2,500 outside urbanized areas in the United States	94
Other rural areas in the United States	106

Table 3.   Age Distribution in 1960 for Corn County, Maizeville, East Town,
           Coal Village, Serviceville, Elm Center, Rural Population of Three Corn
           County Townships, and Selected Other Areas in Per Cent

Area	14 Years and Under	TOTAL 15-64 Years	65 Years and Over
Corn County	29	58	13
Maizeville	27	55	18
East Town	26	61	13
Coal Village	26	60	14
Serviceville	27	56	17
Elm Center	29	52	19
Rural population of three townships	32	57	11
Places of 2,500—10,000 outside urbanized areas in the United States	31	58	11
Places of 1,000—2,500 outside urbanized areas in the United States	31	57	12
Other rural areas in the in the United States	33	59	8

The church membership distribution for the areas examined is summarized in Table 5.

Some General Considerations Regarding Method

The study is descriptive and typological. Because the authors are persuaded that the freedom of man permits him to respond in alternative ways to data given to him, they are skeptical of research efforts in the behavioral sciences to develop models which would, presumably, have high predictive value. This observation is not intended to deny that patterns do exist or that structural elements are significant. It does intend, however, to place a somewhat different emphasis upon research in the social studies. Because, in the writers' judgment, human history and human social organization are a synthesis of freedom and order (or patterning), social studies lack the precision and neatness of predictability apparently available in some of the natural

Table 4. Occupational Groupings for Males for Selected Areas in 1960* Classified by White-Collar, by Blue-Collar Except Farmers and Farm Laborers, and by Farmers and Farm Laborers in Per Cent

Area	OCCUPATIONAL GROUP					Approx. 1960 Total
	White-Collar	Blue-Col., Exc. Farmers	Farmers	Don't Know	Total	
Corn County	22	46	30	2	100	9,900
Corn County rural non-farm	25	65	8	2	100	4,000
Corn County rural farm	3	9	86	2	100	2,900
Maizeville	43	49	5	3	100	1,600
East Town	28	65	1	6	100	1,400
Coal Village†	34	62	3	1	100	162
Serviceville†	38	52	8	2	100	133
Elm Center‡	10	60	21	8	100	53
Rural Farm† population of three townships	8	20	71	2	100	276
Urban population in the U. S. outside standard metropolitan statistical areas	38	56	2	4	100	6,010,000
Rural non-farm population in the U. S. outside standard metropolitan statistical areas	26	61	10	3	100	6,230,000
Rural farm population in the U. S. outside standard metropolitan statistical areas	7	21	70	2	100	3,230,000

* Based on enumerations in this study for Serviceville, Coal Village, Elm Center, and rural-farm population of three townships.
† Based on 50 per cent sample in this study.
‡ Based on a complete enumeration in this study.

Table 5. *Adult Church Membership by Area in Per Cent**

Area	Church	%	Church	%	Church	%
Maizeville	Baptist	6	Lutheran,		Mission Covenant	6
	Catholic	9	Augustana	7	Presbyterian	7
	Christian	4	Lutheran, United	9	Wesleyan	
	Christian Science	1	Lutheran, Other	1	Methodist	1
	Congregational	9	Methodist	16	All other	2
					None	21
					Don't know	1
East Town	Catholic, Total	58	Congregational	14	None	20
	Irish	13	Jewish	1	Don't know	1
	Italian	30	Syrian Orthodox	2		
	Lithuanian	8	All other	5		
	Polish	5				
Coal Village	Catholic	31	Wesleyan			
	Congregational	17	Methodist	1		
	Lutheran	4	All other	4		
	Methodist	16	None	27		
			Don't know	2		
Serviceville	Baptist	12	Methodist	18		
	Catholic	13	Pentecostal	2		
	Episcopal	8	All other	10		
	Mennonite, General		None	28		
	Conference	3	Don't know	1		
	Mennonite, Old	5				
Elm Center	Catholic	13				
	Congregational	36				
	All other	21				
	None	29				
	Don't know	1				

* The Lutheran church in Coal Village is now closed. The Old Mennonite church in Serviceville is in the open country outside of town. Area totals may not sum to 100 because of rounding.

sciences. Therefore, a study such as the present one is designed to illumine feeling tones and to discern cognitive structures and the matrix of interpersonal relations that exist in the communities studied. Because of the authors' concern with religious phenomena, the research has been designed to illumine primarily this area, although the intrinsic interrelatedness of experience limits the effort to do so. Auxiliary data in other areas must be obtained and analyzed. Most of the basic analyses, however, will be couched in terms of interchurch differentials among the phenomena under consideration.

Because verbal expressions and cognitive ideas constitute only a segment of man's experience, it seemed necessary to augment data that might be obtained through the interview method with non-cognitive materials that could be used to illumine the personality structure of the people in the sample. It was felt that the character of a person is molded by a combination of cognitive and emotive dimensions. Therefore, the comparative analysis of such noncognitive material could provide clues to the way in which the various religious traditions did or did not affect the basic character of their adherents. It is assumed, employing the null hypothesis, that negative results indicate that the various religious traditions have been of little significance in affecting the basic personality structure of their adherents. Of course, the problem is compounded by the fact that the American ethos has been partly informed and shaped by the Western tradition, which is nurtured and permeated by Christianity. However, the difference in emphasis between various segments of the Christian tradition ought to provide some variety within the general unity that is the Western cultural heritage if their theological distinctions were internalized by their members.

The relative importance of the institutional churches in the lives of their members and the extent to which the churches are forming the personal relationships and social, economic, and political life of their members were assessed through data dealing with selected questions in these areas. Because of the general inability of the people in the sample to deal with abstract issues and because of their lack of explicitly formulated theological positions, the interview schedule was constructed to elicit feelings and attitudes toward explicit issues and ideas. Probing was undertaken to explore the rationale for the interviewee's initial responses. From these materials, it was possible to discern the respondent's general feeling and to determine the rational or cognitive structure that did or did not underlie the response to a specific question.

No attempt has been made to assess the relative influence among the individuals included in the interview sample. This limitation, intrinsic to the survey method, should be explicitly noted, for it raises but does not resolve the problem of super-

ordination and subordination in a society, however the super-
ordination and subordination are interpreted in the variety of
traditions that consider this problem.[13]

Any attempt to present data involves the use of some type
of conceptual framework which guides its collection, orders its
presentation, and conditions its interpretation. The attempts to
argue for the use of the "scientific" method in social research
in an effort to overcome philosophical or theological biases only
clouds the issue, for there are a variety of "scientific methods,"
the validity of which rests upon the validity of the assumptions
that undergird them. Even the basic categories of analysis reflect
the initial assumptions. For example, in discussing social conflict,
the analyst may talk about harmony and disharmony among
competing elements, about the power configurations evident,
about the stresses and strains exhibited, about the complex of
social, political, and economic factors involved, or about some
combination of these. The language used and the ontology
which that language suggests depend upon these initial decisions.
The relation of these approaches to the data is obtuse. Certainly,
it does not make possible any kind of simple appeal to the
"facts," as some social scientists have suggested.

For what seem to us to be contingent reasons, few writers
in the social sciences today are dialecticians. Therefore, the
language of harmony, disharmony, balance, proportion, hier-
archies of societies, etc. seems, on the one hand, somewhat alien
to the social scientist at present. Almost all Protestant theologians,
on the other hand, are dialecticians and tend to use such terms
when they engage in what they feel is sociological analysis.
Hence, major and continuing disagreements in some areas between the two groups is to be expected.

Our insistence upon the freedom of the human being to respond in a variety of ways to the data received as he becomes

---

13. A valuable correlative study to this one would be the exploration of
the convergences and the divergences between theological elites and
power elites. Unfortunately, the research design employed in this study
and the limitation of resources prevented an extended consideration of top
leadership groups. However, the paucity of theologically knowledgeable
persons suggests that almost no one in top power positions is informed by
an explicit theological perspective.

what he is means that one will look only for configurations and tendencies in the social studies.

From this point of view, the primary purpose of social science is to illumine individuals' attitudes and feelings and to relate them to structures and patterns. Because of the tendency for patterns and structures to persist, these findings will provide the basis for the projections of future behavior and will permit the inference of the influence of various past structures and patterns.[14]

In particular, this study is concerned with the commonalities and the differences that are in evidence among people in the various religious traditions represented in a typical Midwestern area. By the employment of the method of difference, it has been possible to assess provisionally what influences, if any, have been contributed by the differing religious traditions and what influences are a consequence of the American ethos which informs the people of Corn County.

Because of the mutual influence of the religious and secular spheres, and because of the individuality of responses made by people to these various influences, no clearcut causal relationship between the two can be developed in this study. Further, the intrinsic limitation of research instruments to probe the depth of religious experience and the ambiguous relationship existing between words, thoughts, and feelings compound the difficulty.

Generally, the findings dealing with cognitive structures and interactive patterns are most clearcut. The data dealing with the Thematic Apperception Test occupy an intermediate position.

---

14. By structure, we mean those phenomena that can be discerned in various cultures and which are static. By pattern, we mean behavior sequences that tend to recur, partly as related to the feelings that are related to structure. They are dynamic. Thus, in a stratified relationship, the kinds of reciprocal relations that might occur between two people in different strata are the patterns involved that are related to the feelings of the individuals. Man's capacity to respond differently to the same data means that some patterns may transcend posited structures. From this point of view then, "no feeling tone, no structure." Structures may change if the feeling tones of the individuals to which the structures ultimately refer change. In this epoch, it appears unlikely that stratification patterns can be eliminated; at the same time, man's capacity to transcend posited structures may permit intimate personal relationships to exist between persons in different strata and castes.

The illumination of inner religious feelings is in the nature of the case most inadequately examined.

Finally, because of the absence of a full-blown and systematic categorical schema to interpret the data at the highest level of abstraction, critics may legitimately raise questions about the adequacy of the interpretations undertaken. The problem of determining what type of informing structure should be used to order the data and at what level of abstraction the data should be presented constituted a major difficulty. As noted earlier, it is at this level that major divergences may emerge, for the fundamental schema guiding the selection and interpretation of the data may be within or outside the Christian heritage. Because most informing structures in the social studies today fall into the broad tradition of the Sophists and the Atomists of antiquity, whereas most theological formulations fall in the tradition of Plato and Aristotle, it is not surprising that "empirical" data are handled differently by protagonists in each of the two broad groupings.

Investigators dealing with empirical data have two basic options available to them. First, they may systematically explicate an entire categorical schema and set their empirical work within this framework. Second, they may report the data at a relatively low level of abstraction and explicitly interject their categorical schema at appropriate points in the analysis.[15]

It is our hope that the empirical findings reported in this study may be suggestive and may be useful to a variety of people informed by differing cognitive structures—theologians, sociologists, psychologists. If such a hope is to be actualized, the data must be dealt with at a relatively low level of abstraction where theoretical divergences will not be as evident.[16]

It should be noted that this procedure involves provisional affirmation of the Sophistic or what in more modern terms is called the "operational" approach to social studies data. Although

---

15. The expression "level of abstraction" relates to the Platonic heritage that orders this general presentation. Investigators in other heritages would prefer the use of different terminology to describe this phenomenon.

16. Even at this level, divergences clearly emerge. For example, the nature of the "facts" and the "facts" to look for are partially determined by the categorical schema.

the writers reject some of the implications of such a perspective, they know of no other way to present data that can then be employed by persons using different categorical schemata.[17]

Method of Data Collection

The Interview Schedule—The basic instrument employed for collecting data was the interview.[18] In general, open-ended questions were used to obtain data dealing with participation patterns, theological beliefs and attitudes, social and political attitudes, the role definition of the minister, and the personality structure of the individual respondent. Detailed comments dealing with these materials will be presented later in chapters dealing with the substantive findings of the study. At this point, only a few general remarks about the type of instrument that has been used will be made.

For this study, the open-ended interview was deemed preferable both to the unstructured interview and to the scaled instrument. It was felt that an unstructured interview would be too time consuming and would not provide data rich enough to be commensurate with the time expended. On the other hand, the authors exercise considerable reserve about the use of a scaled interview. Their primary objections to such an instrument are four:

1. Its use of mathematical scores to interpret material that tends to be qualitative in character.
2. The strong tendency to force the interviewee to respond in a way conditioned by the categories used.
3. The "flat" or "thin" character of the data—in other words, the difficulty in collecting material that communicates the tone of feeling of the respondent.
4. The great difficulty in constructing a schedule in the field of religion which will collect useful data for people who have different theological viewpoints.

---

17. For a fuller treatment of the issues considered here, see W. Widick Schroeder, "Cognitive Structures and Religious Research," *Review of Religious Research*, III (Fall, 1961), 72-81.

18. See the Appendix for a copy of the interview schedule.

It is felt that the open-ended interview, which may be looked
upon as halfway between the unstructured interview and the
scaled one, enables one to collect the richest amount of data in
the least possible time.[19] The interviewers were instructed to
reword a question in the event that it was not initially understood and to probe for the meaning of the interviewee's response.[20] They were also instructed to record the interviewee's
response verbatim.[21]

Size and Type of Sample—In Maizeville, a 25 per cent sample
was taken of all groups except the Methodist and persons who
were not church members. For each of these groups, a 12½ per
cent sample was selected. In East Town, a 16⅔ per cent sample
of Congregationalists (the only Protestant church group), a 12½
per cent sample of non-church members, and a 6¼ per cent
sample of Catholics were used. In Serviceville, a 50 per cent
sample was drawn for all groups, except for the non-church

19. These comments are not meant to suggest that the unstructured or
scaled instruments do not possess great usefulness. Under some circumstances, both may be very valuable. However, it was not felt that they would
be as useful for gathering the kinds of data that were of primary interest in
this study. It is felt, however, that the scaled interview does possess some
intrinsic difficulties which make it of limited usefulness in investigations
in the social studies. Its nonhistorical character is based on a different
conception of the social studies than that held by these authors. For certain
purposes, such as for discerning the character of a personality or attitudes
and for rather simple problems, it possesses some value. However, because
of the tendency for values and feelings to shift over time due to man's
freedom and creativity and because of the disparity between words, feelings,
and ideas, its value is much less, it seems to these writers, than some of its
proponents might suggest.

20. Contrary to the counsel of some researchers that questions be
phrased identically for each interviewee, we preferred to rephrase questions
to be certain that the interviewee understood the intent of the question. In
our judgment, any loss in precision resulting from such a procedure is more
than compensated for by the richness of the response. Generally, we were
more concerned with feelings and ideas than with the symbols employed
to communicate them. This methodological decision is conditioned by the
cognitive structure that informs our way of looking at the world.

21. With the exception of two interviewers, both of whom were the
wives of theological students, all of the interviewers possessed theological
training. They were particularly sensitive to theological nuances and meanings which respondents might give. The negative character of many of the
findings in the body of this study looms more significant when the extent of
probing by theologically-sensitive interviewers is borne in mind.

members where a 25 per cent sample was taken. A 33⅓ per cent sample was drawn for all groups in the open country.

In Maizeville and East Town, every fourth dwelling unit constituted the original sample. In Serviceville, every other dwelling unit was selected, whereas every third dwelling unit was selected in the open country.

In Maizeville, every other Methodist and every other non-church member among the adults living in the selected houses were interviewed, whereas *all* the adults claiming membership in any of the other churches were interviewed.[22]

In East Town, every fourth adult Catholic in the dwelling unit selected, every other adult non-church member, two out of three adult Congregationalists, and two out of three adult members of all other churches were included in the interview sample. These proportions were established because the approximate membership distribution by denomination had been discovered through earlier work in the area.[23]

In Serviceville, every other non-church member was interviewed, while all church members were interviewed. In the open country, every adult in the dwelling unit selected was approached.

For purposes of this study, an adult was defined as a single person 21 years of age or over or as a married person of any age.

Any person in the sample who refused to be interviewed was approached at least three times, and the nature of the study was explained thoroughly to him. In view of the adamant attitude displayed by those who persisted in their refusal, it would seem reasonable to assume that they are not particularly cooperative in church groups. Some from the marginal group who only grudgingly agreed to be interviewed appeared to be most with-

---

22. In this study, no effort was made to establish whether or not a person who claimed church membership was actually on the church membership rolls. Participation questions were used to assess the degree of involvement in church activities, and they are dealt with in appropriate facets of this study.

23. Some of the findings of this facet of the study are presented in Chapter 2. In each dwelling unit, the ages of adults were listed chronologically from oldest to youngest. The interviewees were selected on the basis of coincidence with preassigned rows on a chart.

drawn and hostile; however, statistical data on this issue are not available.

An examination of selected socioeconomic characteristics for the interview groups and for the groups who refused to be interviewed revealed only minor differences between the two groups. The percentage of refusals ranged from a high of about 14 per cent refusals in Maizeville to a low of about 8 per cent refusals in the open country. The socioeconomic data for refusals were either obtained from neighbors or drawn from data that were gathered during the first phase of this study.

In the presentation of the findings, the refusals are not considered further. This fact should be borne in mind as the interpretation of the data is presented. The main consequence of these refusals probably is to increase slightly the percentage of knowledgeable responses on questions where substantive content was required. However, in light of the small percentage of refusals and the modest differences in selected socioeconomic characteristics between the refusal group and the participating group, variations due to differentials in the two groups are probably most modest.[24]

Coding and Tabulation—The responses were coded, punched on IBM cards, and machine tabulated. A detailed discussion of the categories that were employed in the analysis will be presented in connection with the analysis of the findings in the substantive portions of this book.

Classification of Groups in This Analysis

While most of the categories employed in this study are common and self-evident ones, two of them, intellectual level and status, require some explanation. The evaluation of intellectual level was obtained by an analysis of the stories related by the subjects responding to the Thematic Apperception Test, which was administered as a part of the interview.[25] Because of

24. The socioeconomic characteristics considered included sex, education, occupation, type of house, and frequency of church attendance.

25. A more extensive consideration of the Thematic Apperception Test is given in Chapter 5.

the limited number of cases involved, it was necessary to collapse two categories for this analysis. The interviewees were rated "above average," "average," and "below average" on two classifications related to intellectual capability. The first category employed was "intellectual functioning." The stories were analyzed acording to form, organization, time sequence used, and similar factors to evaluate the subject's overall intellectual functioning. Second, the plot, relation between characters, the novelty of the story, and similar items were considered to evaluate the subject's "imaginative ability." For purposes of the analysis undertaken in this book, subjects who ranked "above average" on either or both of the two classifications noted here were placed in the "above average" category. Persons who ranked "below average" on both or either of the two classifications were placed in the "below average group." The remainder of the interviewees were placed in the "average" group.

The categorization of status into three groupings was undertaken in an analogous manner. Because of limited resources, it was not possible to place the respondents in status groupings which were subjectively determined by residents in the communities studied; rather, some objective criteria had to be employed roughly to establish the status groupings.

After reviewing various criteria that have been employed to discern status ranking, it was decided to use occupation, education, and house type as the criteria of status for this study.[26]

Although finer distinctions had been made in coding the data, sample size suggested that the following classifications be employed. A basic two-fold division by occupation into "white-collar" and "blue-collar" workers was made for males. In the former group were included those occupational groups listed by

---

26. The authors are aware of the imprecise character of these classifications. Because status *per se* was not the primary focus of attention in this study and because of limited resources, the decision to employ these criteria is somewhat arbitrary. On the basis of numerous investigations, however, these criteria do seem to point to distinctions between various groupings.

In this particular area of social science investigation, differences in root categorical schemata are strongly evident. In spite of disagreements between the Warner group and those analysts informed by the analytical schema of Max Weber about the distinctions between class, status, and party, the root meaning of the term "power" that is common to both groups stands in the Sophistic tradition.

the United States Bureau of the Census in the following classes:

1. Professional and semiprofessional workers
2. Proprietors, managers, and officials
3. Clerical, sales, and kindred workers

In the latter group were included all the others (excepting postal employees who were clerks). Craftsmen, operatives, service workers, farmers, and laborers constituted the "blue-collar" classification. Married women's and widows' occupational classifications were determined by the husband's occupation. For single women, their own occupation was used in the classification.

Each of the two groups was then subdivided further into two groups acording to educational level. The "blue-collar" workers who had a high school education or less constituted one group, and the "white-collar" workers who had a high school education or more constituted a second group. A third group emerged from this sorting which consisted of "blue-collar" workers with some college training and "white-collar" workers who had not been graduated from high school.

The "white-collar" group that had a high school education or more was still further subdivided into two groups by house type.[27] One group comprised those persons living in an average house or above and the other comprised those living in a fair house or below. Those in the latter grouping were placed with the residue from the second sort. The "blue-collar" workers with a high school education or less further subdivided into a group living in an average house or below and a group living in a good house or above. The latter group was also placed with the residue from the second sort.

Thus, three status groupings emerged, and are referred to in all the tables that use the status classification. One group, termed "blue-collar" in the tables, consists of "blue-collar" workers and their wives, who had a high school education or less

---

27. The sevenfold house-type classification was modeled after the work done by W. Lloyd Warner and his associates. The houses ranged from excellent, at the top, to very poor, at the bottom. A house ranked as "fair" was one level below "average," while a house ranked as "good" was one level above "average." For a detailed discussion of the method used in developing this scale, see W. Lloyd Warner, Marcia Meeker, and Kenneth Eells, *Social Class in America* (Science Research Associates, 1949).

and who lived in an average or below average house. The second group, termed "white-collar" in the tables, consists of "white-collar" workers and their wives, who had a high school education or more and who lived in an average or better than average type of house. The third group, termed "mixed" in the tables, consists of the remainder. For all the status groups, analysis was confined to the 30–64 age group.

Statistical Tests Employed in This Study

In addition to the descriptive character of this study, differential patterns by church membership were a focus of major attention. To examine these differentials, the chi square test to determine level of significance was used throughout the tables. The 5 per cent level of significance was used throughout the book. The coefficient of contingency, C, was used to assess the degree of association among the selected variables.[28]

---

28. Consistently, data for the Maizeville Christian Church have been excluded from statistical analysis because of the small number of cases involved. In most cases, cells have been combined to insure at least a theoretical frequency of ten per cell, although occasionally exceptions for a few cells were made in some of the larger tables. In those tables in which multiple responses have been given, computations are based on the total number of responses reported.

2. CHURCH PARTICIPATION

PATTERNS AND

INTER-CHURCH FEELINGS

THE FINDINGS outlined in this chapter explore data dealing with church participation and with the differences between churches as understood by the interviewees. In addition, data on friendship patterns are presented to help us discern whether any sharp religious cleavages exist which would appear to affect interpersonal relationships in the area studied and to discover the extent to which one's social life is bound up with the life of a church congregation. In other words, the data are designed to illumine the extent to which one's primary associations are shaped by religious affiliation.[1]

Church Participation Patterns

Introduction—Data dealing with church membership, type of church membership, frequency of attendance at extra-church activities, and the number of memberships in voluntary associations for each of the geographical areas examined are presented for various categories of the population in the following section. In addition, data on inter-church differentials for selected communities and denominations are examined.

The participation patterns reported in this portion of the study are somewhat more inclusive geographically than the attitudinal materials reported in the rest of this book. In addition

---

1. We use the term "primary" in the sense employed by Charles Horton Cooley.

to the four areas already described, participation-pattern data for Coal Village and the hamlet of Elm Center are presented.

Coal Village is a service-center community comparable in population to Serviceville, but with fewer active churches. At the time of the study, the Catholic, Congregational, and Methodist churches were the only ones in the village. Almost 30 per cent of the residents were members of the Roman Catholic church. It was selected for preliminary analysis because it was more heavily Catholic and had fewer churches than Serviceville. It was located about 15 miles from Maizeville on a transcontinental highway and a transcontinental railroad.

The Congregational church was the only church in Elm Center. Elm Center was also located on a transcontinental highway and a transcontinental railroad, about five miles from the county seat of Maizeville, which was the main shopping center for almost all needs.

The interview schedule used was designed to gather quantitative data. It was administered to people in five different types of communities in Corn County and in the open country. A random sample of the population in the selected areas was drawn by taking every nth dwelling unit in which the occupants were interviewed. In the case of a refusal, information was obtained from neighbors whenever possible. In no case were new dwelling units added to the original sample. Because of the quantitative character of the data drawn, any adult informant was used.

In Maizeville and East Town, the two largest towns in which interviews were conducted, a 25 per cent sample was drawn. In the open country, in Coal Village, and in Serviceville, a 50 per cent sample was used, while a 100 per cent enumeration was made in Elm Center, the hamlet. The data were coded on IBM cards and machine-tabulated.[2]

2. For other aspects of the findings of this facet of the study not reported in this book, the reader is referred to the following: Charles Donald England, "A Comparative Sociological Study of Church Participation in Two Illinois Communities" (unpublished B. D. thesis, Hammond Library, The Chicago Theological Seminary, Chicago, 1956); Victor Obenhaus, W. Widick Schroeder, and Charles D. England, "Church Participation Related to Social Class and Type of Center," *Rural Sociology*, XXIII (September, 1958), 298-308; and William Widick Schroeder, "Maizeville:

Church Membership—The distribution of the sample according to church membership is shown in Tables 6, 7, and 8.[3] It should be noted that there were sharp differences both in church membership patterns in Maizeville and East Town and in the status structure of the two towns. Although Coal Village had markedly more Catholics than Serviceville, the two villages had very comparable status structures. The hamlet and the rural population were predominantly Protestant.

Table 6. Church Membership by Geographical Area for Broad Groups in Per Cent

| | CHURCH MEMBERSHIP | | | | |
Area	Protestant	Catholic	None	Total	N =
Maizeville	70	9	21	100	957
East Town*	21	59	20	100	766
Coal Village	41	32	27	100	366
Serviceville	59	13	28	100	286
Elm Center	57	13	30	100	107
Rural Farm Population					
of Three Townships	61	11	28	100	543

* Four Jewish adults excluded from analysis.

In general, the number of non-church members varied inversely with the size of the community. About one-fifth of the population in the two largest communities in the study, East Town and Maizeville, were not church members, whereas the proportion climbed to almost 30 per cent in the hamlet and in the rural farm portion of the sample. Chi square analysis indicated that Maizeville and East Town had significantly higher proportions of church members, whereas the rural farm population had significantly lower proportions than the total sample. The two villages and the hamlet did not differ significantly from the population as a whole. There was no difference in the proportion of non-churched in the two larger communities, despite the sharp difference in the composition of church membership between

A Sociological Study of Participation in Voluntary Associations in a Corn Belt Community with Special Reference to the Churches" (unpublished B. D. thesis, Hammond Library, The Chicago Theological Seminary, Chicago, 1955).

3. It should be emphasized that in all the tables in this section and in subsequent sections dealing with status and intellectual ability, analysis is confined to the 30-64 age group.

Table 7. Church Membership for Broad Groups by Social Status for Geographical Areas in Per Cent

CHURCH MEMBERSHIP

Area	PROTESTANT			CATHOLIC			NONE			TOTAL		
	White-Collar	Blue-Collar	N =	White-Collar	Blue-Collar	N =	White-Collar	Blue-Collar	N =	White-Collar	Blue-Collar	N =
Maizeville	57	43	297	61	39	36	21	79	86	50	50	419
East Town	33	68	83	17	83	221	4	96	68	18	82	372
Coal Village	35	65	66	31	69	49	20	80	35	30	70	150
Serviceville	37	63	76	29	71	21	16	84	38	30	70	135

dominantly Protestant Maizeville and dominantly Catholic East Town.

Table 7 shows the distribution of church membership by social status. The effects of social status upon church membership patterns were more marked in the larger towns, Maizeville and East Town—that is, in areas with the greatest degree of social differentiation—and more marked among Protestants than Catholics.

A chi square analysis of the distributions revealed statistically significant differences at the .001 level among the three broad church-membership groups by social status in Maizeville and East Town. Although the chi squares in Coal Village and Serviceville were fairly high, they were not statistically significant. In none of the areas studied was there any evidence to suggest that the Catholic church drew disproportionately from the white-collar group. However, Protestants drew disproportionately from the white-collar group in all of the communities studied except Coal Village. Similarly, the status selective character of the non-church group manifested itself. Again, with the exception of Coal Village, the non-church members were drawn disproportionately from the blue-collar group.

Although the white-collar workers had contributed disproportionately to the membership of the Protestant churches in almost all of the areas included in this analysis, the several Protestant churches in the largest community were themselves

Table 8.   Distribution for Protestants by Social Status in Maizeville in Per Cent

Church	White-Collar	Blue-Collar	Mixed	N =
		SOCIAL STATUS		
Baptist	19	60	22	37
Christian	19	50	31	16
Congregational	65	19	16	57
Lutheran, Augustana	29	42	29	38
Lutheran, United	32	40	28	57
Methodist	36	31	33	111
Mission Covenant	56	20	24	41
Presbyterian	67	16	16	43
Total	42	32	26	400

status selective, as Table 8, summarizing the findings for Maize-ville, reveals.[4]

The hierarchical character of status structure in the Protestant churches in Maizeville was clear. The Baptists and the Christians had drawn the largest proportion of their members from the blue-collar group. The Congregational and Presbyterian churches had drawn the largest proportion of their members from the white-collar group, whereas the other churches were in inter-mediate positions.[5] Chi square analysis did not reveal that any of the other Protestant churches drew disproportionately from the three social groups, although the chi square for the Methodist approached the .05 level of significance.

Type of Church Membership—In the analysis presented in this book, frequency of church attendance has been used to char-acterize type of church membership. Four types have been delimited:[6]

1. *Nuclear:*   Persons attending church forty-one times per year and over

2. *Modal:*   Persons attending church twelve to forty times per year

3. *Marginal:*   Persons attending church one to eleven times per year

4. *Dormant:*   Persons who do not attend church at all

4. East Town had only one Protestant church, so it was not further examined. Because of the size of the sample, it was not possible to treat the churches in the other communities statistically. The less sharp stratifica-tion in the other areas appeared to militate the status selectivity of the churches, although the data for Serviceville showed some selectivity. In that town, which had seven churches, the Methodist church appeared to have the greatest proportion of white-collar members in the age group examined.

5. Other churches with sufficient membership for statistical analysis included: Augustana Lutheran, United Lutheran, Methodist, and Mission Covenant.

6. The terminology adopted to identify these four groups is identical with that used by Joseph Fichter in his book *Social Relations in the Urban Parish* (University of Chicago Press, 1954). It should be carefully noted, however, that Fichter's criteria included more than frequency of attendance data. The data reported in this study are not directly comparable with his.

A summary of selected data by type of church membership
is présented in Tables 9 through 12. The fewest nuclear members

Table 9. Type of Church Membership by Geographical Area in Per Cent

			TYPE OF CHURCH MEMBERSHIP			
Area	Dormant	Marginal	Modal	Nuclear	Total	N =
Maizeville	22	20	24	35	100	948
East Town	21	15	17	47	100	756
Serviceville	22	24	19	35	100	284
Coal Village	19	19	26	36	100	359
Elm Center	31	11	11	47	100	107
Rural farm population of three townships	24	23	25	27	100	542

were found in the rural farm portion of the population, while the
most nuclear members were found in dominantly Catholic East
Town and in the hamlet of Elm Center. Somewhere between
one-third and one-half of the population were nuclear church
members—that is, members who attended church forty-one times
or more per year—while about 40 per cent of the adult population
consisted of marginal or dormant members, who attended fewer
than twelve times a year.

Because of variations in social status and in religious composition of the several communities examined, gross membership
data are of limited usefulness in analysis. Analysis by social status
and by church membership is more valuable. Table 10 reveals
that while there was some variation in type of church membership in the Catholic church by geographical area, there were
more nuclear Catholic members than nuclear Protestant members
in all of the areas studied.

The very high percentage of nuclear Protestants in the hamlet of Elm Center was atypical. It may largely be accounted for
by two factors: first, the exceptional quality of the minister of
the only church in the hamlet at the time of this study; and second, the truncated character of social stratification in the hamlet.
The overwhelming majority of the residents fell into the blue-
collar classification, which may have contributed to higher participation rates.

Differential membership types were evident among the Prot-

Table 10. Type of Church Membership for Protestants and Catholics by Geographical Area

TYPE OF CHURCH MEMBERSHIP

Area	DORMANT AND MARGINAL		MODAL		NUCLEAR		TOTAL		N =	
	Protestant	Catholic	Protestant	Catholic	Protestant	Catholic	Protestant	Catholic	Protestant	Catholic
Maizeville	34	14	28	10	39	77	100	100	668	81
East Town	39	17	34	15	27	68	100	100	137	445
Coal Village	36	9	44	7	20	84	100	100	150	112
Serviceville	34	13	26	5	40	82	100	100	166	38
Elm Center	16	14	23	0	61	86	100	100	61	14
Rural farm population of three townships	35	18	34	6	32	76	100	100	359	51

Table 11. Type of Church Membership for Protestants and Catholics by Social Status

	TYPE OF CHURCH MEMBERSHIP												N =			
	DORMANT AND MARGINAL				MODAL				NUCLEAR							
	Protestant		Catholic		Protestant		Catholic		Protestant		Catholic		Protestant		Catholic	
Area	White-Collar	Blue-Collar	White-Collar	Blue-Collar	White-Collar	Blue-Collar	White-Collar	Blue-Collar	White-Collar	Blue-Collar	White-Collar	Blue-Collar	White-Collar	Blue-Collar	White-Collar	Blue-Collar
Maizeville	21	43	14	14	36	25	18	7	44	32	68	79	168	129	22	14
East Town	21	47	8	17	38	29	11	18	42	24	81	66	24	55	36	128
Coal Village	22	47	20	12	48	35	0	0	30	19	80	88	23	43	15	34
Serviceville	36	33	0	20	32	35	0	0	32	31	100	80	28	48	6	15
Elm Center	0	21	0	0	0	8	0	0	100	71	0	100	4	24	0	3
Rural farm population of three townships	43	30*	0	25*	43	48*	0	0*	14	22*	100	75*	7	27*	4	4*

* Excluding farmers.

Table 12. Type of Church Membership for Protestant Denominations by Geographical Area and Social Status in Per Cent

TYPE OF CHURCH MEMBERSHIP

Church	DORMANT AND MARGINAL			MODAL			NUCLEAR			N =		
	All Members	White-Collar	Blue-Collar	All Members	White-Collar	Blue-Collar	All Members	White-Collar	Blue-Collar	All Members	White-Collar	Blue-Collar
MAIZEVILLE												
Baptist	32	*	50	26	*	23	42	*	27	57	*	22
Christian	41	*	75	31	*	0	28	*	25	32	*	8
Congregational	32	27	46	43	54	18	25	19	36	81	37	11
Lutheran, Augustana	25	9	27	24	36	27	51	55	47	67	11	15
Lutheran, United	22	17	22	36	22	39	42	61	39	88	18	23
Methodist	32	20	50	35	38	32	33	43	18	154	40	34
Mission Covenant	12	4	25	20	17	25	68	78	50	60	23	8
Presbyterian	36	41	57	34	31	0	31	28	43	62	29	7
EAST TOWN												
Congregational	36	22	44	33	39	27	30	39	29	102	23	34
COAL VILLAGE												
Congregational	26	0	37	46	60	42	28	40	21	61	11	19
Methodist	47	29	46	43	57	46	10	14	8	58	7	13
SERVICEVILLE												
Baptist	40	*	21	20	*	36	40	*	43	35	*	14
Episcopal	36	*	*	18	*	*	46	*	*	22	*	*
Mennonite, General Conference	10	*	*	10	*	*	80	*	*	10	*	*
Mennonite, Old	0	*	*	15	*	*	85	*	*	13	*	*
Methodist	43	31	54	37	62	39	20	8	8	51	13	*
Pentecostal	0	*	*	0	*	*	100	*	*	7	*	*
ELM CENTER												
Congregational	8	*	0	15	*	6	78	*	93	40	*	16

* Too few cases for analysis.

estants and Catholics in the various communities. Among Protestants, a greater range of membership types was noted than among Catholics. Elm Center and Maizeville had a higher proportion of nuclear members than did the Protestants as a group, whereas Coal Village had markedly fewer nuclear members.

Because Coal Village and Serviceville were comparable in population, and because there was a sharp disparity in membership types in the two villages, they were particularly interesting. Including a very small Wesleyan Methodist chapel, Coal Village had three Protestant churches, and Serviceville six. Serviceville had a significantly higher proportion of Protestant nuclear members. The additional churches, requiring the involvement of a larger number of people in the church organization, obviously had a marked effect on membership types.

A further comparison was made between Protestants in Maizeville and Serviceville taken as one group and Protestants in the rural farm population taken as a second group. It was found that there were more nuclear members among city and village Protestants than among the rural farm Protestants.

There was much less difference in membership types among Catholics. East Town had fewer nuclear members than the group as a whole, while Coal Village had more. The rest of the areas did not differ significantly from the total Catholic sample attendance.

Significant variations in type of church membership between white-collar and blue-collar status groups are shown in Table 11. Four observations may be made about these data. First, the Catholic churches in all the communities studied had more nuclear members for both social groupings than did the Protestant churches. Second, there was a remarkably constant percentage of nuclear members among white-collar Protestants in the two largest towns included in this study, Maizeville and East Town. Third, among Protestants there were more nuclear members among the white-collar group than among the blue-collar group with the exception of Serviceville. In that village, the evidence suggested that no differential existed. The large number of churches in this village, which did appear to be stratified, make this finding most interesting. It seems that the greater the number of Protestant churches in a community, the less the degree of differential between the two groups in the nuclear members. Fourth, there was evidence that there were fewer nuclear members among blue-collar Catholics in industrial East Town than among the other blue-collar Catholics. However, in most areas, the differences in membership types between blue-collar and white-collar workers was less than for Protestants. Furthermore, there was no evidence of differences in membership types by geographical area among white-collar Catholics.

Table 12 summarizes the membership types for Protestants in the communities studied. The column "All Members" refers to the total number of respondents in the several communities who said they were members of a specified church. White-collar and blue-collar status groups are the ones that have been used consistently throughout. Because of the paucity of cases, dormant and marginal members were combined for statistical purposes.

The relatively few nuclear members for the dominant Anglo-American churches was evident.[7] In Maizeville, the Continental European churches had the highest proportion of nuclear members among the Protestant churches. The Congregationalists, a high status Anglo-American church, had the lowest participation rates and the lowest percentage of nuclear members.

Sharp variations in membership types by social status seemed evident for almost all of the churches, although in many cases the sample was too small for statistical analysis.

Frequency of Attendance at "Extra-Church" Activities—Almost all the churches in the area included in this study held special extra-church activities, such as bazaars, church dinners, special lectures, festivals, and the like from time to time. If historical records can be trusted, one would infer that in earlier periods such activities were very important, not only in the life of the church, but also in the life of the community as a whole. Their importance today seems to be much less, as Tables 13 through 16 indicate.

---

7. The term "Anglo-American" refers to denominations that developed either in Great Britain or the United States. The term "Continental European" refers to denominations that developed historically on the continent of Europe.

The data shown in Tables 13 and 14 suggest that these activities were much more widespread in rural areas and among Catholics than in larger communities and among Protestants.

Table 13. *Frequency of Attendance at "Extra-Church" Activities by Geographical Area*

	FREQUENCY OF ATTENDANCE				
Area	Less than 25 Per Cent	25-74 Per Cent	75 Per Cent and over	Total Per Cent	N =
Maizeville	64	21	16	100	927
East Town	42	22	36	100	721
Coal Village	44	25	31	100	359
Serviceville	33	28	39	100	283
Elm Center	36	28	36	100	106
Rural farm population of three townships	47	21	32	100	535

In the dominantly Protestant town of Maizeville, participation in extra-church activities was very low among both Catholics and Protestants. In East Town, there was very high participation among Catholics, but it was very low among Protestants.[8] All the smaller communities except Coal Village had higher Protestant participation in extra-church activities than did either Maizeville or East Town. Comparison of Coal Village and Serviceville data revealed that Serviceville had significantly higher attendance at extra-church activities than Coal Village. As was the case with data on type of church membership, the village with the larger number of Protestant churches had the higher participation patterns.

Maizeville had much lower Catholic participation at extra-church activities than had any of the other areas studied. Coal Village had lower participation than Serviceville. In the case of both Maizeville and Coal Village, the patterns for Catholic participation were lower than for the other towns in their population class. The dominant community attitude toward extra-church activities seemed to reduce Catholic participation in such activities in communities where Catholics were in a minority.

---

8. The East Town data are affected by the fact that many respondents reported attendance at once-a-year picnics and the like.

Table 14. Frequency of Attendance at "Extra-Church" Activities for Catholics and Protestants by Geographical Area

| | FREQUENCY OF ATTENDANCE | | | | | | | | | |
| Area | Less than 25 Per Cent | | 25-74 Per Cent | | 75 Per Cent and Over | | Total Per Cent | | N = | |
	Protestant	Catholic	Protestant	Catholic	Protestant	Catholic	Protestant	Catholic	Protestant	Catholic
Maizeville	46	45	26	31	28	24	100	100	648	80
East Town	48	29	30	22	22	49	100	100	130	397
Coal Village	41	33	26	22	33	44	100	100	153	108
Serviceville	26	14	27	22	47	64	100	100	165	36
Elm Center	26	0	28	67	46	33	100	100	61	12
Rural farm population of three townships	35	25	25	13	40	63	100	100	334	48

Table 15. Frequency of Attendance at "Extra-Church" Activities for Catholics and Protestants by Geographical Area and Social Status

	FREQUENCY OF ATTENDANCE PER YEAR												N =			
	Less than 25 Per Cent				25-74 Per Cent				75 Per Cent and Over							
	Protestant		Catholic		Protestant		Catholic		Protestant		Catholic		Protestant		Catholic	
Area	White-Collar	Blue-Collar	White-Collar	Blue-Collar	White-Collar	Blue-Collar	White-Collar	Blue-Collar	White-Collar	Blue-Collar	White-Collar	Blue-Collar	White-Collar	Blue-Collar	White-Collar	Blue-Collar
Maizeville	26	56	38	29	39	21	29	57	35	23	33	14	165	126	21	14
East Town	39	48	11	26	35	32	29	25	26	20	60	49	23	50	35	175
Coal Village	23	51	0	18	36	19	14	29	41	30	86	53	22	43	14	34
Serviceville	36	25	0	7	21	25	0	29	43	50	100	64	28	48	6	14
Elm Center	0	33	0	0	25	21	0	33	75	46	0	67	4	24	0	3
Rural farm population of three townships	29	33*	0	25*	57	30*	0	0*	14	37*	0	75*	7	27*	0	4*

* Farmers excluded.

The influence of social status on participation patterns for extra-church activities is shown in Table 15. Among Protestants, the white-collar group exhibited higher participation patterns than the blue-collar group in all the areas studied except Serviceville. Among Catholics there were no statistically significant variations for the various geographical areas. Unfortunately, there were too few white-collar Catholics in some of the geographical areas to permit a detailed analysis of Catholic participation patterns.

The differential participation patterns in Coal Village and Serviceville were most interesting in that they tend to confirm the observations made above regarding the relationship between the number of churches in a village and the extent of participation in church activities by the various status groups. There was no evidence of differential participation for white-collar groups in the two communities; but there was evidence of higher blue-collar participation in Serviceville, the village with the larger number of Protestant churches.

Variations in participation at extra-church activities for the various Protestant groups are presented in Table 16. In Maizeville, significantly lower than average participation rates were noted for the Baptists and the Methodists, while significantly higher participation rates occurred in the Mission Covenant group. In the white-collar group there was no significant variation among the Congregationalists, Presbyterians, or Methodists, but the Mission Covenant group had higher participation rates than any of the other Continental European origin churches.[9]

Membership in Voluntary Associations—In the past half-century or so there has been a growth and proliferation of innumerable voluntary associations in the communities of the nation. Corn County has participated in this development. Although some of these voluntary associations were special interest groups, the purposes of the majority were rather diffuse. Their primary

9. The primary or communal character of the Mission Covenant Church grouping is evidenced in this finding as in numerous others in the current study. The limited sample prevented an extended analysis in any of the other communities; the results that were obtained are summarized in Table 16.

Table 16. Frequency of Attendance at "Extra-Church" Activities for Protestant Denominations by Geographical Area and Social Status

Church	Less than 25 Per Cent			25-74 Per Cent			75 Per Cent and Over			N =		
	All Members	White Collar	Blue Collar	All Members	White-Collar	Blue-Collar	All Members	White-Collar	Blue-Collar	All Members	White-Collar	Blue-Collar
MAIZEVILLE												
Baptist	67	*	71	16	*	14	21	*	14	52	*	21
Christian	63	*	75	19	*	0	19	*	25	32	*	8
Congregational	40	16	56	37	51	33	23	32	11	78	37	9
Lutheran, Augustana	33	27	25	36	27	38	31	46	38	64	11	16
Lutheran, United	38	17	44	37	50	22	24	33	35	86	18	23
Methodist	60	41	74	22	31	12	20	28	15	149	39	34
Mission Covenant	22	4	25	23	39	38	55	57	38	60	23	8
Presbyterian	37	35	29	27	31	43	37	35	29	60	29	7
EAST TOWN												
Congregational	43	41	39	31	32	42	25	27	19	99	22	31
COAL VILLAGE												
Congregational	28	20	37	28	40	5	43	40	47	60	10	19
Methodist	54	43	62	25	29	23	21	29	15	56	7	13
SERVICEVILLE												
Baptist	31	*	21	34	*	36	34	*	43	35	*	14
Episcopal	36	*	*	27	*	*	36	*	*	22	*	*
Mennonite, General Conference	10	*	*	20	*	*	70	*	*	10	*	*
Mennonite, Old	0	*	*	15	*	*	85	*	*	13	*	*
Methodist	22	31	31	32	15	31	46	54	39	50	13	13
Pentecostal	0	*	*	0	*	*	100	*	*	7	*	*
ELM CENTER												
Congregational	18	*	19	23	*	31	60	*	50	40	*	16

FREQUENCY OF ATTENDANCE PER YEAR

function in many cases was to structure the manner in which leisure time may be used for recreational purposes.

All of these organizations competed with churches for the leisure time of Corn County's inhabitants. It was, however, a select few who provided the major support for the plethora of voluntary associations that existed here. About one-third of the people belonged to no voluntary associations, and another 20 to 30 per cent belonged to only one, as Table 17 reveals.[10] Maizeville, with the highest proportion of white-collar residents, had the highest participation in voluntary associations, while the small dominantly blue-collar hamlet of Elm Center had the lowest.[11]

Table 17. Membership in Voluntary Associations by Geographical Area in Per Cent

Area		NUMBER OF VOLUNTARY ASSOCIATIONS			
	None	One	Two or Three	Four or More	N =
Maizeville	35	21	25	20	923
East Town	31	31	28	11	725
Coal Village	34	22	30	15	355
Serviceville	34	21	28	18	283
Elm Center	44	24	27	5	107
Rural farm population of three townships	33	26	27	14	519

Nonparticipators tended to avoid all types of institutional involvements. As Table 18 reveals, non-church members belonged to the fewest voluntary associations, while the Protestants belonged to the most. Among Catholics and non-church members, there was no evidence to indicate variation in membership patterns for voluntary associations by geographical area. On the other hand, Maizeville had a significantly higher proportion of memberships in voluntary associations than any other area. However, the status-selective character of membership in voluntary associations seems to account for the Maize-

---

10. In this analysis church membership is not included among voluntary associations.

11. This finding, when coupled with the prior finding that the participation in church activities was highest in Elm Center, suggests the less specialized role of the religious institution in that hamlet.

Table 18. Membership in Voluntary Associations by Geographical Area for Broad Church Membership Classification

| | NUMBER OF VOLUNTARY ASSOCIATIONS | | | | | | | | | | | | N = | | |
| | None | | | One | | | Two or Three | | | Four or More | | | | | |
Area	Protestant	Catholic	None	Protestant	Catholic	None	Protestant	Catholic	None	Protestant	Catholic	None	Protestant	Catholic	None
Maizeville	29	35	55	19	21	25	28	30	13	25	14	7	652	77	194
East Town	23	29	45	30	29	38	30	32	14	18	11	4	158	413	154
Coal Village	24	33	51	17	30	20	37	27	21	22	10	8	152	108	95
Serviceville	24	38	51	21	11	24	35	27	15	20	24	10	166	37	80
Elm Center	31	29	75	23	43	19	38	29	6	8	0	0	61	14	32
Rural farm population of three townships	23	29	56	27	27	25	32	29	15	18	15	4	328	48	143

Table 19. Membership in Voluntary Associations by Geographical Area for Broad Church Membership Classification by Social Status in Per Cent

NUMBER OF VOLUNTARY ASSOCIATIONS

| | NONE | | | | | | ONE-THREE | | | | | |
| | Protestant | | Catholic | | None | | Protestant | | Catholic | | None | |
Area	White-Collar	Blue-Collar	White-Collar	Blue-Collar	White-Collar	Blue-Collar	White-Collar	Blue-Collar	White-Collar	Blue-Collar	White-Collar	Blue-Collar
Maizeville	5	36	38	54	18	51	37	48	43	39	53	46
East Town	4	24	24	15	33	37	39	66	49	78	67	60
Coal Village	0	26	0	24	29	32	57	55	50	76	29	61
Serviceville	0	29	0	57	50	44	46	60	17	29	17	56
Rural farm population of three townships	0	19*	0	25*	0	83*	29	67*	50	75*	60	17*

| | FOUR OR MORE | | | | | | N = | | | | | |
| | Protestant | | Catholic | | None | | Protestant | | Catholic | | None | |
Area	White-Collar	Blue-Collar	White-Collar	Blue-Collar	White-Collar	Blue-Collar	White-Collar	Blue-Collar	White-Collar	Blue-Collar	White-Collar	Blue-Collar
Maizeville	59	16	19	8	29	3	169	124	21	13	17	67
East Town	58	11	27	7	0	3	26	55	37	182	3	65
Coal Village	44	19	50	0	43	7	23	42	14	33	7	28
Serviceville	54	10	84	14	33	0	28	48	6	14	6	32
Elm Center	50	8	0	0	0	0	4	24	0	5	0	9
Rural farm population of three townships	71	15*	50	0*	40	0*	7	27*	4	4*	5	18*

* Farmers excluded.

ville findings. When the data for white-collar Protestants were analyzed, it was found that there was no statistically significant variation for them by geographical area.

Statistically significant variations among white-collar Protestants and Catholics were found in the dominantly Protestant county seat town of Maizeville, but not in any of the other areas. Persons of blue-collar status dominated those who belong to no voluntary associations or to a few.[12]

The status-selective character of membership in voluntary associations is also apparent in Table 20. Because of the larger number of cases, the Maizeville data were most interesting and revealing. Although there were too few cases to treat each of the Protestant churches separately, the evidence available strongly suggests the status-selective character of membership in voluntary associations in Maizeville within the same church groups.

Summary of Church Participation Pattern Findings—The salient findings of this section of study may be summarized as follows:

1. The effects of social status upon church membership, type of church membership, and frequency of attendance at extra-church activities were:
   a. More marked in the larger communities, i.e., those with the greatest degree of social differentiation.
   b. More marked among Protestants than among Catholics.
2. There were more nuclear members among members of Continental European origin churches than among members of Anglo-American origin churches for both social groups.
3. Catholics had more nuclear members than Protestants in almost all areas studied for both social groups.
4. Of the two service center communities in the study, the one with the greatest number of churches had most nuclear blue-collar members although there was no statistical evidence of more nuclear white-collar members in the village with the most churches.

---

12. Labor unions, although often a union shop exists, were counted as voluntary associations. Data for East Town, particularly, and Maizeville to a lesser degree, were affected by this fact.

Table 20. Membership in Voluntary Associations for Protestants by Denomination and Social Status for Geographical Areas in Per Cent

Church	NONE			ONE TO THREE			FOUR OR MORE			N =		
	All Members	White-Collar	Blue-Collar	All Members	White-Collar	Blue-Collar	All Members	White-Collar	Blue-Collar	All Members	White-Collar	Blue-Collar
					MAIZEVILLE							
Baptist	51	*	57	42	*	38	7	*	5	55	8	21
Christian	38	*	38	50	*	38	13	*	25	32	3	8
Congregational	25	11	33	39	30	67	35	60	0	84	37	9
Lutheran, Augustana	26	0	25	58	64	50	17	36	25	66	11	16
Lutheran, United	21	6	19	54	28	57	25	67	24	85	18	21
Methodist	26	3	50	45	35	35	29	63	14	148	40	34
Mission Covenant	15	4	13	57	35	75	29	61	13	62	23	8
Presbyterian	10	3	14	42	31	57	48	66	29	60	29	7
					EAST TOWN							
Congregational	22	0	29	55	38	56	23	63	15	105	24	34
					COAL VILLAGE							
Congregational	20	0	32	49	55	47	31	46	21	61	11	19
Methodist	29	0	0	68	100	92	4	0	8	56	7	12
					SERVICEVILLE							
Baptist	46	*	43	40	*	36	14	*	21	35	*	14
Episcopal	18	*	*	50	*	*	32	*	*	22	*	*
Mennonite, General Conference	30	*	*	70	*	*	0	*	*	10	*	*
Mennonite, Old	0	*	*	83	*	*	17	*	*	12	*	*
Methodist	14	0	23	54	54	62	32	46	15	50	13	13
Pentecostal	0	*	13	100	*	*	0	*	*	7	*	*
					ELM CENTER							
Congregational	20	0	13	70	33	81	10	67	6	40	3	16

* Too few cases for analysis.

5. Membership in voluntary associations was status selective. No significant variation in membership in voluntary associations was noted among white collar Protestants by geographical area, although white collar Protestants in the dominantly Protestant county seat town had more memberships than the comparable Catholic group.

Church Attendance

Reasons for Church Attendance—Each of the interviewees was asked, "When you attend church, what are the main reasons that prompt you to go?" Each of the respondents was given the opportunity to answer the question as he saw fit. In the event of no response, the interviewer probed further.

The basic patterns of the responses were divided into two categories that have been termed "internal" and "external." Although the validity of the decision may be debated, the data did suggest this type of ordering. Further, the logically exhaustive character of the classification enhances its usefulness.

The "internal" responses referred to those in which the respondent cited some aspect of the worship service. Although the implicit inter-relatedness of elements classified as internal may limit their usefulness, the responses were further divided into three kinds. The first type of internal response was that in which the respondent expressed a duty or obligation to attend church. The element of worship was explicitly cited in these responses. This type of response could be considered "objective" in the sense that the respondent was responding to a form or experience eliciting attendance as a duty or obligation.

The following response from a middle-aged Catholic man who was a service worker illustrates the type: "Why does anybody go to church? To worship the Lord."

The second type of internal response was classified as "subjective." The respondent explained that he derived some psychological benefit from the service. Often, the response was couched in terms such as the following from a middle-aged, middle-class Methodist man: "Oh, I don't know why I attend church. You might say it is just because I feel better when I go. It kinda makes me feel good."

Or again, an older lower-middle class Baptist woman responded:

"It gives me peace of mind. I feel relieved when I go to church." It may be that these types of responses were vestigial remains of the classical Christian motifs of repentence and forgiveness.[13]

The third type in this classification was called a "mixed" type in which it was not possible to decide on the "objective" or "subjective" character of the response. Here is an example of this type of response. The respondent was a young, lower-class Lutheran woman: "Well, I don't know. I kinda want to go. You should and you want to. That's all I can say."

The second major type of classification that was employed was called "sociological" or "external." Persons who reported that they attended from custom or habit represented one of the categories employed here. The second category was friendship. Persons reported they went because they enjoyed the fellowship and liked to see their friends.

Here is an example of the kind of response which was classified in the habit or tradition category. The respondent was a middle-aged Presbyterian shop-owner: "Well, I really don't know. I never gave it much thought. We've always gone and that's about all I can say."

This response from an elderly United Lutheran woman was classified in friendship or fellowship category: "For fellowship.

---

13. In light of the lack of comparable studies in earlier times, the authors are not inclined to say that church members in this epoch have a less vivid sense of the classical notions of sin, repentence, and forgiveness than was the case in earlier epochs. Written documents and historical judgments are of relatively little value in aiding the assessment of such conditions. The written document almost always is written by a person who is deeply involved in the Christian tradition and who is superior in intelligence and sensitivity to the majority of the people. It is indisputable, however, that the root assumptions which inform the writings of the literati of our epoch are significantly less informed by the Christian heritage than the literati of other epochs of Western culture. Such widespread and subtle shifts are very difficult to assess by the kind of research tools employed in this study. An adequate treatment would demand a work of a somewhat different character than the present one.

No doubt about it. Course, I know a person ought to go for other reasons; but to be real honest with you, the main reason I go is to see my friends that I haven't seen all week."

Obviously, not all the responses were the relatively pure types reported here. In the event that a respondent gave two or more reasons for church attendance, they were all coded and reported in the analysis.

The difficulty that an investigator confronts in attempting to penetrate the depth of religious experience is clearly evident in the process of coding the responses. It is not at all evident that a respondent can verbalize the inner feelings prompting him to attend divine services or express the meaning that he derives from them. Of primary concern in this analysis are the differential responses offered. Hence, the efficacy of various patterns of service and ecclesiastical organization, as well as the theological undergirding for the pattern and organization, can in part be assessed from these responses despite their limitations. However, the authors categorically reject the notion that the innermost meaning of religious experience can be discerned through the type of question here employed.

The Findings—The findings are summarized in Tables 21-25. Probably the most significant single finding was the relatively minor variation in motivation for church attendance between broad membership groupings (see Table 21). Although somewhat more Protestants than Catholics cited subjective internal reasons for church attendance in all of the areas except Maizeville, most variations between groups were not large. The rural sample revealed a much higher percentage of responses in the category of objective psychological reasons, i.e., that it was one's duty or obligation to attend worship services. Later data which illustrate the cognitive weakness of the responses of this group suggest that these responses were largely tradition-oriented.

Table 22 reveals the variations among the several churches in Maizeville. Again, the most striking thing about these responses was the modest intra-Protestant and inter-Catholic-Protestant variations. With the exception of the Mission Covenant group, which showed a significant deviation on many of the phenomena examined in this study, there were not wide variations between the various denominations.

Table 21.   *Reasons for Church Attendance by Broad Membership Groups and Residential Areas*

REASONS CITED

Church Membership of Respondent	N =	INTERNAL			EXTERNAL		All Others and Don't Know[a]
		Objective	Mixed[a]	Subjective	Tradition	Fellowship[a]	
			MAIZEVILLE				
Catholic[b]	52	52	8	35	29	8	6
Protestant	490	48	12	34	28	15	8
None[c]	111	27	10	20	13	14	16
			EAST TOWN				
Catholic	100	36	3	22	30	2	18
Protestant	82	38	12	34	9	7	17
None[c]	49	20	10	8	8	4	50
			SERVICEVILLE				
Catholic[b]	23	9	13	30	17	0	30
Protestant	133	35	14	38	19	12	12
None[c]	31	16	7	10	19	6	42
			OPEN COUNTRY				
Catholic[b]	14	86	0	7	14	14	14
Protestant	62	73	8	34	13	18	11
None[c]	31	29	13	19	0	13	26

$$\chi^2 = 32.72 \qquad p < .01 \qquad C = .16$$

a. Columns combined in chi square analysis.
b. Rows combined in chi square analysis.
c. Rows excluded in chi square analysis.

Table 22.   *Reasons for Church Attendance for Selected Denominations, Maizeville, in Per Cent*

REASONS CITED

Church Membership of Respondent	N =	INTERNAL			EXTERNAL		All Others and Don't Know[a]
		Objective	Mixed[a]	Subjective	Tradition	Fellowship[a]	
Baptist	44	55	14	25	23	25	7
Catholic	52	52	8	35	29	8	6
Christian[b]	20	35	5	40	40	5	20
Congregational	73	47	12	43	26	16	7
Lutheran, Augustana	42	36	14	36	46	12	10
Lutheran, United	81	46	20	33	21	9	7
Methodist	82	46	11	42	18	17	4
Mission Covenant	54	61	9	28	37	20	6
Presbyterian	44	46	3	32	36	16	14
None[b]	111	27	10	20	13	14	16

$$\chi^2 = 9.02 \qquad p < .98$$

a. Columns combined in chi square analysis.
b. Rows combined in chi square analysis.

A hypothesis had been entertained that those church groups which emphasized liturgical patterns and formal worship services would have significantly more people indicating worship as their reason for attending church. In the tabulation presented here, one would have expected a higher proportion of responses in the first category, the objective internal response, for churches emphasizing liturgical patterns. The Catholic-Protestant comparisons in Table 21 and the detailed denominational analysis in Table 22 do not support this hypothesis, and it has been rejected. There was no evidence that the Catholic or Lutheran traditions—the two traditions included in our sample which laid the greatest emphasis on liturgical worship patterns—did, in fact, encourage a more significant recognition of the nature and purpose of the worship service.

While apologists for these two traditions probably would be inclined to question the adequacy of this question for probing the depths of the worship experience, the authors would suggest that there seems to be no empirical justification for claims that particular forms of worship serve to produce more devout laymen. As a matter of fact, the varying forms of worship employed seemed to have negligible effect on motivation to become such. The one qualification to this observation is that almost all the churches studied had a reasonably formal worship pattern if contrasted with a group of Pentecostal churches. These findings might vary if a sufficient sample of this group had been drawn from a radically different sustaining environment. However, it should be noted that the responses for Pentecostal groups in Maizeville did not vary significantly from responses for the total group.

In order to discern whether the rather gross classifications employed in Tables 21 and 22 might obscure differences actually extant between subgroups in the various traditions, further types of analyses were made.

Further analysis of modal and nuclear respondents of above average intellectual functioning has been undertaken. These church members have been divided into four major subgroupings which we have called the perfectionist wing of the Calvinist tradition, the transforming wing of the Calvinist tradition, the Lutherans, and the Catholics. While the last two categories are self evident, some explanation of the first two groupings is necessary.[14]

Because the number of cases in the sample was insufficient to permit detailed statistical analysis of each of the churches in the broad Calvinist heritage, members of several churches were grouped together. The Baptist, Christian, and Mission Covenant churches were grouped under the general heading of the perfectionist wing of the Calvinist tradition, whereas the Congregationalists, Methodists, and Presbyterians were grouped under the transforming wing of the Calvinist tradition.[15]

The second grouping employs the same church membership categories but examines the data for members of average intellectual functioning by type of church membership.

The reasons for the selection of these factors is readily explicable. Type of church membership, characterized in this study by frequency of attendance at Sunday morning worship services, is an index of involvement in church life, while the ability to appropriate cognitive forms and to internalize emotive feelings is related to intellectual functioning. Thus, it seemed reasonable to suppose that persons of above average intellectual functioning who were most involved in church activities ought to reflect significant differences in how they internalize their heritage, assuming that such differences do, in fact, exist.

An examination of Table 23 reveals no significant variations between the members of the four major traditions categorized by reasons cited for church attendance. Further, a comparison with Table 24, which examines the same categories for persons of average intellectual functioning, reveals only very modest differences between the above average and average intellectual groups on this question. When the data were examined by type of church membership (see Table 25), a somewhat higher proportion of nuclear members of average intellectual functioning cited objective reasons for church attendance. With the exception

---

14. See also pp. 198ff.

15. The rigorous historical accuracy of these classifications is obviously not defensible. It is our intent here to provide groupings that seem consistent with the major contemporary emphases in the denominations cited. Other facets of the rationale for and implications of these classifications are considered in the chapter "Some Psychological Correlates of Religious Affiliation."

Table 23. Reasons for Church Attendance for Selected Membership Groups of Nuclear and Modal Members of Above Average Intellectual Ability, Maizeville, in Per Cent

| Church Membership of Respondent | N = | INTERNAL | | | EXTERNAL | | All Others and Don't Know[a] |
		Objective	Mixed[a]	Subjective	Tradition[a]	Fellowship[a]	
Perfectionist Wing Calvinist Tradition	40	35	2	28	28	7	0
Transforming Wing Calvinist Tradition	75	31	4	32	16	15	2
Lutheran[b]	20	35	5	35	15	10	0
Catholic[b]	17	41	6	29	6	18	0
Total	152	34	4	31	18	12	1

$$\chi^2 = 1.06 \qquad .95 < p < .90$$

a. Columns combined in chi square analysis.
b. Rows combined in chi square analysis.

Table 24. Reasons for Church Attendance for Selected Membership Groups of Nuclear and Modal Members of Average Intellectual Ability, Maizeville, in Per Cent

| Church Membership of Respondent | N = | INTERNAL | | | EXTERNAL | | All Others and Don't Know[a] |
		Objective	Mixed[a]	Subjective	Tradition[a]	Fellowship[a]	
Perfectionist Wing Calvinist Tradition	62	35	10	21	24	8	2
Transforming Wing Calvinist Tradition	75	35	2	35	11	15	2
Lutheran[b]	48	36	15	31	8	8	2
Catholic[b]	45	45	4	20	18	4	9
Total	230	37	7	27	15	10	4

$$\chi^2 = 6.07 \qquad .10 < p < .20$$

a. Columns combined in chi square analysis.
b. Rows combined in chi square analysis.

of the persons classified as church members who reported that they never attended, most variations were quite modest. The data for this last group must be treated with considerable reserve because of the very small number of cases in the cell.

In summary, the data did not reveal any striking variations in reasons cited for church attendance for any of the groups on which detailed analysis has been undertaken.

Although they are not presented in tabular form here, analysis was undertaken of responses by sex for broad membership groups in Maizeville, responses by intellectual ability for the 30-64 age group in Maizeville, and responses by social status for the 30-64 age group in Maizeville.

There was not much difference in the responses either between sexes or between Protestants and Catholics. As one would expect, the non-church members had uniformly lower percentage responses than either Catholics or Protestants. The factors responsible for this phenomena were two-fold. First, there was a greater disinterest in the institutional church in this group; second, the status and intellectual ability selectivity involved in the non-church group produced a lower degree of articulation among this group of respondents.

There was a direct relationship between the intellectual ability of the interviewee and the number of responses that were cited, although the rank order of the responses remain almost the same for each of the intellectual ability groupings. These data

Table 25. Reasons for Church Attendance by Type of Church Membership for Persons of Average Intellectual Ability, Maizeville, in Per Cent

Type of Church Membership of Respondent	N =	REASONS CITED					All Others and Don't Know[a]
		INTERNAL			EXTERNAL		
		Objective	Mixed[a]	Subjective	Tradition[a]	Fellowship[a]	
Nuclear	138	41	5	27	16	8	3
Modal	92	32	11	27	14	12	4
Marginal[b]	75	32	13	19	13	10	13
Dormant[b]	22	18	5	32	18	9	18
Total	327	35	9	25	15	9	7

$$\chi^2 = 14.26 \qquad .05 < p < .10$$

a. Columns combined in chi square analysis.
b. Rows combined in chi square analysis.

suggest that the pattern of reasons cited for church attendance was relatively constant although the level and complexity of feelings increased with an increase in intellectual ability. The variations in the reasons cited for church attendance by social status for the 30-64 age group in Maizeville were not significant.

Lack of Church Attendance

Reasons for Lack of Church Attendance—There was no widespread alienation from the churches in any group in the sample. The reasons that most persons offered for failure to attend church services were external factors such as illness, trips, or guests, or the internal factor of indifference. It should be noted, however, that indifference did not mean hostility. Most of those in the sample who offered reasons of this kind prefaced them with the observation that they knew they ought to be in church and that they had nothing against the church. Here is the response of a young working-class man who had not belonged to a church but who had preference for the Methodist Church: "I ain't got nuthin' agin' the church. I know I ought to go, but somehow, after workin' all week I kinda like to take it easy around the house on Sunday."

The Findings—The responses for broad membership groups are summarized in Table 26 by geographical area. It should be observed that there were no wide variations between Catholic and Protestants in most geographical areas. Among the group of non-church members, about half attributed their nonattendance at church services to lack of interest. Even among this group, however, only about one person in every ten interviewed expressed overt hostility toward some facet of church activity.

The reasons for nonattendance at church services for selected denominations in Maizeville are shown in Table 27. The data for Protestants disclosed some very interesting interdenominational differences in reasons cited for lack of attendance at church services. Especially noteworthy was the very low percentage of members of the Augustana Lutheran, Baptist, and Mission Covenant churches that reported internal reasons for failure to attend church services. Conversely, the same group gave sig-

Table 26. **Reasons for Nonattendance at Church Services by Broad Membership Groups and Residential Areas in Per Cent**

Church Membership of Respondent	N =	REASONS CITED			Don't Know[a]
		EXTERNAL		INTERNAL	
		Illness, Travel, Company, etc.	Lack of Interest	Hostility Toward Some Aspect of Church[a]	
MAIZEVILLE					
Catholic[b]	52	79	27	4	8
Protestant	478	99	24	8	6
None	103	57	51	13	8
EAST TOWN					
Catholic	100	87	26	3	8
Protestant	82	90	20	4	10
None	47	36	53	11	19
SERVICEVILLE					
Catholic[b]	18	72	22	17	11
Protestant	122	88	14	2	3
None[c]	27	56	48	11	7
OPEN COUNTRY					
Catholic[b]	13	100	0	8	15
Protestant	65	99	28	3	5
None[c]	28	36	57	10	4

$$\chi^2 = 124.67 \qquad p < .01 \qquad C = .28$$

a. Columns combined in chi square analysis.
b. Rows combined in chi square analysis.
c. Rows combined in chi square analysis.

Table 27. **Reasons for Nonattendance at Church Services for Selected Denominations, Maizeville, in Per Cent**

Church Membership of Respondent	N =	REASONS CITED			Don't Know[a]
		EXTERNAL		INTERNAL	
		Illness, Travel, Company, etc.	Lack of Interest	Hostility Toward Some Aspect of Church[a]	
Baptist	44	114	9	5	9
Catholic	52	79	27	4	8
Christian[b]	20	80	25	15	5
Conregational	65	83	32	15	9
Lutheran, Augustana	42	119	9	7	0
Lutheran, United	79	92	29	5	6
Methodist	81	96	37	10	6
Mission Covenant	54	133	9	4	2
Presbyterian	44	95	21	7	7
None[b]	103	57	51	13	8

$$\chi^2 = 41.02 \qquad p < .01 \qquad C = .25$$

a. Columns combined in chi square analysis.
b. Rows excluded in chi square analysis.

nificantly higher responses of external reasons for failure to attend church services. It should be noted that all of these groups exhibited some cultural, status and/or ethnic isolation from the community. These factors seem to be more significant in affecting attitudes toward church attendance than the type of worship service practiced. In spite of the wide difference in form of services, the Baptists and the Augustana Lutheran groups had very similar responses to this question.

This problem of cultural, status, and ethnic isolation poses significant questions for Protestantism. As data so far exhibited and additional data to be presented will show, the most vigorous institutional participation and loyalty seemed to be displayed by these culturally isolated groups. These groups did not possess cognitive structures to understand, to explicate, and to relate the Christian faith to culture in any greater degree than other groups. In fact, some of the data that will be presented suggest an even greater degree of cognitive impoverishment for these groups than for some of the other church groupings.

The responses by intellectual ability for the 30-64 age group in Maizeville are shown in Table 28. In general, these findings

Table 28. Reasons for Nonattendance at Church Services by Intellectual Ability for the 30-64 Age Group, Maizeville, in Per Cent

		REASONS CITED			
		EXTERNAL	INTERNAL		
Intellectual Ability of Respondent	N =	Illness, Travel, Company, etc.	Lack of Interest*	Hostility Toward Some Aspect of Church*	Don't Know
Below average	74	85	28	4	5
Average	225	82	36	16	8
Above average	117	93	31	9	9

$$\chi^2 = 4.05 \qquad .30 < p < .50$$

* Columns combined in chi square analysis.

were negative; the evidence did not suggest that there were marked differences in reasons for lack of church attendance by intellectual ability. As a matter of fact, the findings suggested rather close agreement. About one-third of the respondents reported that they were not interested, i.e., preferred to engage in alternative types of activity to church attendance.

There was no evidence to suggest that the type of program undertaken had differential appeal for different levels of intellectual ability. The data did not suggest that persons of above average intellectual ability are alienated from the church in large numbers. On the contrary, as Table 28 shows, only nine per cent of the respondents of above average intellectual ability cited hostility toward some aspect of the church or church program as a reason for failure to attend.

Similarly, there was no evidence to suggest differential status alienation from the church, as Table 29 indicates. The white-

Table 29. *Reasons for Nonattendance at Church Services by Social Status for the 30-64 Age Group, Maizeville, in Per Cent*

Social Status	N =	REASONS CITED EXTERNAL Illness, Travel, Company, etc.	INTERNAL Lack of Interest*	Hostility Toward Some Aspect of Church*	Don't Know
Blue-collar	119	89	32	4	12
Mixed	147	78	35	13	8
White-collar	149	91	31	15	5

$$\chi^2 = 7.99 \qquad .05 < p < .10$$

* Columns combined in chi square analysis.

collar group had about three times as many respondents critical of some aspect of the churches than had the blue-collar group, although responses in this area were quite low for all the status groupings.

Although the data are not presented here, it can be noted that males indicated significantly higher lack of interest among Protestants, Catholics, and non-church members than females. Not surprisingly, the non-church group had the highest proportion of respondents who indicated that they were not interested in church activities. There was no sex differential with respect to hostility toward some aspect of the church or church program.

Summary of Church Attendance Findings—Most of the findings dealing with reasons for church attendance were negative. Only very modest intra-Protestant and interfaith differentials in reasons cited for church attendance were discernible. Similarly, the variations in reasons cited for church nonattendance were also very modest.

There was no evidence to suggest that the more elaborate liturgical patterns of worship, manifest in the Catholic and Lutheran traditions in Corn County, encouraged a more significant recognition of the nature and purpose of a worship service. Similarly, an examination of the data by type of church membership and broad historical tradition, by sex, and by social status revealed no positive findings.

An examination of the data on the reasons the interviewees gave for not attending church indicated that there was no widespread disaffection from the church among any group for which analysis was undertaken. Casual indifference rather than any kind of militant opposition seems the best explanation for nonparticipation, although participation was status conditioned, as the data in previous sections of this chapter have indicated.

Geographically, the rural sample had a higher proportion of "objective" responses for church attendance, but the data on the cognitive weakness of the respondents in this geographical area suggests that these responses were probably tradition oriented.

There was a direct relationship between the intellectual ability of the interviewee and the number of responses cited for church attendance, but the rank order of the responses remained almost the same for each of the intellectual groupings. This finding would suggest that a common pattern of reasons for church attendance is manifest, although the level and complexity of the feelings involved increases with an increase in intellectual ability.

Feelings and Attitudes Toward Other Religious Institutions

Introduction—The denominational pattern of institutional church life in the United States has a history extending back to early European settlement. The waves of immigrants that periodically came across the Atlantic brought with them their own religious institutions and customs. The development of numerous religious traditions related to these migrations, coupled with the emergence of indigenous religious groupings in this nation, has resulted in the development of a considerable number of Protestant religious groups, many of which were represented by churches in the area included in this study.[16]

It has been hypothesized by one writer[17] that in contemporary America one's social identity is, in part, determined by his relation to one of the three major religious traditions extant in the United States. Historically both Protestanism and Judaism are very complex entities within themselves. They are composed of varying traditions with different emphases and beliefs. While the number of Jews included in the sample drawn in this study was too small to treat statistically, the county seat town did provide an opportunity to explore the sense of commonality that might be manifested among the existing Protestant bodies, and the data for the entire study permitted some Roman Catholic-Protestant comparisons.

The Schema Employed in the Analysis—The problem of devising a satisfactory instrument to explore this whole area of inter- and intra-faith attitudes was a difficult one. It was decided that the question be raised as to which religious institution the respondents thought was most like their own and which one was least like their own. From the polarities that emerged some notion of the way in which the respondents related themselves to the other religious institutions in the community might be inferred. While such a procedure does not permit the development of highly discriminated groupings, it does illumine the feeling tones extant among members of the community studied.

The distinctions and commonalities that emerged as the respondents attempted to describe the ways in which churches were similar to or different from their own were grouped into five classifications. Two of these classifications referred to the service of worship, one referred to the qualities or characteristics of the group, and one was a catch-all category including all other efforts at substantive responses. The final classification employed was "Don't Know." The two subclasses under service of worship were responses referring to the content and to the form of the worship service. As has been done for most of the other responses, multiple responses were given multiple coding.

16. See chapter one for a brief discussion of the impact of these migrations upon Corn County.

17. See Will Herberg, *Protestant, Catholic, Jew.* (Doubleday, 1956).

This response from a middle-aged Lutheran woman who had cited the Lutheran church of another synod as most like her own illustrates the type of response which referred to both the form and content of the worship service: "Well, sir, I think that their service is pretty much like ours. I went there once, and it seemed like ours. 'Course, I think they believe pretty much like we do, too."

This response from a Presbyterian proprietor who had cited the Congregational church as most like his own illustrates all three categories: "We meet with them [Congregational parishioners] during the summer. Our services are quite similar though we're a bit more formal, you might say. I think our beliefs are about the same. Then, too, the people are pretty much alike. You know, they used to be one church here."

This response from the Methodist wife of a truck driver illustrates the type of response coded as one citing a similar form of worship: "Well, they [the Presbyterians] have about the same service as we do. [Interviewer: anything else?] No, guess that's about it—the same kind of service."

The Findings—*Churches most like one's own*—Table 30 shows the patterning of responses to the question "What church do you think is most like your own?" for Maizeville for selected denominations. Several significant factors deserve observation.

First, there was an extremely sharp Protestant-Catholic cleavage. In Maizeville only seven Protestant church members (five of them United Lutheran) out of a total of 515 reported that the Catholic church was most like their own. Catholics in Maizeville felt that the Lutheran and Episcopal churches were most like their own. Significantly, when Catholics were asked why the church they named was most like their own, 37 per cent responded that the church selected had a similar form of worship. Lutherans also cited this factor relatively frequently, as Table 31 reveals.[18]

---

18. A high proportion of the responses are indicated "other" in Table 31. The reason for this phenomenon is that this category includes responses which indicated that there was little or no distinction between the church of which the respondent was a member and the church cited by the respondent as most like his own.

Table 30. Church Most Like Own for Selected Denominations, Maizeville, in Per Cent

Church Membership of Respondent	N =	CHURCH CITED AS MOST LIKE RESPONDENT'S										
		Baptist	Catholic	Christian	Congregational	Lutheran, Augustana	Lutheran, United	Methodist	Mission Covenant	Presbyterian	Other	Don't Know
Baptist	47	4	0	21	4	4	4	13	9	2	17	21
Catholic	56	2	0	0	0	9	21	0	2	0	45	21
Christian	22	41	0	9	9	0	0	23	5	5	0	9
Congregational	75	5	1	5	7	1	0	13	0	48	7	16
Lutheran, Augustana	42	0	0	0	0	2	62	2	14	2	0	17
Lutheran, United	82	2	6	0	1	49	4	13	2	6	7	9
Methodist	91	4	0	3	29	3	8	4	8	21	4	15
Mission Covenant	58	12	0	2	5	28	12	19	0	7	3	12
Presbyterian	46	0	0	0	57	4	4	17	0	4	7	7

Table 31. Reasons Church Is Most Like Own for Selected Denominations,
           Maizeville, in Per Cent

| Church Membership of Respondent | N = | SERVICE OF WORSHIP | | Charac- teristics of Group | Other | Don't Know |
		Similar Creed	Similar Form of Worship			
Baptist	44	16	25	14	39	23
Catholic	52	19	37	6	35	33
Christian*	20	15	25	20	50	5
Congregational	73	19	32	29	25	22
Lutheran, Augustana	42	50	38	12	17	12
Lutheran, United	81	25	42	20	21	15
Methodist	82	15	32	21	28	20
Mission Covenant	54	30	26	35	17	15
Presbyterian	44	9	18	48	39	16
None*	111	8	13	21	19	49

$$\chi^2 = 54.98 \qquad p < .01 \qquad C = .29$$

* Rows excluded in chi square analysis.

Second, feelings of likeness were usually reciprocal and these feelings were related to social status. For example, the most frequently cited church by Baptists was the Christian church (21 per cent), while the most frequently cited church by Christians was the Baptist church (41 per cent). Similarly, each of the Lutheran churches was cited most frequently by the members of the other. The Congregationalists felt that the Presbyterian church was most like their own and vice versa.

An interesting situation emerged among the Methodist respondents. Respondents from this church cited the Congregationalists most frequently (29 per cent) and the Presbyterians second most frequently (20 per cent). These data are particularly interesting when one considers the relative status structure of the membership of these churches. The data presented earlier indicated that the Presbyterian and Congregational churches had the highest proportion of people in the "white-collar" group that is employed in this analysis as a measure of social status. The Methodists were somewhat lower; hence, in a society dominated by upwardly mobile values it could be suggested that the Methodists tend to look toward the Presbyterian and Congregational churches rather than toward the Baptist, Christian, or other

Anglo-American origin churches that might be considered by Methodists if they were differentiating primarily on the basis of belief or form of worship.

A further observation should be made about Table 31, which summarizes the reasons why the interviewee cited a given church as most like his own. Most interviewees possessed only a minimum of knowledge about churches other than their own. Of the 1,200 people interviewed in Corn County, fewer than ten displayed any penetrating understanding of other religious institutions. This generalized ignorance could, under certain circumstances, fan the fires of bigotry. Two other factors should be noted, however, which might counteract potential bigotry as a consequence of such ignorance. First, friendship patterns in Corn County tended to transcend religious (but not status) lines. Second, most people seemed to be committed to a position of tolerance, if not indifference, toward other churches which would suggest that the general lack of perceptivity discerned is probably not too crucial in the present epoch. It is clear, however, that deep seated differences between Protestant and Catholic churches were experienced at the feeling-tone level and that in situations where religious issues were explicitly involved (such as in the 1960 United States presidential campaign or the controversy about public aid to parochial schools), intense feelings may be expected to develop.

Churches least like one's own—The interviewees were all asked the question "What church in town do you think is least like your own?" Table 32 indicates the distribution of churches which respondents said were least like their own for selected groupings by geographical area. The most significant finding was the way in which polar groups were most frequently cited by most respondents. Non-Pentecostal Protestants almost always cited either Pentecostal-type churches or the Catholic church.

The responses of East Town Protestants to this query were illuminating. Although there were four Roman Catholic churches in East Town, only 20 per cent of non-Catholic respondents answering "Catholic" cited a specific Roman Catholic church. The churches were simply categorized as a group with no further differentiation undertaken by the respondents. Such categorical thinking seemed to characterize most respondents. Because of the character of Pentecostal expressive behavior, it was relatively easy for most respondents to characterize small Pentecostal groups as least like their own. However, as noted earlier, very few of the respondents possessed the kind of detailed understanding necessary for finer discriminations.

The very high percentage of "Don't Know" responses among Roman Catholics in all geographical areas points up both the relative isolation and the categorical thinking of many members

Table 32.　Church Least Like Own by Selected Denominational Groupings and Residential Areas in Per Cent

Church Membership of Respondent	N =	Catholic	Pentecostal-type Protestant	All other Protestant	Don't Know
			MAIZEVILLE		
Baptist	47	57	9	21	13
Catholic	55	0	29	24	47
Christian[a]	21	71	5	19	5
Congregational	78	63	8	23	6
Lutheran, Augustana	42	38	31	7	24
Lutheran, United	84	33	23	18	26
Methodist	83	69	8	10	13
Mission Covenant	56	62	4	14	20
Presbyterian	44	63	16	5	16
			EAST TOWN		
Catholic	102	16	31	29	24
Congregational	52	73	15	6	6
Other Protestant except Pentecostal	33	36	27	21	16
			SERVICEVILLE		
Catholic[b]	23	0	44	12	44
Protestant except Pentecostal[c]	158	51	22	11	16
			OPEN COUNTRY		
Catholic[b]	14	0	21	36	43
Protestant except Pentecostal[c]	65	72	15	5	8

Maizeville:	$\chi^2 = 120.83$	$p < .01$	$C = .48$
East Town:	$\chi^2 = 58.14$	$p < .01$	$C = .49$
Serviceville and Open Country:	$\chi^2 = 44.75$	$p < .01$	$C = .38$

a. Row excluded in chi square analysis.
b. Rows combined in chi square analysis.
c. Rows combined in chi square analysis.

of that faith. Catholics tended to group all non-Catholics together and to undertake no further discrimination between them. This relative isolation was also evidenced by the fact that 16 per cent of the Catholics in East Town cited one of the other Catholic nationality parishes as the church least like their own. Respondents were also asked why the church cited was least like their own church. Although they are not reproduced here, it should be noted that the responses were vague and general. As was true for most other responses, differences in practice or ritual were cited much more frequently than were differences in belief. However, respondents again generally were in no position to offer penetrating reasons for the differences between churches. For example, here is the response of a young Baptist man of lower-middle status and average intelligence: "Well, I think the Catholics are least like us because they don't conduct their services anything like we do, I don't think."

Again, here is the response of a middle-aged East Town Catholic woman of average intelligence whose husband was the proprietor of a small store: "I really don't know anything about the other churches. We just don't talk about things like that here."

And an elderly Congregational woman of middle status and average intelligence noted simply: "The Catholics. They are worlds apart from ours."

These findings are very important, for they underscore the noncognitive, emotive feeling-tone character of the distinctions between churches which most church members displayed. While there is increasing likelihood of rapproachement between several of the Protestant groupings, it is most unlikely that inter-faith conversations between Protestant and Catholic theologians, evident in some quarters at the present time, will in the near future materially alter the deep cleavages between Protestant and Catholic laymen, so evident in these data. These cleavages are based on emotive feelings and not upon rational considerations.

An examination of the data by frequency of church attendance and by intellectual functioning did not reveal any marked variations from the patterns revealed in Table 32. Further, a comparison of the data for nuclear and modal members of av-

erage and of above average intellectual functioning revealed
only most minor variations in responses.

Feelings and Attitudes Toward Own Church

Introduction—Although feelings and sentiments expressed by
respondents toward other religious institutions are a useful tool
for assessing inter-group feelings about the relative importance
of the various dimensions of institutional religious life, it was
deemed desirable to supplement such findings with data focusing directly on the feelings and sentiments reflected toward the
respondent's own church. Such data are also helpful in assessing
dimensions of strength and weakness in local church programs.

Consequently, respondents were asked to indicate those things
which they particularly liked about their own church and those
things which they disliked. In the latter case, if the respondent
seemed diffident at first, he was told that such items as he might
suggest need not indicate strong disapproval; rather, he should
simply point to those areas in which he felt improvement in the
church or church program could be made.

The Findings—*Things liked most about own church*—The responses to the question, "What things do you like most about
your church?" were divided into seven categories. The first group
of responses included those referring to aspects of the worship
service or other aspects of the church program. The initial intention was to categorize separately those responses referring to the
belief or the doctrine of the church; however, so few cases fell
into this category that it was not employed. In practice it proved
very difficult to separate responses referring obliquely to beliefs
from the responses referring to the fact that the respondent liked
the worship program.

This response from a middle-aged Methodist woman in Serviceville illustrates this first group of responses: "I'd say probably
over-all the worship service. Yeah, that's what I'd say I liked
best."

The second category employed was one in which the quality
of the present minister was cited as the thing which the respondent liked most about his church. The following response

Table 33. Things Liked Most About Own Church by Broad Membership Groups and Residential Areas, in Per Cent

Church Membership of Respondent	N =	Worship and/or Program	Quality of Present Minister or Priest	Character of Some Church Members	ELEMENTS CITED No Outstanding Element[a]	Everything Liked[a]	Other[a]	Don't Know
MAIZEVILLE								
Catholic[b]	52	58	13	8	2	15	38	8
Protestant	490	54	20	32	5	2	25	6
None	111	29	13	21	8	2	11	32
EAST TOWN								
Catholic	102	22	29	29	2	8	24	11
Protestant	83	54	19	23	0	2	18	18
None	49	35	2	10	2	2	6	55
SERVICEVILLE								
Catholic[b]	23	39	9	9	4	4	43	4
Protestant	133	50	17	29	4	0	26	4
None[c]	31	23	16	6	3	0	19	39
OPEN COUNTRY								
Catholic[b]	14	86	14	7	0	0	14	0
Protestant	65	54	26	54	0	0	20	6
None[c]	31	39	16	23	3	0	3	39

$\chi^2 = 386.89$ $p < .01$ $C = .43$

a. Columns combined in chi square analysis.
b. Rows combined in chi square analysis.
c. Rows combined in chi square analysis.

from a middle-aged Methodist woman, the wife of a postal employee in Maizeville, is an example of this type of response: "Right now I'd say the best thing I like about our church is our minister. He's a cracker-jack. He's real friendly and preaches real good sermons."

The third substantive category included responses referring to the personal qualities of some of the members of the church. Most frequently, the respondent cited the fact that the people were always so friendly. Here are the words of a young craftsman who was a member of the United Lutheran Church in Maizeville: "I suppose if I had to pick out one thing I liked most, I'd have to say it is the friendly people that we meet there. 'Course, I've been a member of that church all my life, and it is always good to see my friends on Sunday."

Although they did not provide substantive notions, two other classifications were employed to indicate the type of response that was given to this question. The first case was a rather negative one in which the respondent indicated that he could think of no outstanding qualities or characteristics. The second group included the responses of those interviewees who liked everything about the church. All other substantive responses were included in the "other" classification. The final group included respondents who said they simply didn't know.

The responses to this question by broad membership groups and residential areas are summarized in Table 33. Perhaps the findings of greatest interest were the differentials in the percentage of respondents who cited the character of some church members as the favorite aspect of their church. In Maizeville, Serviceville, and the open country, all dominantly Protestant areas, much higher proportions of Protestants than Catholics cited the character of church members as one of the factors they liked most about their church.

By contrast, in East Town more Catholics cited this quality than did Protestants. The variation in responses seems readily explicable when it is recalled that in Maizeville, Serviceville, and the open country the Catholic church was a geographical parish with only one Catholic church in the area in contrast to East Town where there were four nationality parishes.

In each of the dominantly Protestant areas, members of the

Catholic church had no choice with respect to the church they should attend. Hence, these churches were inclusive by class and by style of life, while in East Town a Catholic could select the Catholic church most congenial to him. Thus, in East Town, the kinds of people that were members of the Catholic church loom as important as the basis for liking one's church as they did for most of the Protestant churches. Under these conditions, social rather than theological factors were important for an individual's choice of membership affiliation.

It may further be noted in Table 33 that the per cent of Catholics in East Town citing some facet of the worship or church program as the thing they liked most about their own church was markedly lower than in any of the other areas. It would seem that this phenomenon was related to the minority status of Roman Catholics in the other areas; apparently this minority status tended to heighten their religious self-consciousness and to dramatize the contrast between their worship pattern and that of other religious groupings.

It had been hypothesized that the well-defined liturgical pattern of the Catholic church, the clear and distinct ecclesiastical structures extant, and the objective character of the office of the priest would condition Catholic responses so that fewer Catholics than Protestants would cite the personality of the current religious leader as one of the things which they liked most about their own church.

While the differentials here were not nearly as great as they were on the character of some church members as a best-liked feature about the church, a similar pattern seemed to emerge. Once again, the personality and the quality of the priest were cited more frequently by Catholics in East Town than by Catholics in any of the other areas. When the Catholic had church membership options available, he was more sensitive to the personal qualities of his religious leader than when his parish membership was defined geographically.

An analysis of the responses for selected denominations in Maizeville is shown in Table 34. It should be noted that very wide and seemingly idiosyncratic variations appeared. It is clear that there was no consistent pattern of response by church polity, type of service, or type of religious emphasis.

Table 34. Things Liked Most About Own Church for Selected Denominations, Maizeville, in Per Cent

				ELEMENTS CITED				
Church Membership of Respondent	N =	Worship and/or Program	Quality of Present Minister or Priest	Character of Some Church Members	No Outstanding Elements[a]	Everything Liked[a]	Other	Don't Know[a]
Baptist	42	40	10	55	7	0	36	5
Catholic	52	58	13	8	2	15	38	8
Christian[b]	20	25	20	65	5	5	20	5
Congregational	73	62	11	26	3	0	23	14
Lutheran, Augustana	42	79	12	2	5	7	17	2
Lutheran, United	81	57	23	31	5	2	19	7
Methodist	82	52	28	29	7	1	17	6
Mission Covenant	54	63	15	28	2	7	13	4
Presbyterian	44	45	36	39	9	0	32	2
None[b]	111	29	13	21	8	2	11	32

$\chi^2 = 75.02$ $p < .01$ $C = .32$

a. Columns combined in chi square analysis.
b. Rows excluded in chi square analysis.

Although they are not reproduced here, an analysis of the responses by broad membership groups and by sex did not reveal wide variations by sex. Generally, males cited fewer factors that they liked most about their own church, but the rank order remained about the same for both sexes.

Further, an examination of the respondents by social status for the 30-64 age group in Maizeville did not reveal significant variations between the three status groupings used in this study.

While slightly below the level of significance, the responses by intellectual ability for the 30-64 age group in Maizeville suggested that the above average group cited the worship or church program more frequently than did any of the other intellectual ability groups. Approximately two-thirds of the respondents of above average intellectual ability indicated that the worship and church program were things they liked most about their own church. Further, the data suggested an increase with intellectual ability in the per cent of respondents citing the character of some church members as one of the things they liked most about their own church. Nineteen per cent of the below average intellectual ability respondents cited this quality, while 29 per cent of the average intellectual ability respondents and 34 per cent of the above average intellectual ability respondents cited the character of some church members as a factor.

Analysis of data for nuclear and modal members of above average and average intellectual ability in Maizeville revealed that for both intellectual ability groups members of the perfectionist wing of the Calvinist tradition cited the quality of church members as one of the things they liked most about their own church significantly more frequently than did any of the other groups. Catholics cited this factor much less frequently. Fifty-seven per cent of the nuclear and modal members of the perfectionist wing of the Calvinist tradition of average intellectual ability cited the quality of church members as one of the aspects they liked most about their church, while only 3 per cent of the comparable Catholic group cited this factor. Forty per cent of the comparable group for the Lutheran tradition and for the transforming wing of the Calvinist tradition cited this factor. Perhaps no single finding in the entire study more dramatically contrasts the social character of the Catholic and Protestant traditions in Maizeville.

An examination of the data for dormant, marginal, modal, and nuclear members of average intellectual ability in Maizeville revealed only modest variations in responses for all items except the quality of church members, where the dormant group cited this factor much less frequently than did any of the other membership types.

In substantiation of the observation made earlier that dormant church members reflected very little hostility toward the institutional churches, it should be noted that 59 per cent of the dormant church members indicated that the worship service or church program was the thing that they liked most about their church; 55 per cent of the marginal group, 45 per cent of the modal group, and 67 per cent of the nuclear group cited this factor.

Similarly, there was only modest variation in frequency of response citing the quality or character of the minister as the aspect members liked most about their church by type of church membership.

Things liked least about own church—The responses to the question "What things do you like least about your own church?" were also divided into seven groups.

The first category included those responses which criticized some aspect of the church program or plant facilities. These responses did not include those that were explicitly critical of the service of worship. So few interviewees gave the latter response that the responses were included with the "other" group.

This response, drawn from the schedule of a Presbyterian, the wife of a proprietor in Maizeville, illustrates the first type: "Well, the thing I think we need most at our church is improvement in the Sunday School facilities. They're pretty bad right now. [Interviewer: "Anything else?"] No, I'm afraid that's about it right now."

The second and third categories, the quality of present minister or priest and character of some church members, respectively, were identical with the categories employed in the analysis of the responses to the preceding question.

The fourth classification included responses that were explicitly critical of some aspect of the belief or doctrine of the church. Almost without exception, the criticisms were non-systematic and focused on rather specific beliefs, doctrines, practices and prohibitions.

This response, drawn from the schedule of an elderly Baptist woman in Maizeville, illustrates the type: "Some of our members try to tell me that Baptists shouldn't go to movies. Maybe they shouldn't go on Sunday, but I can't see anything wrong with going to the show now and then."

The fifth group included those responses of persons who affirmed, even after considerable probing, that they were unable to think of anything they did not like about their church. This response from the wife of a Catholic schoolteacher in East Town illustrates the type: "I like everything about our church. There isn't a thing that they could do to improve it. [Interviewer: "You can't think of anything you don't like or anything that might be done to improve your church?"] No, I just don't have any criticisms about it at all."

The sixth group included all other substantive responses, while the final group included "Don't Know" responses.

The responses by broad membership groups and residential areas are indicated in Table 35. Three patterns that emerged from the examination of data in this table deserve observation.

First, it should be noted that a very significant proportion of the respondents in all geographical areas and among both Catholics and Protestants cited no negative elements. Further, Catholics in all geographical areas cited fewer negative elements than Protestants. In most cases, the difference was about 10 per cent. While this finding, by itself, was not unduly significant, it did suggest a less critical attitude toward the church by Catholic laymen.

Second, and undoubtedly related to the level and frequency of interaction among church members, Protestants in all geographical areas more frequently cited the character of some church members as one of the things they liked least about their own church than did Catholics.

Third, it should be noted that the aspects of doctrine or belief were mentioned very infrequently by the respondents of all the churches as one of the factors which they liked least about

Table 35. Things Liked Least About Own Church by Broad Membership Groups and Residential Areas in Per Cent

ELEMENTS CITED

Church Membership of Respondent	N =	Aspect of Program or Plant Facilities	Quality of Present Minister or Priest[a]	Character of Some Church Members	Aspect of Belief or Doctrine[a]	No Negative Elements	Other[a]	Don't Know
MAIZEVILLE								
Catholic[b]	52	17	2	12	12	48	10	4
Protestant	490	17	9	22	5	39	13	6
None	111	10	3	6	5	23	6	52
EAST TOWN								
Catholic	102	18	2	2	4	65	10	5
Protestant	83	12	0	11	4	54	12	8
None	49	8	2	6	2	29	4	51
SERVICEVILLE								
Catholic[b]	23	0	0	0	13	35	35	22
Protestant	133	8	2	29	1	22	26	15
None[c]	31	3	3	16	0	23	6	48
OPEN COUNTRY								
Catholic[b]	14	7	14	0	0	72	0	7
Protestant	65	22	5	23	6	38	15	2
None[c]	31	3	0	6	3	32	6	48

$\chi^2 = 379.33$ $p < .01$ $C = .48$

a. Columns combined in chi square analysis.
b. Rows combined in chi square analysis.
c. Rows combined in chi square analysis.

their own church. Thus, a theme which recurs again and again through the analysis of the data—the minimum of concern with or understanding of cognitive structures—is demonstrated here. Interdenominational differences are illustrated in Table 36.

Aside from the Catholic-Protestant differentials noted earlier, the evidence did not suggest significant deviations in elements cited from denomination to denomination. The relatively high proportion of Presbyterians who cited the need for improvement in some aspect of program or plant facilities is explained by the discussion of additional Sunday School facilities that was under way when this study was in process.

The quality of the present minister or priest was singled out so infrequently that it was not possible to make meaningful Catholic-Protestant comparisons. In spite of the controversies that emerged from time to time over ministerial leadership in Corn County, the data strongly suggest that usually only a very small minority of any congregation was dissatisfied with the type of ministerial leadership they were getting.

An analysis by sex of comparable broad membership groups— Catholic, Protestant, and non-church members—revealed no variation in response. The data suggested that, at least in the eyes of the respondents, the church was adequately meeting the needs of both sexes. This finding is significant in the light of the frequent charge that a matriarchal organizational structure is characteristic of many churches. If this is the case in Corn County, there was no evidence to suggest criticisms of the pattern by church members.

Persons of above average intellectual ability in the 30-64 age group and persons of white-collar social status in the 30-64 age group in Maizeville were somewhat more critical of their church than were persons of average or below average intellectual ability or of mixed or blue-collar social status. For example, 42 per cent of the persons of below average intellectual ability cited no negative elements while only 28 per cent of persons of above average intellectual ability cited no negative elements. Similarly, 38 per cent of persons of blue-collar social status did not cite negative elements while only 25 per cent of persons of white-collar social status cited no negative elements.

Examination of the responses for nuclear and modal members

Table 36. Things Liked Least About Own Church for Selected Denominations, Maizeville, in Per Cent

Church Membership of Respondent	N =	ELEMENTS CITED						
		Aspect of Program or Plant Facilities	Quality of Present Minister or Priest	Character of Some Church Members	Aspect of Belief or Doctrine[a]	No Negative Elements	Other[a]	Don't Know[a]
Baptist	42	14	10	24	7	40	10	7
Catholic	52	17	2	12	12	48	10	4
Christian[b]	20	35	0	20	0	30	15	10
Congregational	73	8	12	18	3	44	18	5
Lutheran, Augustana	42	19	2	31	5	29	14	10
Lutheran, United	81	14	14	19	2	44	9	5
Methodist	82	21	17	23	4	33	20	5
Mission Covenant	54	13	0	30	7	41	6	11
Presbyterian	44	30	14	23	11	27	11	2
None[b]	111	10	3	6	5	23	6	52

$\chi^2 = 27.04$ $.10 < p < .20$

a. Columns combined in chi square analysis.
b. Rows excluded in chi square analysis.

of average and above average intelligence for the four broad traditions extant in Maizeville revealed no marked deviations from the findings reported in Table 36. Variations in response by persons of average intelligence in Maizeville by type of church membership were not significant. Nuclear, modal, marginal, and dormant members had common patterns of responses.

Church Membership and Friendship Patterns

It is common knowledge that different segments of the population participate in the several activities of religious organizations in varying degrees. It is also generally known that members of some types of religious groupings participate more frequently in the religious and social activities of their own group than do members of some other types of religious groupings.

In order to discern how church affiliation was related to the respondent's total pattern of social interaction, each interviewee was asked to indicate the church membership of his three closest friends. It was felt that members of those churches who reported that a high proportion of their closest friends were members of the same church would display a stronger measure of group cohesiveness and group self-consciousness than would members of churches in which this was not the case. Consequently, those churches whose members reported a significantly higher than average percentage of members' closest friends in the same church would indicate a relatively high degree of group cohesiveness while those citing significantly lower percentages of closest friends being members of the same church would indicate less cohesiveness and self-consciousness. In the former situation, one's associational and communal groupings would tend to converge; in the latter situation, they would not.[19] The findings are summarized in Tables 37 and 38.

In Table 37 the church membership of the interviewees' three closest friends is tabulated by church membership. In Maizeville, Serviceville, and the rural area (all dominantly Protestant), be-

---

19. By communal interaction the authors mean interaction that is informal and diffuse. By associational interaction, they mean interaction that is formal and specific.

Table 37. Church Membership of Three Closest Friends by Broad Membership
Groups and Residential Areas, in Per Cent

Church Membership of Respondent	N =	CHURCH MEMBERSHIP OF THREE CLOSEST FRIENDS			
		Catholic	Same	Protestant* Other	None
		MAIZEVILLE			
Catholic	156	38		52	10
Protestant	1,459	8	32	55	5
None	321	15		72	13
		EAST TOWN			
Catholic	300	82	8	7	3
Congregational	143	62	24	13	1
Other Protestant	98	31	9	57	3
None	139	63	14	17	6
		SERVICEVILLE			
Catholic	72	35		48	17
Protestant	471	14	25	56	5
None	88	19		63	18
		OPEN COUNTRY			
Catholic	43	35		60	5
Protestant	196	14	26	55	5
None	93	13		83	4

* In East Town, columns are "Congregational" and "Other Protestants."

tween one-quarter and one-third of the interviewees' closest friends were members of the same church as the respondent. While the Roman Catholic respondents reported slightly more of their closest friends were Roman Catholics than was the case for Protestants, the differences were not large. Although communal interaction among Catholics was more intense, there was a relatively large amount of Protestant-Catholic communal interaction.

In Maizeville, the sample was sufficiently large to provide a more detailed analysis by church membership. These data are summarized in Table 38. It should be noted that only one denomination varied significantly from the 30-40 per cent range in which most church groups fell on the percent of friends who were of the same denomination. The Mission Covenant sample, a closely knit group descended from Swedish ancestors, reported that 60 per cent of their closest friends belonged to the Mission Covenant church. This finding is not surprising in the light of comments made by interviewees. For example, one middle-aged

Congregationalist housewife, the wife of a local businessman, commented: "Most of the Protestant churches here are pretty much alike. Of course, some of them are kinda clannish. The Mission Covenant people, for example, tend to stick by themselves."

The data support her observation, although some recent developments in Maizeville indicate that this pattern is now less significant. For example, in contrast to an earlier practice of calling ministers trained in a seminary of their denomination, the congregation recently called a minister educated at one of the major Protestant interdenominational educational centers. Further, the status of the group, as measured by the objective indices of education, occupation, and house type, was high.

These data suggested that religious groupings were relatively insignificant in determining friendship patterns in these communities. With the exception noted for the Mission Covenant group in Maizeville, and with the exceptions to be noted for selected groups of nuclear church members, it did not appear that the various religious traditions contributed to significant cleavages in the population. Rather, there was a large degree of interdenominational and Roman Catholic-Protestant friendship

Table 38.   Church Membership of Three Closest Friends for Selected Denominations, Maizeville, in Per Cent

| Church Membership of Respondent | N = | CHURCH MEMBERSHIP OF THREE CLOSEST FRIENDS | | | |
| | | Catholic | Protestant | | None |
			Same	Other	
Baptist	135	4	30	59	7
Catholic	156	38	52		10
Christian*	60	7	25	57	11
Congregational	224	6	32	57	5
Lutheran, Augustana	126	3	41	51	5
Lutheran, United	237	8	33	55	4
Methodist	242	12	32	50	6
Mission Covenant	162	2	60	36	2
Presbyterian	132	7	29	59	5
None*	321	15	72		13

$$\chi^2 = 50.20 \qquad p < .01 \qquad C = .19$$

* Rows excluded in chi square analysis.

overlapping, generally proportional to the population distribution in the communities examined.[20]

Although the tables are not reproduced here, data for respondents of average and above average intellectual ability for the 30-64 age group in Maizeville were further examined. An over-all view of the data suggested a slight tendency for closest friends of nuclear church members to be drawn from the same broad tradition.

Particularly significant was the high proportion of nuclear church members of the transforming wing of the Calvinist tradition of both average and above average intellectual ability who indicated that their closest friends belonged to churches of the same broad tradition. While the data do not permit an explanation of this phenomenon, one may speculate that status factors involving a common style of life and value affirmations were related to this phenomenon.

Significantly fewer Lutheran members indicated that their closest friends were members of the same tradition. These data supported evidence drawn from other sources that the Lutheran tradition in the United States is in process of becoming more inclusive and less ethnic.

Data not presented here on the analysis by broad membership groups and sex in Maizeville indicated only minor deviations between males and females. The differentials were not statistically significant.

Further data to document the observation that religious groupings were not of major importance in shaping friendship patterns differentially are shown in Table 39, which examined the proportion of interviewees' closest friends who were met at church activities.

That church affiliation did play some role in ordering friendship patterns is seen by the fact that a significantly higher proportion of the respondents reported having closest friends of their own denomination than reported having met their friends

20. This finding supports the thesis advanced by Herberg, Marty, and others that the various religions of America are becoming increasingly amalgamated in a religion of America. It does not accord with the findings by Lenski in *The Religious Factor*, although our data excluded interaction between relatives. Unfortunately, data for prior periods are not available, so trends cannot be assessed.

through church activities. A generally positive disposition toward members of one's own denomination, the opportunity the church context provided for further meetings, or both, undoubtedly contributed to producing a significantly higher friendship pattern among people of the same church membership than among the population as a whole.

It should further be noted that higher proportions of Protestants than Catholics reported that they met their closest friends through church activities in all of the areas studied. Whatever the negative aspect of status differentiation by denomination may be, it did, apparently, serve to foster friendships.[21]

Detailed data for the method of meeting closest friends by denomination for Maizeville are shown in Table 40. Again, with the exception of the Mission Covenants, there was not a wide variation between denominations, although the relative differences are of some interest. In the light of the rather strong emphasis that the Methodist church places on "fellowship," it is somewhat surprising to find that so few of its members reported that they met their closest friends through church activities. This finding is probably related to the status distribution of the Methodist church. Next to the Roman Catholic church, the Methodist church was the most inclusive in status. It seems highly unlikely that it is a coincidence that these two groups had the lowest proportion of respondents who met their closest friends through church activities.

Although the data are not presented here, an examination of responses by broad membership groups and sex for the Maizeville sample revealed that there was no differential between males and females for the broad Protestant-Catholic groupings.

While the percentage of persons meeting their closest friends through a church activity was relatively small for all groups, twice as many persons of above average intellectual ability reported that they met their closest friends through church activities than did persons of below average intellectual ability (16 per cent of the above average and 8 per cent of the below aver-

---

21. It should be emphasized that the authors are not arguing that church membership did not contribute to the formation of friendship patterns. What they are arguing is that there was a minimum of differential contribution by the various church traditions.

age). This phenomenon is undoubtedly related to differential participation in church activities by the two intellectual ability groupings.

Summary of Inter-Church and Intra-Church Findings—The data reported in the last three sections of the study revealed deep feelings of Catholic-Protestant church differences. When Protestants were asked to name the church least like their own, the responses polarized about Pentecostal types of churches on the one hand and the Catholic church on the other.

At the same time, the data on friendship patterns indicated a considerable number of close interfaith friendships. These findings, coupled with those just noted, suggest that a considerable measure of adjustment and accommodation between Protestants and Catholics has been effected in Corn County, although awareness of differences was still strong.

The basis of differentiation among various churches was largely emotive, since the interviewees possessed only minimal understanding of churches other than their own.

The interviewees' assessments of the similarities among

Table 39. Method of Meeting of Three Closest Friends by Broad Membership Groups and Residential Areas in Per Cent

Church Membership of Respondent	N =	METHOD OF MEETING Through Church Activities	Other
		MAIZEVILLE	
Catholic	150	8	92
Protestant	1,391	16	84
None*	309	3	97
		EAST TOWN	
Catholic	288	5	95
Protestant	290	8	92
None*	75	3	97
		SERVICEVILLE	
Catholic	65	4	96
Protestant	387	21	79
None*	84	10	90
		OPEN COUNTRY	
Catholic	43	0	100
Protestant	186	10	90
None*	92	3	97

$$\chi^2 = 69.16 \qquad p < .01 \qquad C = .14$$

* Rows excluded in chi square analysis.

churches were usually reciprocal. These assessments were related both to social status and to the broad historical traditions to which the churches were related.

Where voluntarism was the basis of church selection, social factors were cited more frequently as one element the respondent liked most about his church than was the case when the respondent had no option of church selection within his broad tradition. Similarly, those of average and above average intellectual ability and who were nuclear and modal members of the churches in the perfectionist wing of the Calvinist tradition in Maizeville, churches in which the data suggested high member-member interaction, cited the quality of church members as one thing they liked most about their own churches significantly more often than did members of any of the other groups examined.

A large proportion of the respondents in all geographical areas and among both Catholics and Protestants cited no negative elements in their churches. Catholics displayed a less critical attitude than Protestants, a difference that is predictable, given the differing conceptions of the Church in the two facets of the Christian tradition.

Similarly, Protestants in all geographical areas cited the character of some church members as one of the things they liked least about their churches more frequently than did Catholics, a

Table 40. Method of Meeting Three Closest Friends for Selected Denominations, Maizeville, in Per Cent

Church Membership of Respondent	N =	METHOD OF MEETING Through Church Activities	Other
Baptist	130	19	81
Catholic	150	8	92
Christian*	53	21	79
Congregational	213	11	89
Lutheran, Augustana	109	24	76
Lutheran, United	222	10	90
Methodist	232	7	93
Mission Covenant	159	38	62
Presbyterian	129	14	86
None*	309	3	97

$$\chi^2 = 100.93 \qquad p < .01 \qquad C = .26$$

* Rows excluded in chi square analysis.

phenomenon that probably resulted from the greater member-member interaction in activities other than the worship service among Protestants.

Aspects of doctrine or belief and the quality of present professional religious leadership were cited very infrequently as sources of discontent by respondents in all of the churches in all the geographical areas examined in this study. Common ethnic and status churches reported the highest proportion of friendships established through church activities; inclusive status churches reported the lowest proportion.

When the responses for the elements liked least and those liked most by church members were examined by sex, social status, and intellectual ability, the findings were negative.

3. CHURCH MEMBERSHIP AND COGNITIVE STRUCTURES

MANY of the churches in Corn County have been in existence for a century or more. All of the major churches were established prior to World War I. The type of ministerial leadership which they have had over the years has been similar to that available in most counties in the north central portion of the country. It seems reasonable to assume that the cognitive characteristics of the churches of this county established over the past century or so are comparable to those which have been found elsewhere in this area.[1]

In general, apprehension of cognitive elements of the Christian faith was minimal for the members of all of the denominations in the county studied. There was evidence that some members of the Congregational, Methodist, and Presbyterian churches in the county seat town of Maizeville and some members of the Congregational church in East Town had a vague acquaintance with some facets of Biblical criticism and desired a minister who was not a Biblical fundamentalist; but even among these members, no serious effort had been made to relate the faith to theological fashions in these areas.

Pretesting of the interview schedule and a knowledge of

---

1. While the findings reported in this investigation have been explicitly generalized to typify religious life extant in the town and country sections of the Corn Belt area of the United States, a variety of data drawn from other sources would suggest that the general patterns described here reflect religious life in most of the country. Data drawn from public opinion polls, a *Catholic Digest* series in 1952-1954, Yoshio Fukuyama's study, "The Major Dimensions of Church Membership" (Unpublished Ph.D. dissertation, University of Chicago, 1960), and Gerhard Lenski's study in the Detroit metropolitan area (*The Religious Factor, op. cit.*) all point to the minimum cognitive structures that inform members of churches in the United States.

the findings of other workers investigating this area had indicated that the general level of conceptual understanding was going to be relatively low. Therefore, instead of asking directly for the informing cognitive structures, it was decided to employ specific content questions. It was felt, and subsequent analysis confirmed this judgment, that those persons who possessed substantial cognitive understanding would reveal it by the manner in which they responded to the specific questions that were asked.

Although any neat division of content was not possible, the interview schedule was designed to explore the extent and depth of cognitive understanding in three general areas. First, certain questions were included to illumine the level of understanding of the Bible which the respondents possessed. It was felt that probably the most extensive effort made in religious education among the churches of this area had been devoted to the Bible, since, at a minimum, most of the churches had Bible-centered Sunday schools. Second, questions were asked which explicitly probed five areas of theological interest and concern. Third, questions were included that were designed to probe the respondent's understanding of the relationship between the Christian faith and the social order. In this presentation, the three areas will be considered sequentially.

Biblical Knowledge and Comprehension

Introduction—Three questions in the interview schedule that was employed dealt explicitly with the area of Biblical knowledge and comprehension.

The first question sought to discern the respondent's general way of looking at the Bible by asking him what he considered to be the main differences between the Old Testament and the New Testament. The second question was designed to explore a facet of the Old Testament. Each respondent was asked what the meaning of the Old Testament Hebrew Prophets was for him. The final question, designed to discern the level of comprehension of Biblical themes, focused on the story of the Good Samaritan.

Differences Between the Old Testament and the New Testament—
Responses to the first question, about differences between the
Old and New Testaments, were divided into five general categories. The first group included responses of a subjective or
psychological nature, in which the respondent observed that the
New Testament was easier to understand. This response, taken
from the schedule of a Serviceville Baptist woman, the wife of
a clerk, illustrates the type: "Well, I would say the New Testament is more modern. It's easier to understand. Less wars and
stuff like that."

The second general group of responses were categorized as
theological. This general group was further subdivided into
three subgroups. The first subgroup contrasted the Old Testament and the New Testament in terms of prophecy or preparation as the key to the Old Testament and fulfillment of prophecy
or preparation as the key to the New Testament. The second
subgroup offered a contrast between law as the major motif in
the Old Testament and love as the major motif in the New
Testament. The last subgroup included responses that stated
that the New Testament provided the means to attain salvation.[2]

This response, drawn from the schedule of a Methodist proprietor in Maizeville, illustrates the first subgroup: "Well, I
always heard that the Old Testament was prophesying the coming of the Lord."

This response of a middle-aged Mission Covenant woman
illustrates the second subgroup: "The Old Testament teaches us
to live by law, but the New Testament teaches us to live by
love."

A Catholic woman, the wife of an East Town factory machinist, gave this response, illustrative of the third subgroup: "Well,
that is sure a hard one. I haven't thought much about that. These
are some questions. Oh, gee, I'd say that the New Testament
shows us we'll have eternal life if we believe in Jesus."

The last major substantive grouping included responses that
referred to historical differences between the Old Testament
and the New Testament. This response, drawn from the schedule

---

2. Efforts by interviewers to probe the respondents' understanding of
salvation proved fruitless. Hence, no subdivision of responses by type of
salvation was undertaken.

of a Baptist farmer, depicts the type: "I'd say that the New Testament tells us about the life and times of Jesus."

In order to provide an exhaustive categorization, two other groupings were employed. One included all other substantive responses, while the other included the "Don't Know" responses. The responses to this question are summarized in Tables 41-48.

The broad membership group and residential area analysis shown in Table 41 revealed sharp differences between Protestants, Catholics, and non-church members and between dominantly Catholic, industrial East Town and the other residential areas included in the study. Roman Catholic church members were least knowledgeable on this question, as, in fact, they were on all of the questions dealing with Biblical content. In light of systematic reasons for the lack of emphasis on the Bible in the Roman Catholic church, this finding is not surprising.

In this connection, an examination of Table 43 is suggestive, although unfortunately the number of Catholics falling into the appropriate category was so small that serious questions are raised about the statistical significance of the finding. This table does suggest, however, that Roman Catholic church members of above average intellectual ability had appropriated as much substantive material as had either comparable Lutheran or transforming wing Calvinist church members. Thus, it might follow that Catholics of superior ability may have received more advanced instruction, as on systematic grounds they should have.

Protestants had markedly fewer "Don't Know" responses to this question than any of the other broad membership groups in all of the residential areas examined. Thus, the data did suggest that the Protestant emphasis upon the Bible had succeeded, at least at this level, in communicating some cognitive notions about the Bible.[3]

When it is noted that some respondents cited more than one theological distinction between the two Testaments, it is clear that less than one-third of the respondents in any of the areas focused upon theological distinctions between the two Testaments.

---

3. The problems of the depth of appropriation and its relation to the theological structures which form the various traditions and of the differential ability of people to appropriate cognitive structures will be discussed in greater detail later in this study.

Table 41. Differences Between Old Testament and New Testament by Broad Membership Groups and Residential Areas in Per Cent

Church Membership of Respondent	N =	Subjective[a] (N.T. Easier to Comprehend)	Prophecy-Fulfillment Couplet[a]	Law-Love Couplet[a]	Salvation in N.T.[a]	Historical[a]	Other[a]	Don't Know
				MAIZEVILLE				
Catholic	52	14	6	12	12	12	10	68
Protestant	488	23	15	12	21	15	14	38
None	63	11	8	2	8	6	11	67
				EAST TOWN				
Catholic	100	0	0	2	6	5	2	92
Protestant	80	13	10	5	20	13	4	63
None	48	8	2	0	4	4	0	90
				SERVICEVILLE				
Catholic[b]	23	9	0	0	0	0	4	87
Protestant	177	8	14	12	14	11	11	31
None	34	0	0	9	3	0	3	85
				OPEN COUNTRY				
Catholic[b]	14	7	7	0	0	0	7	86
Protestant	64	16	23	34	28	14	11	27
None	31	20	3	3	13	10	3	61

$\chi^2 = 205.45$ $p < .01$ $C = .39$

a. Columns combined in chi square analysis.
b. Rows combined in chi square analysis.

The differential responses for selected denominations in Maizeville are shown in Table 42; those for selected membership groupings of nuclear and modal members of above average and average intellectual ability are shown in Tables 43 and 44. Differential responses by type of church membership for persons of average intellectual ability are shown in Table 45.

As noted earlier, consistent with their lack of emphasis upon the Scriptures for the majority of laymen, Roman Catholics recorded by far the highest percentage of "Don't Know" responses of any church members in Maizeville. The groups that have been categorized as the perfectionist wing of the Calvinist tradition consistently had the lowest percentage of "Don't Know" responses and the highest proportion of theological responses to this question. The differences between the Lutheran tradition, with its characteristic catechetical instruction, and the transforming wing of the Calvinist tradition were negligible.

When the various traditions were examined, holding type of member and intellectual functioning constant, as shown in Tables 43 and 44, some interesting differentials emerged. The members of churches in the perfectionist wing of the Calvinistic tradition gave a much higher percentage of substantive responses for both average and above average intellectual functioning groups, whereas the differences between the transforming wing of the Calvinist tradition, the Catholic tradition, and the Lutheran traditions were quite small for persons of above average intellectual functioning. However, an examination of Table 44 reveals marked differences between the three traditions for persons of average intellectual ability.[4]

The evidence clearly suggested that there was differential substantive appropriation by type of membership, as revealed in Table 45. Although there were only modest differences between nuclear and modal members, there was a sharp increase in the percentage of "Don't Know" responses for the marginal and dormant church members.

In general, one could say that, even in church groups that

---

4. As noted earlier, data of nuclear and modal members of above average intellectual ability in Maizeville for Catholics must be treated with great reserve because of the small number of cases in the sample. The finding is most suggestive, however, and warrants further investigation.

Table 42. Differences Between Old Testament and New Testament for Selected Denominations, Maizeville, in Per Cent

Church Membership of Respondent	N =	Subjective (N. T. Easier to Comprehend)	THEOLOGICAL DIFFERENCES CITED					Don't Know
			Prophecy-Fulfillment Couplet[a]	Low-Love Couplet[a]	Salvation in N. T.[a]	Historical[b]	Other[b]	
Baptist	44	27	16	14	25	30	16	25
Catholic	52	14	6	12	12	12	10	68
Christian[c]	20	15	10	5	40	20	15	30
Congregational	71	17	6	4	18	13	14	48
Lutheran, Augustana	42	31	21	14	17	14	12	36
Lutheran, United	81	22	10	7	15	9	9	51
Methodist	82	35	4	10	7	6	11	45
Mission Covenant	54	19	44	35	43	24	9	11
Presbyterian	44	18	25	14	23	21	27	27
None[c]	63	11	8	2	8	6	11	67

$\chi^2 = 130.60$ $p < .01$ $C = .41$

a. Columns combined in chi square analysis.
b. Columns combined in chi square analysis.
c. Rows excluded in chi square analysis.

Table 43. Differences Between Old Testament and New Testament for Selected Membership Groups of Nuclar and Modal Members of Above Average Intellectual Ability, Maizeville, in Per Cent

Church Membership of Respondent	N =	DIFFERENCES CITED THEOLOGICAL						
		Subjective[a] (N. T. Easier to Comprehend)	Prophecy-Fulfillment Couplet[b]	Law-Love Couplet[b]	Salvation in N. T.	Historical[a]	Other[c]	Don't Know[c]
Perfectionist Wing Calvinist Tradition	24	17	42	58	33	25	17	4
Transforming Wing Calvinist Tradition	41	24	15	19	29	22	12	29
Lutheran[d]	15	33	33	7	27	33	13	27
Catholic[d]	12	17	8	33	50	50	17	33
Total	92	23	24	29	33	28	14	23

$\chi^2 = 14.61$ $p < .05$ $C = .29$

a. Columns combined in chi square analysis.
b. Columns combined in chi square analysis.
c. Columns combined in chi square analysis.
d. Rows combined in chi square analysis.

Table 44. Differences Between Old Testament and New Testament for Selected Membership Groups of Nuclear and Modal Members of Average Intellectual Ability, Maizeville, in Per Cent

DIFFERENCES CITED
THEOLOGICAL

Church Membership of Respondent	N =	Subjective[a] (N.T. Easier to Comprehend)	Prophecy-Fulfillment Couplet[b]	Law-Love Couplet[b]	Salvation in N.T.[b]	Historical[a]	Other[c]	Don't Know[c]
Perfectionist Wing Calvinist Tradition	35	11	26	31	51	31	11	14
Transforming Wing Calvinist Tradition	44	27	20	5	25	16	18	32
Lutheran	29	41	28	21	24	7	14	21
Catholic	32	9	9	3	3	6	6	84
Total	140	22	21	14	26	16	13	37

$\chi^2 = 45.23$ $p < .01$ $C = .42$

a. Columns combined in chi square analysis.
b. Columns combined in chi square analysis.
c. Columns combined in chi square analysis.

Table 45. Differences Between Old Testament and New Testament by Type of Church Membership for Persons of Average Intellectual Ability, Maizeville, in Per Cent

DIFFERENCES CITED
THEOLOGICAL

Type of Church Membership of Respondent	N =	Subjective[a] (N. T. Easier to Comprehend)	Prophecy-Fulfillment Couplet[b]	Law-Love Couplet[b]	Salvation in N. T.[b]	Historical[a]	Other[c]	Don't Know[c]
Nuclear	87	18	25	17	26	13	9	38
Modal	53	28	13	9	26	21	19	36
Marginal[d]	56	27	5	2	4	11	20	50
Dormant[d]	24	17	4	0	0	4	8	79
Total	220	23	15	10	18	13	14	45

$\chi^2 = 44.15$ $p < .01$ $C = .36$

a. Columns combined in chi square analysis.
b. Columns combined in chi square analysis.
c. Columns combined in chi square analysis.
d. Rows combined in chi square analysis.

had a relatively high proportion of members responding substantively to this question, the depth of the response was limited quite sharply. For example, once a respondent had cited a response such as "The Old Testament teaches us to live by law, but the New Testament teaches us to live by love," he was most frequently unable to put any additional content into such words. Probing queries such as "What is law?" or "How would you distinguish between law and love?" almost invariably failed to elicit a substantive response.

Differences in the percentage of substantive responses by sex were statistically significant, but the percentage difference was not large. For example, 35 per cent of Protestant females responded that they did not know the difference between the Old Testament and the New Testament, and 44 per cent of the Protestant males in Maizeville responded in the same way. Although they are not reproduced systematically, differences in the percentage of "Don't Know" responses by sex ranged from about 5 to 10 per cent for most of the cognitive questions. These data suggested that so far as the cognitive dimensions of the faith were concerned there was only a modest differential in appropriation in favor of females.

Much greater differentials in response occurred when the differences cited were examined by intellectual ability and social status, as shown in Tables 47 and 48. Not surprisingly, there was a direct relationship between intellectual level and substantive response. Similarly, there was a sharp difference between the white-collar social status group and the other two status groupings. The percentage of theological responses was greater for the above average intellectual grouping and for the white-collar status grouping than for any of the other groups. These findings are consistent with numerous other studies which show that the white-collar group sustains much of the intellectual tradition of the culture.[5]

Meaning of the Old Testament Prophets—Because of the preeminent place which the prophetic writings occupy in the Old

---

5. Because the patterns reported here are consistent for all of the findings dealing with cognitive structures, tables dealing with differentials by sex, intellectual ability, and social status will not be presented systematically. Only a few tables dealing with matters of special interest will be presented in the rest of this chapter for these groupings.

Table 46. Differences Between Old Testament and New Testament by Broad Membership Groups and Sex, Maizeville, in Per Cent

Church Membership of Respondent	N =	Subjective	Prophecy-Fulfillment Couplet[a]	Law-Love Couplet[a]	Salvation in N.T.[a]	Historical[b]	Other[b]	Don't Know
				FEMALES				
Catholic	38	13	8	11	11	11	8	68
Protestant	300	27	16	10	23	14	13	35
None	34	12	9	0	6	9	15	65
				MALES				
Catholic	14	14	0	14	14	14	14	57
Protestant	188	16	14	14	18	18	16	44
None	29	10	7	3	10	3	7	69

$\chi^2 = 54.21$ $p < .01$ $C = .25$

a. Columns combined in chi square analysis.
b. Columns combined in chi square analysis.

Table 47. Differences Between Old Testament and New Testament by Intellectual Ability for 30-64 Age Group, Maizeville, in Per Cent

Intellectual Ability of Respondent	N =	Subjective	Prophecy-Fulfillment Couplet[a]	Law-Love Couplet[a]	Salvation in N.T.[a]	Historical[b]	Other[b]	Don't Know
Below average	74	12	5	1	12	11	11	53
Average	235	19	15	7	16	12	14	38
Above average	119	20	19	24	28	23	16	25

$\chi^2 = 42.77$ $p < .01$ $C = .26$

a. Columns combined in chi square analysis.
b. Columns combined in chi square analysis.

Table 48.   Differences Between Old Testament and New Testament by Social Status for 30-64 Age Group, Maizeville, in Per Cent

Social Status of Respondent	N =	Subjective	Prophecy-Fulfillment Couplet[a]	Law-Love Couplet[a]	Salvation in N. T.[a]	Historical[b]	Other[b]	Don't Know
			THEOLOGICAL DIFFERENCES CITED					
Blue-collar	122	27	4	3	14	11	12	43
Mixed	153	11	14	11	16	14	10	43
White-collar	154	18	23	16	25	19	18	26

$\chi^2 = 46.68$ $p < .01$ $C = .28$

a. Columns combined in chi square analysis.
b. Columns combined in chi square analysis.

Testament, it was decided to focus upon the respondents' under-standing of the meaning of the Old Testament prophets as an index of their general grasp of the Old Testament. The responses to this question fell into four major groups.

The first group included those responses which suggested that the Old Testament prophets were predicting the future. Some specified that the Old Testament prophets were predicting the coming of Jesus.

This response, taken from the interview schedule of a Serv-iceville Methodist, the wife of a farmer, illustrates the type: "The Old Testament prophets, huh? Gee, I haven't thought about them since I was in the Sunday School. They always said that they were predicting the coming of the Lord, prophesying the future."

The second substantive grouping included responses that indicated a theological or moral interpretation of the role of the prophets. It comprised responses indicating that the prophets were preparing the world for the coming of the Messiah, that they were developing the idea of monotheism, that they were emphasizing a moral life, and that they were expressing God's judgment upon their people. This response, drawn from the schedule of a Presbyterian schoolteacher in Maizeville, is illus-trative of this type: "I think a lot of people missed the real point of the story of the Old Testament prophets when they think they were just trying to predict the future. From my way of thinking, that isn't right. What they were really doing was expressing God's judgment upon the people for their evil ways and were calling upon them to repent. That's it. They were judging the people."

The final substantive grouping included all other responses except "Don't Know." That response constituted the final cate-gory. The findings are summarized in Tables 49 through 56.

The most salient finding in this analysis was the extremely high proportion of interviewees who were unable to respond in any way at all to this question. The percentage of the inter-viewees who were unable to respond to the question ranged from a low of 61 per cent in the rural area to a high of 87 per cent in the industrial community of East Town. Of the persons who did respond with an interpretation of some kind, less than half gave a theological or moral interpretation of the meaning of the prophets. The actual percentage of the total sample giving a theological or moral interpretation ranged from a low of 6 per cent in East Town to a high of 20 per cent in Maizeville. Only an extremely small segment of the residents of Corn County were able to give a profound theological interpretation of the meaning of the Hebrew prophets.

As Table 49 reveals, in all of the communities studied Protestants gave considerably higher proportions of responses citing a theological or moral interpretation. However, only about one Protestant in five was able to give such a response.

Although the absolute differences between Protestants and Catholics were not as great on this question as on the previous one, Protestants consistently had fewer "Don't Know" responses than had Catholics or non-church members.

Tables 50, 51, 52, and 53 present data for respondents in Maizeville by selected membership groupings.

Table 49. *Meaning of Old Testament Prophets by Broad Membership Groups and Residential Areas in Per Cent*

Church Membership of Respondent	N =	Prophecy[a]	MEANING CITED Theological and/or Moral[a]	Other[a]	Don't Know
			MAIZEVILLE		
Catholic	52	10	14	2	77
Protestant	481	15	22	7	64
None	67	5	8	3	87
			EAST TOWN		
Catholic	101	3	6	1	90
Protestant	82	11	7	2	81
None	49	2	2	4	92
			SERVICEVILLE		
Catholic[b]	22	5	0	9	86
Protestant	131	21	17	6	62
None[c]	31	0	3	3	94
			OPEN COUNTRY		
Catholic[b]	14	0	0	7	93
Protestant	71	31	17	11	41
None[c]	33	13	3	13	77

$$\chi^2 = 99.11 \qquad p < .01 \qquad C = .29$$

a. Columns combined in chi square analysis.
b. Rows combined in chi square analysis.
c. Rows combined in chi square analysis.

The data in Table 50 revealed a wide interdenominational difference in responses in Maizeville. The percentages of "Don't Know" ranged from a low of 33 per cent among the Mission Covenant church members to a high of 77 per cent among the Roman Catholics. The Presbyterians had the highest proportion of respondents who gave a theological-moral interpretation of the role of the prophets. The Augustana Lutherans had the lowest percentage (10 per cent).[6]

Table 50. Meaning of Old Testament Prophets for Selected Denominations, Maizeville, in Per Cent

Church Membership of Respondent	N =	Prophecy[a]	MEANING CITED Theological and/or Moral	Other[a]	Don't Know
Baptist	43	12	30	12	56
Catholic	52	10	14	2	77
Christian[b]	19	5	11	16	74
Congregational	69	12	22	7	65
Lutheran, Augustana	42	26	10	5	62
Lutheran, United	80	10	15	6	74
Methodist	81	6	17	6	74
Mission Covenant	54	43	33	0	33
Presbyterian	44	16	36	14	60
None[b]	67	5	8	3	87

$$\chi^2 = 95.72 \qquad p < .01 \qquad C = .40$$

a. Columns combined in chi square analysis.
b. Rows excluded in chi square analysis.

Because of the strong relationship between intellectual ability, social status, and substantive response to this question, an analysis of the data for nuclear and modal church members by selected membership groupings in Maizeville for the above average intellectual ability group was undertaken. The findings, presented in Table 51, suggested that somewhat different conclusions about the relationship between denominational affiliation and substantive response to this question should be given than the data in Table 50 might imply. For the groups of above

6. Perhaps the most significant point to be made here is that none of the denominations exhibited even a modest proportion of members who had more than a minimum of theological grasp of the role of the prophets.

average intellectual ability, it was the members of the transforming wing of the Calvinist tradition (Congregationalists, Methodists, and Presbyterians) who appeared to be least involved with the problem of the meaning of the Hebrew prophets. Well over half of these respondents, more than double the percentage in any of the other groupings, were unable to give a substantive response to this question. At the same time, however, the second highest percentage of members of this tradition gave a theological or moral interpretation of the meaning of the Hebrew prophets. Unfortunately, the number of respondents in the Lutheran tradition and in the Catholic tradition of above average intellectual ability was so small that these data must be interpreted with caution. However, the percentage of "Don't Know" responses for members of these two traditions was proportionately so much higher for persons of average intellectual functioning than for persons of above average intellectual functioning that this finding deserves attention.

As Table 52 reveals, the percentage of "Don't Know's" among nuclear and modal members of average intellectual ability was considerably higher than for those of above average intellectual ability for all the membership groups except the transforming wing of the Calvinist tradition. In the case of this group, the percentages were about the same.

Table 51. Meaning of Old Testament Prophets for Selected Membership Groups of Nuclear and Modal Members of Above Average Intellectual Ability, Maizeville, in Per Cent

Church Membership of Respondent	N =	Prophecy	Theological and/or Moral	Other[a]	Don't Know[a]
Perfectionist Wing Calvinist Tradition	24	42	54	4	17
Transforming Wing Calvinist Tradition	41	12	39	5	56
Lutheran[b]	16	31	31	13	25
Catholic[b]	13	31	23	8	5
Total	94	26	39	6	39
		$\chi^2 = 16.55$	$p < .01$	$C = 35$	

a. Columns combined in chi square analysis.
b. Rows combined in chi square analysis.

It is clear that persons who were modal and nuclear church members did appropriate a richer cognitive structure than those who were marginal or dormant members. As Table 53 indicates, about twice as many nuclear church members of average intellectual ability in Maizeville cited a theological and/or moral meaning in the Old Testament prophets than did the members of any of the other groups. The differences between modal and marginal church members seem especially sharp.

The very strong relationship between the ability of the respondent to give a substantive answer to this question and the variables of intellectual ability and social status are revealed in Tables 54 and 55. Over two-fifths of the above average group in intellectual ability in Maizeville cited a theological and/or moral meaning of the Old Testament prophets, while only 3 per cent of the below average group did so. Further, an examination of Table 55 reveals that the blue-collar group was the group that was dominantly lacking substantive responses to this query. Over four-fifths of the blue-collar group responded that they were unable to give a meaning to the work of the Old Testament prophets, while only two-fifths of the white-collar group responded in such a fashion.

While the differences in response by sex were not great, as Table 56 shows, it is interesting to note that the percentage of males citing a theological or moral meaning for the Old Testament prophets was higher than that of females. These data, coupled with a consideration of the other responses in this section, strongly suggested that males had probably appropriated as much—if not more—of a cognitive structure to inform their faith than women, in spite of the latter's generally higher rate of participation in all church activities.

Meaning of the Story of the Good Samaritan—The last question in the section designed to discern the level of comprehension of Biblical themes asked the interviewees what they thought was the meaning of the story of the Good Samaritan. Insofar as the parable has become a part of folklore, it was believed that it would be one story which would be widely known.

The responses were divided into three main groups, interpretations of it as exemplary, other interpretations, and "Don't Know."

Table 52. Meaning of Old Testament Prophets for Selected Membership Groups of Nuclear and Modal Members of Average Intellectual Ability, Maizeville, in Per Cent

Church Membership of Respondent	N =	Prophecy*	MEANING CITED Theological and/or Moral	Other*	Don't Know
Perfectionist Wing Calvinist Tradition	34	35	32	15	32
Transforming Wing Calvinist Tradition	47	13	36	15	53
Lutheran	30	17	23	7	67
Catholic	35	9	3	11	80
Total	146	18	25	12	58

$$\chi^2 = 24.01 \qquad p < .01 \qquad C = .36$$

* Columns combined in chi square analysis.

Table 53. Meaning of Old Testament Prophets by Type of Church Membership for Persons of Average Intellectual Ability, Maizeville, in Per Cent

Church Membership of Respondent	N =	Prophecy[a]	MEANING CITED Theological and/or Moral	Other[a]	Don't Know
Nuclear	89	20	30	7	58
Modal	57	14	16	21	56
Marginal[b]	57	7	5	5	86
Dormant[b]	25	16	8	0	76
Total	228	15	18	9	67

$$\chi^2 = 25.97 \qquad p < .01 \qquad C = .31$$

a. Columns combined in chi square analysis.
b. Rows combined in chi square analysis.

Table 54. Meaning of Old Testament Prophets by Intellectual Ability for 30-64 Age Group, Maizeville, in Per Cent

Intellectual Ability of Respondent	N =	Prophecy*	MEANING CITED Theological and/or Moral	Other*	Don't Know
Below average	65	9	3	2	86
Average	210	15	21	7	67
Above average	114	21	41	9	41

$$\chi^2 = 48.80 \qquad p < .01 \qquad C = .32$$

* Columns combined in chi square analysis.

Table 55. Meaning of Old Testament Prophets by Social Status for 30-64 Age Group, Maizeville, in Per Cent

Social Status of Respondent	N =	Prophecy	MEANING CITED Theological and/or Moral	Other	Don't Don't
Blue-collar	99	13	14	7	83
Mixed	134	14	19	6	69
White-collar	146	20	38	8	40

$$\chi^2 = 37.02 \qquad p < .01 \qquad C = .29$$

Table 56. Meaning of Old Testament Prophets by Broad Membership Groups and Sex, Maizeville, in Per Cent

Church Membership of Respondent	N =	Prophecy*	MEANING CITED Theological and/or Moral*	Other*	Don't Know
			FEMALES		
Catholic	38	5	13	0	84
Protestant	303	16	17	6	63
None	35	6	3	3	88
			MALES		
Catholic	14	21	14	7	57
Protestant	186	13	29	9	61
None	32	3	13	3	84

$$\chi^2 = 21.27 \qquad p < .01 \qquad C = .19$$

* Columns combined in chi square analysis.

The group interpreting it as an exemplary story was further subdivided into three subgroups. The first subgroup equated the meaning of the story with the Golden Rule. Included in the second subgroup were responses indicating that the story contained a mandate to give unqualified help to others. All other interpretations of it as exemplary were included in the third subgroup.

This response, drawn from the schedule of a Lutheran craftsman's wife in Maizeville, is illustrative of the first type: "That I would say is—a—'Do unto others as you would have them do unto you.'"

This response, drawn from the schedule of a middle-aged Christian church member in Maizeville, demonstrates the second type: "To me that means you should give help to others no matter what." The most frequently cited exemplary meaning included in the third subgroup interpreted the parable as suggesting qualified help to others. This response of an Episcopalian woman in Serviceville demonstrates the type: "Well, to me it means you should help others. 'Course, I don't mean you should go around helping just to be helping, but you should do as much as you can."

The second group, although numerically very small, contained a wide variety of substantive responses. Theologically, the interpretation which was considered most adequate by the authors was that the story reflected God's giving of Himself to man with no insistence on repayment. In fact, no one suggested such an interpretation.

Of the responses that were cited, probably the most adequate interpretation suggested was that one should give unqualified help to others.[7] In fact, somewhat less than one-third of the respondents said that the parable suggested that one should give unqualified help to others. A portion of the findings are summarized in Tables 57-61.

In all of the areas studied except Maizeville, the Roman Catholics and the non-church members had the highest percentage of "Don't Know" responses for the different geographical areas. Among Protestants, greater substantive knowledge was exhibited in most rural areas, Serviceville, and the open country. The Sunday school-centered church program of such areas, and the folklore status of the story may account for this relatively better showing by rural areas. Similarly, the exceptionally high percentage of Roman Catholics in East Town who did not know the meaning of the story suggested the limited acculturation of this group in the American ethos.

The range of respondents in Maizeville citing an unqualified help-to-others meaning of the parable—the response considered normatively the most adequate among those that were given—was from a low of 25 per cent for Baptists and Congregationalists to a high of 61 per cent for members of the Mission Covenant

---

7. Had the respondent further suggested the impossibility of following such a dictum and had he then explored this issue, we would have found evidence of greater theological understanding and sensitivity. Again, in fact, no one explored the problems related to the impossibility of fulfilling the injunction.

Table 57. Meaning of Good Samaritan Story by Broad Membership Groups and Residential Areas in Per Cent

Church Membership of Respondent	N =	MEANING CITED				
		EXEMPLARY				
		Golden Rule[a]	Unqualified Help to Others[a]	Other Exemplary	Other[a]	Don' Know
		MAIZEVILLE				
Catholic	52	6	33	21	8	37
Protestant	499	10	33	8	6	41
None	99	5	16	18	8	64
		EAST TOWN				
Catholic	100	1	3	9	4	83
Protestant	82	5	23	17	9	51
None	49	2	4	12	2	80
		SERVICEVILLE				
Catholic[b]	22	0	14	5	14	68
Protestant	133	5	38	13	14	32
None[c]	31	7	16	0	13	65
		OPEN COUNTRY				
Catholic[b]	14	7	7	21	0	64
Protestant	65	5	39	28	9	18
None[c]	31	3	6	42	10	39

$$\chi^2 = 132.44 \qquad p < .01 \qquad C = .32$$

a. Columns combined in chi square analysis.
b. Rows combined in chi square analysis.
c. Rows combined in chi square analysis.

Table 58. Meaning of Good Samaritan Story for Selected Denominations, Maizeville, in Per Cent

Church Membership of Respondent	N =	MEANING CITED				
		EXEMPLARY				
		Golden Rule[a]	Unqualified Help to Others	Other Exemplary	Other[a]	Don' Know
Baptist	44	11	25	22	9	34
Catholic	52	6	33	21	8	37
Christian[b]	20	15	50	15	5	25
Congregational	73	8	25	22	11	34
Lutheran, Augustana	41	15	36	20	5	22
Lutheran, United	81	6	27	24	4	42
Methodist	82	10	33	18	5	37
Mission Covenant	54	6	61	5	7	17
Presbyterian	44	25	36	14	11	16
None[b]	99	5	16	18	8	64

$$\chi^2 = 28.88 \qquad .10 < p < .20$$

a. Columns combined in chi square analysis.
b. Rows excluded in chi square analysis.

church. There appeared to be no consistent patterns by social status of the church or by the type of church service. There was no evidence of statistically significant variation in response by church membership in Maizeville, as shown in Table 58.

When the Maizeville data were considered by other selected variables, as shown in Tables 59, 60, and 61, some interesting differentials did emerge. While a large majority of nuclear and modal church members of above average intellectual ability was able to give a substantive response to this question, the members of the transforming wing of the Calvinist tradition had significantly more "Don't Know" responses than the members of any of the other broad membership groupings considered in this analysis. This pattern was not found for the comparable group of members of average intellectual ability. (See Table 60.) The evidence strongly suggested that the intellectually superior group of members in the transforming wing of the Calvinist heritage was not as deeply involved in some facets of its religious heritage as were the intellectually superior groups of the other traditions. (Also see Table 51.)

Once again, the data did suggest differential appropriation of cognitive structures by type of church membership. As Table 61 reveals, nuclear church members had only half as many "Don't Know" responses as any of the other groupings. The

Table 59. Meaning of Good Samaritan Story for Selected Membership Groups of Nuclear and Modal Members of Above Average Intellectual Ability, Maizeville, in Per Cent

| | | MEANING | CITED | | | |
| | | | EXEMPLARY | | | |
Church Membership f Respondent	N =	Golden Rule[a]	Unqualified Help to Others	Other Exemplary[a]	Other[a]	Don't Know[a]
Perfectionist Wing Calvinist Tradition	24	12	71	4	13	4
Transforming Wing Calvinist Tradition	42	17	38	17	2	26
Lutheran[b]	16	19	50	25	6	0
Catholic[b]	13	23	31	15	23	15
Total	95	17	47	15	8	15
	$\chi^2 = 6.34$		$p < .05$	$C = .25$		

a. Columns combined in chi square analysis.
b. Rows combined in chi square analysis.

lack of variation in "Don't Know" responses for the other groups suggested the embodiment of this story in folklore. However, it should be noted that a much higher percentage of nuclear and modal church members cited the normatively most satisfactory response, i.e., unqualified help to others.

Although they are not presented here, an examination of the data in per cent by broad membership groups and sex for the Maizeville sample indicated that Protestant males had somewhat more "Don't Know" responses (37 per cent) than Protestant females (28 per cent) and that for non-church members the patterns were very similar (59 per cent "Don't Know" for females and 56 per cent "Don't Know" for males).

When the data were examined for variation by intellectual ability and by social status for the 30-64 age group in Maizeville, patterns common to the findings in the other portions of this section emerged. The percentage of "Don't Know" responses ranged from a high of 60 per cent for the below average intellectual ability group to 18 per cent for the above average intellectual ability group. Similarly, the percentage of "Don't Know" responses ranged from a high of 44 per cent for the blue-collar social status group to a low of 21 per cent for the white-collar social status group.

It seems clear that the 15-20 per cent of the population who

Table 60. Meaning of Good Samaritan Story for Selected Membership Groups of Nuclear and Modal Members of Average Intellectual Ability, Maizeville, in Per Cent

Church Membership of Respondent	N =	Golden Rule*	Unqualified Help to Others	Other Exemplary*	Other*	Don't Know
			MEANING CITED EXEMPLARY			
Perfectionist Wing Calvinist Tradition	36	6	50	28	6	14
Transforming Wing Calvinist Tradition	48	17	42	8	8	25
Lutheran	31	16	23	13	23	35
Catholic	36	3	22	22	11	42
Total	151	11	35	17	11	28

$$\chi^2 = 13.04 \qquad p < .05 \qquad C = .28$$

* Columns combined in chi square analysis.

were of low intellectual ability had appropriated almost none of the cognitive structure sustaining the Christian faith, while one-third to one-half of the population of average intelligence had not dealt with the cognitive structure at any length. A relatively high proportion of the high intellectual functioning population evidenced some appropriation of what we have called here cognitive dimensions of the faith.

Table 61. Meaning of Good Samaritan Story by Type of Church Membership for Persons of Average Intellectual Ability, Maizeville, in Per Cént

Church Membership f Respondent	N =	Golden Rule[a]	EXEMPLARY Unqualified Help to Others	Other Exemplary[a]	Other[a]	Don't Know
Nuclear	92	13	32	22	15	21
Modal	59	7	41	10	5	41
Marginal[a]	63	10	13	19	13	48
Dormant[a]	26	12	12	23	12	46
Total	240	10	27	18	12	35

$$\chi^2 = 28.68 \qquad p < .01 \qquad C = .32$$

a. Columns combined in chi square analysis.
b. Rows combined in chi square analysis.

Summary of Biblical Knowledge and Comprehension—The data presented in this portion of the study showed clearly the minimal character of the cognitive precipitate of the Christian faith in Corn County. Perhaps more important than the differentials in the responses for the various groups we have considered was the discovery of a minimal understanding of the Bible evidenced in almost all the churches examined and in almost all of the subgroups considered.[8] For example, somewhat less than half of the nuclear and modal church members of above average intellectual ability in Maizeville were able to give a meaning for the story of the Good Samaritan that was normatively considered reasonably adequate.

Ministers who use Biblical imagery in their sermons and who refer to Biblical stories in their presentations are undoubtedly failing to communicate with the majority of members in the con-

8. The only church members who possessed a relatively high understanding of Biblical material were the Mission Covenant church members in Maizeville.

gregations who have no context in which to place such references. The Sunday schools seemed to have been quite ineffective in communicating cognitive material to their students.[9] The depth of penetration of cognitive dimensions of the Christian tradition in this country seems to be much less than is often suggested.[10]

Theological Understanding and Religious Life

Introduction—We note again that although it is not possible to make any clear delineation between Biblical knowledge and theological understanding, some distinction between the two areas has been made for purposes of analysis and presentation.

Five areas were selected to explore the manner in which respondents understood certain crucial Christian doctrines and to illumine the feeling tones of the respondents in certain areas of their personal religious lives. The areas that were chosen were broad and rich enough to enable the respondent to react to a range of issues. The areas were:

1. Importance of Easter
2. Distinctive aspects of Christianity
3. Characterization of God
4. Circumstances under which a person is most religious
5. Reasons for prayer

The first two areas focus upon the respondents' understanding of the Christ, while the third attempts to illumine the respondents' understanding of God. The fourth and fifth areas are designed to illumine the interior religious life of the respondent. The areas will be considered sequentially and a summary will be given at the end of this section.

---

9. It should be noted, however, that numerous studies of cross sections of adults on other issues indicate a very high degree of ignorance for the adult population on most substantive matters.

10. The problem of differentials in wisdom, understanding, and/or power is a recurrent one in all historical epochs. American Protestantism has experienced considerable difficulty, both theoretically and practically, with this problem. Our effort to deal constructively with this issue will be deferred until later in this book.

The Importance of Easter—The responses to this query were categorized into two broad groups. The first group included responses that were descriptive in nature. The second group included responses that involved some type of theological interpretation of the descriptive response. Some persons responded with answers that would be included in both groups; such responses would then be classified in the appropriate category of each group.

Three subgroups in the first category were established. The first subgroup was one in which the respondents equated the meaning of Easter with the Resurrection without effort at theological interpretation. The response of a middle-aged, lower-class woman in Maizeville was typical when she simply said: "Resurrection of Christ."

When the interviewer asked her to explain what that meant she said: "Oh, I don't know. That's what I always heard. I really never gave it much thought."

Of the remaining two others which were tabulated, the number of people responding in each was negligible. One classification was "Death of Christ"; the other was "Birth of Christ." In the tables, the responses in these last two subgroups were placed in the "other" column in the descriptive category.

The responses that incorporated theological material were divided into two subgroups. The first subgroup included responses that were considered to be more classical or traditional, while the second group included responses which were obviously an attempt to reformulate traditional beliefs.[11] Included in the first subgroup were responses such as the following answer drawn from the schedule of a young, middle-class Mission Covenant church member in Maizeville: "The importance of Easter? Everybody knows that. It was when Christ died for our sins."

A somewhat different emphasis, but one which also was included in the traditional-belief classification, was the following response given by a middle-aged Methodist man who was em-

---

11. As is the case with other of the analyses undertaken here, systematic theologians would be unhappy with the looseness of the classifications here employed. The relatively unstructured theological thought of laymen has encouraged the use of these kinds of typologies. For our purposes, these subgroups enable us to assess the extent to which persons in the various religious traditions attempt to appropriate their heritages.

ployed as an assistant manager in a local store: "That would be that Easter guarantees eternal life to believers."

Or again, consider this response of an elderly, lower-middle class United Lutheran woman: "Proof that Jesus was God."

The second type of theological response was one which indicated that the respondent was attempting some type of reformulation of classical doctrine.

Illustrative of the type, a 32-year-old Congregational woman whose husband was a professional man responded: "Well, to me Easter symbolizes the possibility of immortality." Again, a middle-aged Methodist proprietor said: "Oh, I don't know. Easter has always meant a message of renewal or rebirth—the coming of Spring."

Some responses were explicitly negative. This response from a mechanic in Maizeville who did not belong to a church is illustrative: "It is the day when all the hypocrites show off their clothes. That's all it means to me."

The classification "other" included responses that were vague and impossible to classify. Here is an example drawn from the interview schedule of a retired Lutheran farmer: "Well, it is mighty important, all right. I sure do think it's important." Such responses might have been included in the "Don't Know" classification. However, in this analysis it was decided to include in that category only those persons who explicitly stated that they did not know how to answer the question. The findings are reported in Tables 62-66.

While there were significant variations in response by broad membership groups and residential areas, in each area Protestants more frequently cited a theological meaning of Easter than did Roman Catholics.

The minimal ideological alienation from the churches was once again evidenced by the very small percentage of negative responses to this question. Almost no church members and only a very small segment of the non-church members gave a negative interpretation for the meaning of Easter.

The detailed denominational analysis given in Table 63 revealed a remarkable uniformity among Protestants insofar as a theological meaning was concerned. With the exception of the members of the Christian church, of whom a very low per-

Table 62. Meaning of Easter by Broad Membership Groups and Residential Areas in Per Cent

Church Membership of Respondent	N =	DESCRIPTIVE		MEANING CITED THEOLOGICAL				
		Resurrection of Jesus	Other[a]	Traditional or Classical	Reformulative Effort	Negative[a]	Other[a]	Don't Know
MAIZEVILLE								
Catholic	52	69	6	15	17	0	15	6
Protestant	490	56	6	21	26	3	13	9
None	111	34	5	10	12	14	15	21
EAST TOWN								
Catholic	102	52	5	7	5	4	18	15
Protestant	82	46	12	6	12	4	18	11
None	49	22	8	0	0	6	29	33
SERVICEVILLE								
Catholic[b]	24	57	4	0	4	4	17	17
Protestant	169	51	11	4	18	2	14	5
None[c]	31	45	10	0	3	7	3	32
OPEN COUNTRY								
Catholic[b]	14	42	8	17	17	8	17	8
Protestant	65	60	4	42	12	2	11	8
None[c]	31	58	0	16	10	3	3	23

$\chi^2 = 220.56$ $p < .01$ $C = .36$

a. Columns combined in chi square analysis.
b. Rows combined in chi square analysis.
c. Rows combined in chi square analysis.

Table 63. Meaning of Easter for Selected Denominations, Maizeville, in Per Cent

Church Membership of Respondent	N =	DESCRIPTIVE		MEANING CITED THEOLOGICAL				
		Resurrection of Jesus	Other[a]	Traditional or Classical	Reformulative Effort	Negative[a]	Other[a]	Don't Know[b]
Baptist	44	61	2	25	23	0	14	9
Catholic	52	69	6	15	17	0	15	6
Christian[c]	20	60	0	20	5	2	20	5
Congregational	73	43	1	15	44	8	12	10
Lutheran, Augustana	42	74	12	26	26	0	5	5
Lutheran, United	81	52	10	16	20	0	11	19
Methodist	82	51	6	27	24	7	12	4
Mission Covenant	54	76	6	20	24	0	13	2
Presbyterian	44	52	11	23	27	5	18	7
None[c]	111	34	5	10	12	14	15	21

$\chi^2 = 29.50$ $.10 < p < .20$

a. Columns combined in chi square analysis.
b. Column excluded in chi square analysis.
c. Rows excluded in chi square analysis.

centage gave theological responses, and the Congregationalists, of whom a relatively high proportion gave this type of response, the range among Protestant groups was remarkably constant.[12]

On the other hand, some interesting relationships emerged when the data for the descriptive response "Resurrection of Christ" were considered.

If one ranks percentage responses in descending order for this response, the following rank order emerges:

1.	Mission Covenant	76 per cent
2.	Augustana Lutheran	74
3.	Catholic	69
4.	Baptist	61
5.	Christian	60
6.	Pentecostal type	54
7.	Presbyterian	52
8.	United Lutheran	52
9.	Methodist	51
10.	Congregational	43
11.	Non-church members	34

The order corresponds closely to the inverse of the status structure (except for non-church members and Roman Catholics) and is roughly proportional to the ordering of closest friends. Those church groups which had the greatest doctrinal emphasis and the greatest degree of intergroup contacts displayed the larger percentage of traditional descriptive responses to the question "What is the importance of Easter?"

Although data are not presented here, an examination of responses by broad membership groups and sex in Maizeville revealed that females had significantly more substantive responses for both Protestants and non-church members. For example, 55 per cent of Protestant females cited a theological meaning of Easter while only 34 per cent of the Protestant males cited a theological meaning of Easter.

In Table 64, the responses are summarized by intellectual

---

12. Because of the small number of cases involved, data for the Christian church should be treated with great reserve. The data are included only because they may be suggestive. They have not been examined statistically, as noted earlier.

Table 64. Meaning of Easter by Intellectual Ability for 30-64 Age Group, Maizeville, in Per Cent

Intellectual Ability of Respondent	N =	DESCRIPTIVE		MEANING CITED THEOLOGICAL		Negative*	Other*	Don't Know
		Resurrection of Jesus	Other*	Traditional or Classical	Reformulative Effort			
Below average	74	50	11	22	8	8	8	15
Average	235	52	4	17	26	6	15	7
Above average	119	58	6	17	44	3	18	3

$\chi^2 = 29.61$ $p < .01$ $C = .22$

* Columns combined in chi square analysis.

ability for the 30-64 age group in Maizeville. The findings were most illuminating and indicated the type of role that intelligence plays in cognitive theological formulations. The category "Theological Formulations" included responses which attempted to put some content into the observation that the meaning of Easter was the Resurrection of Christ. Only 30 per cent of the respondents of below average intelligence cited a theological meaning while twice that percentage of above average intellectual ability cited a theological meaning. It is clear that the attempt to move beyond descriptive statements about the meaning of Easter—and possibly about many theological matters—was closely related to the intellectual ability of the respondent. Although they are not presented here, similar patterns emerged when the analysis of the data by the social status of the respondent was undertaken.

An analysis of the responses to this question for selected membership groups of nuclear and modal members of above average intellectual functioning and of average intellectual functioning are presented in Tables 65 and 66. Broadly speaking, differences between the three Protestant traditions were relatively modest for the above average intellectual ability group. Among members of average intellectual ability, respondents in the transforming wing of the Calvinist tradition had a noticeably higher percentage of theological responses while members of the Roman Catholic church had markedly fewer theological responses to this question than average.

Nuclear and modal church members clearly cited a theological meaning of Easter more frequently than marginal or dormant church members. It was evident that involvement in church activities did increase theological sensitivity, at least so far as it can be assessed by questions of the type employed in this study.

Distinctive Aspects of Christianity—Most theologians have maintained that in the revelation of Christ the character of God has been disclosed in a special and unique way. Reinhold Niebuhr, for example, has maintained that in the Christ the character of God as Redeemer has become clear;[13] man knows that the

---

13. See Reinhold Niebuhr, *The Nature and Destiny of Man* (Charles Scribner's Sons, 1949), *passim*, especially Vol. I, Chapter v, and Vol. II, Chapters i-iii.

Table 65. **Meaning of Easter for Selected Membership Groups of Nuclear and Modal Members of Above Average Intellectual Ability, Maizeville, in Per Cent**

Church Membership of Respondent	N =	DESCRIPTIVE		MEANING CITED THEOLOGICAL				
		Resurrection of Jesus	Other[a]	Traditional or Classical[b]	Reformulative Effort[b]	Negative[a]	Other[a]	Don't Know[a]
Perfectionist Wing Calvinist Tradition	23	74	9	22	35	0	9	4
Transforming Wing Calvinist Tradition	42	45	2	21	48	5	14	0
Lutheran[c]	15	67	7	13	60	0	7	7
Catholic[c]	12	92	8	25	17	0	8	8
Total	92	62	5	21	42	2	13	3

$\chi^2 = 3.45$ $.30 < p < .50$

a. Columns combined in chi square analysis.
b. Columns combined in chi square analysis.
c. Rows combined in chi square analysis.

Table 66. Meaning of Easter for Selected Membership Groups of Nuclear and Modal Members of Average Intellectual Ability, Maizeville, in Per Cent

Church Membership of Respondent	N =	DESCRIPTIVE		THEOLOGICAL				
		Resurrection of Jesus	Other[a]	Traditional or Classical[b]	Reformulative Effort[b]	Negative[a]	Other[a]	Don't Know[a]
Perfectionist Wing Calvinist Tradition	35	74	3	34	23	3	11	3
Transforming Wing Calvinist Tradition	47	47	2	43	36	4	23	2
Lutheran	29	52	10	31	38	0	10	7
Catholic	34	50	0	9	9	0	18	9
Total	145	55	3	30	27	2	17	5

$\chi^2 = 12.85$ $p < .05$ $C = .25$

a. Columns combined in chi square analysis.
b. Columns combined in chi square analysis.

Table 67. Meaning of Easter by Type of Church Membership for Persons of Average Intellectual Ability, Maizeville, in Per Cent

Church Membership of Respondent	N =	DESCRIPTIVE		THEOLOGICAL				
		Resurrection of Jesus	Other[a]	Traditional or Classical[b]	Reformulative Effort[b]	Negative[a]	Other[a]	Don't Know[a]
Nuclear	89	70	2	30	22	1	12	4
Modal	56	50	5	30	34	4	23	5
Marginal[c]	56	52	9	13	23	7	16	14
Dormant[c]	25	56	4	4	32	8	12	4
Total	226	59	5	23	27	4	16	7

$\chi^2 = 13.85$ p < .01   C = .20

a. Columns combined in chi square analysis.
b. Columns combined in chi square analysis.
c. Rows combined in chi square analysis.

ultimate fact about God is not that He is a Creator or a Judge, but, rather, that He is loving and forgiving. Other theologians have desired to ascribe more to the special revelation of God in the Christ; a few have wanted to ascribe less.[14]

In an effort to discern how much of this conversation among theologians had been communicated to laymen, the interviewees were asked the question, "If you were talking with a non-Christian, what would you say was special or distinctive about Jesus and Christianity?"

The responses were categorized into three broad classes. The first class included responses which referred to the role of Jesus. This group was further divided into two subgroups. The first subgroup included those statements which ascribed a theological role to Jesus. The second subgroup included responses which ascribed an exemplary role to Jesus.

Three examples of the type of response which ascribed a theological role to Jesus follow.

A middle-aged Methodist service worker responded: "Well, I don't know. That is pretty hard to say. I guess you'd have to say that He was the Son of God."

A young Congregational woman, the wife of a proprietor, answered: "I would simply say, Jesus was perfect."

A Lutheran man who was a carpenter replied: "Jesus forgave us for our sins. We're saved because of Him."

The following are some responses which ascribed an exemplary role to Jesus.

A Methodist deacon responded: "Jesus led a wonderful life. We should all follow the example He set."

Similarly, a Presbyterian professional man in Maizeville observed: "I always have said that the most important thing about Jesus was the kind of life He led. He has set an example which all of us should try to follow."

Not all responses could be so simply categorized. Consider, for example, this response from a well-educated, middle-class Lutheran housewife, whose husband was a proprietor in the

---

14. Formally, there are three possibilities to be considered in the context of the discussion of special and general revelation. All, some, or none of the content of revelation may be derived from the unique or distinctive element of special revelation. In our considerations here only minimal attention is paid to doctrine. The structure of the argument is ignored.

county seat town of Maizeville: "Well, that is a pretty difficult question to answer. We Lutherans like to say that Jesus died for our sins. I mean that man needs forgiveness and he can't be assured of it by himself. Jesus takes the sins of the world unto Himself. While Jesus in a way shows us what we should be, we know we can't. Still, He is a kind of example, too."

A response of this type was classified both as "theological" and as "exemplary." It should be noted that this response was an extremely high level one. Only a very small number of the respondents gave a response as complex and as theologically sensitive as the one just cited.

The second broad category comprised responses reporting that all religions were the same. Although not stated explicitly, it was implied that there was nothing distinctive about Christianity.

A very small segment of the sample refused to attribute anything distinctive to Christianity. None of the responses in this category indicated any awareness of the epistemological implications of such an affirmation. Here is an example of this type of response. The speaker was a craftsman in Serviceville and was not a church member: "Well, I'll tell you. It seems to me that there really isn't any difference between the various religions. They are all tryin' to do the same thing."

The interviewer asked what they were all trying to do and the respondent said: "Get to heaven."

The third broad category comprised responses which did not answer the question. These responses were further subdivided into three subgroups. The respondents in the first subgroup said that they never discussed religion with anyone. The second subgroup attempted to respond, but their answer was in no sense addressed to the question asked. The third subgroup simply said they did not know.

The last major group of responses was classified as "Don't Know." The respondents were simply unable to respond to the question in any substantive manner. The findings are summarized in Tables 68 and 69.

Three areas of interest related to the data deserve special observation. First, it should be noted that a high proportion of the respondents was unable to give a substantive answer to this question. At the same time, a high proportion of those persons

Table 68. *Distinctive Aspects of Christianity by Broad Membership Groups and Residential Areas in Per Cent*

| | | DISTINCTIVE ELEMENTS CITED | | | | | |
| | | ROLE OF JESUS | | | NO SUBSTANTIVE RESPONSE | | |
Church Membership of Respondent	N =	Theological	Exemplary[a]	All Religions the Same[a]	Never Discusses Religion[a]	Response Does Not Answer Question	Don't Know
			MAIZEVILLE				
Catholic	52	62	1	8	17	15	10
Protestant	390	79	15	3	7	13	22
None	111	48	19	1	3	11	25
			EAST TOWN				
Catholic	101	45	3	0	10	10	37
Protestant	83	39	13	2	10	10	25
None	49	25	2	4	16	14	47
			SERVICEVILLE				
Catholic[b]	23	61	4	4	4	9	18
Protestant	133	57	12	1	2	20	18
None[c]	31	26	3	7	0	19	45
			OPEN COUNTRY				
Catholic[b]	14	29	7	0	29	21	43
Protestant	65	83	14	0	8	6	18
None[c]	31	26	7	7	10	16	42

$\chi^2 = 103.97$ $p < .01$ $C = .27$

a. Columns combined in chi square analysis.
b. Rows combined in chi square analysis.
c. Rows combined in chi square analysis.

Table 69. *Distinctive Aspects of Christianity for Selected Denominations, Maizeville, in Per Cent*

| | | DISTINCTIVE ELEMENT CITED | | | | | |
| | | ROLE OF JESUS | | | NO SUBSTANTIVE RESPONSE | | |
Church Membership of Respondent	N =	Theological	Exemplary[a]	All Religions the Same[a]	Never Discusses Religion[a]	Response Does Not Answer Question[a]	Don't Know
Baptist	44	71	16	0	5	5	27
Catholic	52	62	1	8	17	15	10
Christian[b]	20	75	15	0	5	5	25
Congregational	73	73	8	1	1	4	15
Lutheran, Augustana	42	64	7	2	7	12	17
Lutheran, United	81	47	12	3	11	14	22
Methodist	82	65	9	1	2	16	11
Mission Covenant	54	83	9	0	4	11	9
Presbyterian	44	50	23	5	11	11	14
None[b]	111	48	19	1	3	11	25

$\chi^2 = 22.68$ $.05 < p < .10$

a. Columns combined in chi square analysis.
b. Rows excluded in chi square analysis.

who did respond cited multiple reasons. The percentage of respondents failing to give a substantive answer ranged from a low of 32 per cent among open-country Protestant interviewees to a high of 77 per cent among non-church members in East Town (see Table 68).

Second, the percentage of persons who gave an exemplary interpretation of the role of Jesus was quite low in almost all of the denominations and in almost all of the geographical areas studied. In light of the emphasis of this motif, the exemplary role of Jesus, in the so-called "liberal" Protestant movement of the post World War I period in the United States, it is especially interesting to note that the impact of this emphasis had not been strong among church members. Members of the higher status churches in Maizeville, the Congregational and the Presbyterian, have probably had a greater exposure to this tradition than have the members of any of the other churches. Yet, only 8 per cent of the Congregationalists in Maizeville who were interviewed gave an exemplary interpretation of the role of Jesus, while 23 per cent of the Presbyterians did so. Even though the latter group had the largest proportion of such respondents in the entire sample, the percentage of respondents so replying was still quite low.

Third, there was no evidence to indicate that churches emphasizing a liturgical form of service conveyed a greater sense of the theological significance of Jesus. Responses of Lutheran and Catholic church members, the two traditions in Corn County having the greatest emphasis on liturgical services, were not significantly high on this response, as Table 69 reveals.[15]

An examination of the data by broad membership groups and sex in Maizeville indicated no differences in response by sex for comparable membership groups. The customary relationship

---

15. Although they are not presented here, data for nuclear and modal members of above average and of average intelligence for the four major traditions extant in Corn County have been examined. These data did not suggest significantly higher proportions of theological responses to this question for the traditions emphasizing a liturgical form of service.

Data for dormant, marginal, modal, and nuclear church members of average intellectual ability in Maizeville revealed the usual pattern of increased substantive responses among modal and nuclear church members.

between intellectual ability and substantive response emerged. The proportion of respondents in the 30-64 age group in Maize- ville who cited an exemplary role for Jesus was twice as high for the group of above average intellectual ability as for the groups that were ranked as average and below average, although the proportion so responding was not large for any of the groups.[16] Although the direction was suggestive, the differences by social status were not statistically significant.

Characterization of God—The inability of almost all the de- nominations to transmit any sort of systematic cognitive structure by which their members could interpret their faith has been in- dicated in the analysis of responses in the preceding sections of this study. It was not surprising to discover that the same phe- nomenon occurred when the interviewees were asked to describe or characterize God.

Because of the desire to permit a person to respond to the question without suggesting categories of analysis, the question was open-ended. The difficulty of the question was attested to by most of the respondents. Most were able to offer only a vague or elusive response.[17] These responses were coded by general type and analyzed in Tables 70-75.

The analysis divided the responses into seven general classes. Although much greater precision in a normative theological analysis would be demanded, the typology employed here is quite broad. This type of grouping was made necessary by the vague character of the responses given in the interviews. Very few people were able to give a reasonably coherent analysis. The seven general classes that were devised were partially suggested

---

16. Ten per cent of the below average intellectual ability group, 11 per cent of the average intellectual ability group, and 21 per cent of the above average intellectual ability group cited an exemplary role of Jesus.

17. Because of the theological bias involved in coding the responses, and because of the ambiguous character of the words used in the statements, the authors found scaled and coded forced answers to an investigation in this area to be of very limited value.

At the same time, because the investigators affirmed the reality of the Living God, transcending words and the forms to which those words point, they were much impressed by the respondents' attempts to deal with this question, even though the cognitive structures that informed these efforts were generally most limited.

by the traditional discussion of the issues, and partially suggested by the responses given in the interview schedules. A discussion of each class follows.

Traditional characterization—Some of the respondents answered the question by referring explicitly to specific doctrinal descriptions of God. Responses that were contained in this class included the following explicit characterizations of God:

1. Supreme Being
2. Trinity
3. Omnipresent or "God is everywhere"
4. Omnipotent or "God is all powerful"
5. Omniscient or "God knows everything"

Because of the explicitness of the categories, no difficulty was encountered in coding this type of response. Typical of the responses in this classification was that of a middle-aged, Roman Catholic, lower-middle class woman who said simply: "God's every place."

Or again, a young Roman Catholic man in East Town who was employed as a machine operator said: "Well, I'd say one thing. He is Almighty."

Analogical responses—While, in any rigorous discussion of theological method, most theologians would arrive at the formulations outlined in the first class by analogy, it seemed appropriate in our analysis to distinguish between those persons who used traditional classifications and those who appealed to an explicit analogy. Our decision to make this distinction was prompted by an interest in discerning whether or not differential responses were related to the type of confirmation or catechism class maintained by the several churches.

Two types of responses emerged that were included in this classification. The first—and by far the most frequently employed —response made reference to the fact that God is "like a father." This response, drawn from the schedule of an elderly Baptist woman, the widow of a farmer, illustrates the type: "Well, that's a pretty hard question. You sure can ask them, can't you? I'd say that God is like a father."

The second type of response noted that God was seen through

nature.[18] This response from a middle-aged Methodist man, who clerked in a store in Maizeville, is an example of the second type of response: "I'd say that the way you can know that there is a God is by looking at the wonders of nature around you."

A much more complex response, and one which was given a multiple coding, was this response from a young farmer's wife who was a member of the Christian (Disciples of Christ) church: "Well, God is a Spirit. And He's a God of love. And He's forgiving. And I'd say that He is a Father in Heaven; He is the Father of all, and He has divine power over everything."

Quasi-anthropomorphic responses—A third type of category included those who gave an anthropomorphic characterization of God, such as in the following response from a truck driver who was not a church member: "He is somebody who watches over you. That is what I would say."

Characterizations by reference to attributes—The fourth and most varied category included responses in which God was characterized by reference to His attributes. Included were the following:·

1. Spirit
2. Love, kindness, goodness
3. Creator
4. Governor of the universe
5. Eternal
6. Perfect
7. Judge
8. Forgiving

Whenever a respondent indicated one of these characteristics in his answer to the question, it was coded in this classification.

---

18. The classification of this response in the analogical response group illustrates the difficulty involved in this kind of coding. The decision to focus on method rather than on characterization by reference to attributes, the fourth class that was employed, is more or less arbitrary. Our way of attempting to deal with the problem of method and content in response to the question was to use a multiple code.

The constructive issue involved is whether method and content can be separated. Those persons affirming the unity of the Trinity and denying the legitimacy of the separation between method and content will be inclined to look for a pervasive unity underlying or related to all the differentiations that we have made here.

Often such attributes would be mentioned as part of a relatively complex response, as was shown in the case of the answer given by the young farmer's wife quoted earlier, in the discussion of the analogical classification.

Here are two other examples of responses that would be coded in this classification. The first and relatively simple response came from a Lutheran warehouse stock man: "God is love. That's about all I can say." The second response is that of a middle-aged Presbyterian woman whose husband was a professional man: "That is a hard question. I would have to say that God is a Spirit and that He is love. He is kind and forgiving to us even though we offend Him at times. He is simply perfect."

Quasi-psychological and relational responses—The fifth classification that was used was called "quasi-psychological and relational." Included in this group as relational were the responses indicating the respondent's view of God related to him as helper or protector; included as psychological were responses referring to a feeling one has, to an image in the mind, and to the conscience of man.

Here is an example of a response placed in this general category. The respondent was a middle-aged, lower-class Methodist woman whose husband was a painter: "God is a feeling. You've got to have a feeling to have God. When you go to church you can feel it as something right there [pointing to her heart]."

Other responses—The sixth type of classification included all other responses. They possessed some content, but they were too vague to classify. The following response from a middle-aged Methodist farmer in Serviceville illustrates the type: "God, He isn't no man, that's for sure. That's pretty hard for me to explain. You have to believe in the Lord, if you want anything, far as that goes. If you're awfully sick."

Don't know—The final type of classification included responses of persons who were unable to answer the question at all. The response of this elderly Congregational woman, the wife of a proprietor in Maizeville, is illustrative of the type: "That would be hard to say."

The findings—As Table 70 indicates, the type of response most frequently given in all of the communities studied was the type in which God was characterized by His attributes. The per cent

Table 70. Characterization of God by Broad Membership Groups and Residential Areas in Per Cent

CHARACTERIZATION OF GOD

Church Membership of Respondent	N =	Traditional Characterization	Analogical[a]	Quasi-Anthropomorphic[a]	Characterized by Attributes	Quasi-Psychological[a]	Other[a]	Don't Know
				MAIZEVILLE				
Catholic	52	50	4	12	60	10	15	10
Protestant	490	28	16	9	58	12	13	19
None	111	14	6	6	38	14	20	31
				EAST TOWN				
Catholic	102	27	6	14	40	7	9	22
Protestant	82	24	12	16	41	6	7	18
None	49	14	0	12	25	2	20	38
				SERVICEVILLE				
Catholic[b]	23	13	4	17	48	9	13	30
Protestant	133	14	12	8	61	13	11	20
None[c]	31	3	7	13	32	3	16	36
				OPEN COUNTRY				
Catholic[b]	14	50	0	21	64	0	36	7
Protestant	65	35	20	6	51	15	18	5
None[c]	31	26	23	13	29	19	10	23

$\chi^2 = 82.45$ $p < .01$ $C = .21$

a. Columns combined in chi square analysis.
b. Rows combined in chi square analysis.
c. Rows combined in chi square analysis.

of responses that were so categorized ranged from a high of 56 per cent of the responses in Maizeville to a low of 37 per cent in East Town.

By wide margins, the most frequently mentioned characterizations of God were "love" and "a spirit." Theologians in the Protestant tradition dominant in the areas studied have frequently characterized God by describing Him as Creator, Judge, and Redeemer. The last dimension of His character usually emphasizes that the redeeming love of God transcends His judgment. It is significant that only a few people stated that God is Creator and even fewer characterized God as Judge. Indeed, the fact that very few respondents characterized God as Judge suggested strongly that the doctrine of sin was of minor explicit significance in Corn County.[19] It should be noted further that there was no difference between those denominations which had maintained a more tradition-oriented doctrinal emphasis and those denominations which were most influenced by the Protestant "liberal" tradition. The data suggested that neither tradition had served to maintain the judgmental aspect of God's character in the understanding of church members. Insofar as this phenomenon reflected the understanding of the nature of sin and of the nature of redemption, as vaguely entertained by the respondents, it strongly suggested that the understanding reflected by church members was markedly different than that held by the major theologians of the dominant Protestant tradition. It appears that a Pelagian notion of sin was a dominant one. A God who judges man, both in his defiance of structures and in his idolatrous activity, seemed to be remote to the ideas of most Corn County church members, regardless of denominational affiliation, social status, sex, intellectual ability, or type of church membership.

About one-third of the adults in the sample were either unable to respond to the question or else responded in a manner that

---

19. The actual number of respondents reporting that God is a Judge were:

Maizeville	15	Serviceville	3
East Town	2	Open Country	2

The number of respondents who stated that God is a Creator were:

Maizeville	61	Serviceville	17
East Town	22	Open Country	9

Table 71. Characterization of God for Selected Denominations, Maizeville, in Per Cent

Church Membership of Respondent	N =	Traditional Characterization	Analogical[a]	Quasi-Anthropomorphic[a]	Characterized by Attributes	Quasi-Psychological[a]	Other[a]	Don't Know
					CHARACTERIZATION OF GOD			
Baptist	44	11	20	7	68	9	18	34
Catholic	52	50	4	12	60	10	15	10
Christian[b]	20	10	20	5	45	15	5	30
Congregational	73	34	12	8	44	18	12	16
Lutheran, Augustana	42	33	7	14	62	7	14	17
Lutheran, United	81	26	14	5	46	19	14	24
Methodist	82	28	13	11	55	13	17	16
Mission Covenant	54	24	30	11	87	6	7	9
Presbyterian	44	34	23	11	75	9	11	14
None[b]	111	14	6	6	38	14	20	31

$\chi^2 = 39.44$ $p < .01$ $C = .22$

a. Columns combined in chi square analysis.
b. Rows excluded in chi square analysis.

Table 72. Characterization of God by Type of Church Membership for Persons of Average Intellectual Ability, Maizeville, in Per Cent

Type of Church Membership of Respondent	N =	CHARACTERIZATION OF GOD						
		Traditional Characterization	Analogical*	Quasi-Anthropomorphic*	Characterized by Attributes	Quasi-Psychological*	Other*	Don't Know
Nuclear	89	18	18	12	90	9	10	16
Modal	56	39	5	7	64	13	20	14
Marginal	56	30	13	13	39	20	13	27
Dormant	25	16	8	8	28	16	28	24
Total	226	26	12	11	64	13	15	19

$\chi^2 = 28.17$ $p < .01$ $C = .27$

* Columns combined in chi square analysis.

was so vague as to defy classification. The very high proportion of non-church members so responding, as indicated in Tables 70 and 71, revealed the cognitive impoverishment of this group. While the authors would not be inclined to interpret this finding as evidence of a lack of religious experience, it was clear that the lack of cognitive structures isolated these people from the churches. It is very difficult to imagine that such persons would become involved in the kind of church programs characterizing most of the churches in Corn County.

This phenomenon was further reflected in Table 72 which indicates the percentage of responses to this question by type of church membership for persons of average intellectual ability in Maizeville. Dormant church members responded much less frequently with substantive responses which could be categorized. Once again both nuclear and modal church members had internalized more substantive material related to the Christian heritage than had marginal and dormant church members of comparable intellectual ability.

It was hypothesized that those traditions which emphasized liturgical patterns and doctrinal statements would show a higher proportion of their members responding to the question with traditional theological formulations, such as omniscience, omnipotence, or omnipresence, and by reference to the Trinity and the Supreme Being. An examination of the data presented in Tables 70, 71, 73, and 74 suggested that persons of above average intellectual ability in these traditions did respond more frequently with a traditional characterization, but not at the expense of fewer responses characterizing God by His attributes. While the small number of cases suggested that the data for Lutherans and Catholics of above average intellectual functioning in Maizeville must be treated with reserve, the Maizeville data in Table 73 clearly suggested that the traditions emphasizing traditional doctrinal formulations did succeed in communicating these to laymen of above average intellectual functioning. However, as Tables 70 and 74 reveal, no such differential existed for persons of average intellectual ability.

It should be noted that no one who was interviewed in the sample responded with overt expression of atheism. However, as the data revealed, it is one thing to affirm theism or a positive

Table 73. **Characterization of God for Selected Membership Groups of Nuclear and Modal Members of Above Average Intellectual Ability, Maizeville, in Per Cent**

CHARACTERIZATION OF GOD

Church Membership of Respondent	N =	Traditional Characterization	Analogical[a]	Quasi-Anthropomorphic[a]	Characterized by Attributes	Quasi-Psychological[a]	Other[a]	Don't Know[b]
Perfectionist Wing Calvinist Tradition	24	54	33	4	114	0	8	12
Transforming Wing Calvinist Tradition	41	37	24	7	66	22	12	2
Lutheran[c]	15	67	27	7	60	13	13	13
Catholic[c]	12	133	8	0	58	8	17	17
Total	92	62	25	5	76	13	12	9

$\chi^2 = 13.05$ $p < .02$ $C = .26$

a. Columns combined in chi square analysis.
b. Column excluded in chi square analysis.
c. Rows combined in chi square analysis.

Table 74. **Characterization of God for Selected Membership Groups of Nuclear and Modal Members of Average Intellectual Ability, Maizeville, in Per Cent**

Church Membership of Respondent	N =	Traditional Characterization	Analogical[a]	Quasi-Anthropomorphic[a]	Characterized by Attributes	Quasi-Psychological[a]	Other[a]	Don't Know[b]
Perfectionist Wing Calvinist Tradition	35	17	20	6	89	6	6	23
Transforming Wing Calvinist Tradition	47	36	17	11	81	9	15	6
Lutheran	29	31	14	3	72	21	17	17
Catholic	34	18	0	21	76	9	18	18
Total	145	26	13	10	80	10	14	15

$\chi^2 = 4.73$ $.50 < p < .70$

a. Columns combined in chi square analysis.
b. Column excluded in chi square analysis.

Table 75. **Characterization of God by Intellectual Ability for 30-64 Age Group, Maizeville, in Per Cent**

Intellectual Ability of Respondent	N =	Traditional Characterization	Analogical*	Quasi-Anthropomorphic*	Characterized by Attributes	Quasi-Psychological	Other	Don't Know
Below average	74	22	11	8	43	16	16	20
Average	235	26	10	9	56	12	14	23
Above average	119	48	21	7	72	13	16	11

$\chi^2 = 20.83$ $p < .05$ $C = .17$

* Columns combined in chi square analysis.

feeling toward the divine and quite another thing to command the concepts necessary to articulate any ideas about God.

Although the data are not reported here, an examination of responses by sex and by broad membership groups in Maizeville revealed that females responded more frequently with some type of substantive answer to this question than did males. The greatest difference occurred among those responses in which God was characterized by His attributes. This finding was suggestive when one recalls that females had been somewhat more responsive to questions demanding explicit understanding of religious matters. Although the interpretation must be made with great caution, it would seem that the data may point to the idea that women had a more intuitive awareness of some religious dimensions than did men. However, this situation was undoubtedly related to the types of tasks in which women engage, particularly the care and instruction of the young. Many women who were interviewed responded that it had been necessary to try to answer this question for their children.

The responses to this question by intellectual functioning for the 30-64 age group in Maizeville are presented in Table 75. Once again, variations by intellectual ability were much greater than variations by church membership. The group having superior mental ability gave significantly more substantive responses than did either of the other groups. The average group generally occupied an intermediate position between the below average and the above average groupings. It should be observed, however, that differences by the variable of intellectual ability and by that of church membership were not as great for this question as they were for some other areas. From our point of view such a finding is not surprising, for it would be affirmed that religious experience is more fundamental than the words used to describe it.

Although the findings are not reproduced here, an examination of responses by social status for the 30-64 age group in Maizeville revealed patterns very similar to the responses by intellectual ability.

Circumstances under which a Person is Most Religious—It has frequently been noted that in certain types of circumstances a heightened interest in religion is manifest. Most frequently, crisis situations threatening the life of the individual or situations involving internal disharmony for the individual seem to invoke feelings which are identified by the individual as religious.[20]

Three positive types of responses and a "Don't Know" category were employed in the analysis of responses to this question. The positive responses were categorized as follows:

1. Internal—involves the internal character of the individual often evoked by the possibility of imminent death of self.
2. Internal-External—involves a situation created in part by external circumstances. The individual is not threatened by immediate death, but certain circumstances have arisen which prompt the respondent to think in some way about the meaning of existence.
3. External—refers either to religious attitudes reported in response to explicit behavior or to a stage of life (such as "old age") in answer to the question.

The primary intent of this classification was to assess the differential religious sensitivities of the respondents. It was felt that those persons whose answers fell in the first or second type of response probably possessed a greater sensitivity to life and its religious dimensions than did persons whose responses fell in the third type and in the "Don't Know" groupings.[21]

Included in the first classification were responses which were explicit in their reference to situations which threatened the life of the individual. This response to the question of when one

---

20. The interpretation given to this response by the analyst is dependent upon his theoretical understanding of the nature of religion. From the point of view entertained by the writers, it is entirely reasonable to give credence to the validity of this type of response. Consideration of the ultimate validity of this type of response is deliberately ignored in the body of the study because of our desire to present the empirical findings at a relatively low level of abstraction. As we have indicated previously, such a procedure should serve to make the findings useful to persons entertaining a variety of theoretical interpretations.

21. In addition to the problem of the validity of the inference posited here, a further problem emerges in the internal-external classification employed in this analysis. If it is the case that every event is internally related to every other event, then the classifications used here must be looked upon as polar types which are only approximated in reality. From our point of view, it is the inter-related character of reality which ultimately makes a rigorous internal-external categorization impossible.

is most religious by an elderly, lower-middle status non-church member with a Lutheran church preference illustrates the type: "Probably before he dies."

In addition to references to death, responses which referred to sickness or to situations of great physical danger were included in this classification.

The second type of response, illustrated by this quotation taken from the interview schedule of an elderly Congregational wife of a proprietor in Maizeville, pointed to some type of crisis other than possible death: "In time of trouble or need."

Many of the responses included items which referred to both of the above classifications. Here is an example of this type of response, drawn from the schedule of an elderly, middle-class Episcopalian woman in Serviceville: "Death and sickness or baby being born or things like that. Well, when seriously ill and think you won't get well—that's the time when you feel He is very near—our priest emphasizes that when anyone's ill."

The dominant type of response in the third group referred to some explicit time or event as the situation in which one is more religious. For example, here is the response of a young Methodist woman, the wife of a truck driver in Serviceville: "Well, I think more so at Christmas."[22]

The findings by broad membership groups and residential areas are presented in Table 76. The customary pattern of a significantly higher proportion of "Don't Know" responses by non-church members emerged. In East Town, Serviceville, and the Open Country, significantly more Protestants than Catholics cited the internal-external circumstance grouping.

Although they are not presented here, an examination of the Maizeville data for nuclear and modal church members of average intellectual ability revealed only modest variations between the four broad traditions extant in Corn County. The percentage

---

22. The difficulty of coding and of adequately representing responses to questions focusing upon the area of religion is clearly illustrated in this response. Whether the respondent actually referred to an external event, Christmas, or to the internal meanings associated with that event, is not clear from this response. This ambiguity, however, should extend in an unbiased way to all the groupings employed in this study. Hence, while the absolute responses must be treated with reserve, the differential patterns that are extant are unaffected by these difficulties.

of respondents citing an "internal-external" response ranged from a low of 61 per cent of the perfectionist wing of the Calvinist tradition so responding to a high of 75 per cent of the transforming wing of the Calvinist tradition. For nuclear and modal church members of average intellectual functioning, the tradition in which the person stood apparently had no differential effect upon his response to this question. However, one very significant finding did emerge when the comparable group of above-average intellectual ability in Maizeville was studied. A much higher proportion of respondents of above average intellectual functioning in the perfectionist wing of the Calvinist tradition responded to this question with an "internal-external" response than was the case for any of the other groups. It was this group which strongly emphasized the notion that their members should seek the will of God for themselves in periods of need and crisis. The data strongly suggested that persons of superior intellectual ability who were nuclear and modal members of churches in this tradition did in fact so respond. At the same

Table 76. Circumstances Under Which a Person is Most Religious by Broad Membership Groups and Residential Areas in Per Cent

CIRCUMSTANCES CITED

Church Membership of Respondent	N =	Internal	Internal-External	External	Don't Know
		MAIZEVILLE			
Catholic	52	40	58	25	12
Protestant	490	48	63	26	8
None	111	35	41	32	18
		EAST TOWN			
Catholic	102	55	39	18	12
Protestant	82	54	57	26	2
None	49	43	18	18	31
		SERVICEVILLE			
Catholic[a]	23	61	52	17	17
Protestant	133	49	78	20	8
None[b]	31	29	55	19	26
		OPEN COUNTRY			
Catholic[a]	14	50	21	36	7
Protestant	65	65	55	23	3
None[b]	31	45	61	23	10

$$\chi^2 = 97.98 \qquad p < .01 \qquad C = .24$$

a. Rows combined in chi square analysis.
b. Rows combined in chi square analysis.

time, differences in response between persons of average and above average intellectual ability for the other three traditions were negligible.

When the data were examined by type of church membership for persons of average intellectual ability in Maizeville, no differentials emerged between the four types of church members. These findings are particularly significant when contrasted with the responses for non-church members in Maizeville, as shown in Table 76. Only 8 per cent of the dormant members of average intellectual ability in Maizeville responded with a "Don't Know" response to this question, in contrast to 18 per cent of the non-church members in Maizeville. Similarly, only 16 per cent of the dormant church members of average intellectual ability responded with an "external" response, in contrast to 32 per cent of the non-church members. The data suggested that dormant and marginal church members did have a somewhat greater sensitivity to some facets of religious experience than did non-church members.

Although the data only approached the level of statistical significance, analysis of the responses by intellectual ability for the 30-64 age group in Maizeville showed a marked increase in "external-internal" responses as one moved from the below average to the above average intellectual ability groupings. It was in this category that variations between the three intellectual ability groupings occurred. The data suggested that the ability to appropriate experience and to respond to it in a way which the respondent identifies as religious was correlated with intellectual ability; the common character of human finitude and its relation to religious feelings independent of intellectual ability seemed to be reflected in the extremely modest variations in the internal response. This type of response, it was indicated earlier, suggested a threat to the organism in which death was a possibility. The variations among responses for the three intellectual groups in this category were minimal. Apparently, at this root level, intellectual ability was not determinative; rather, the common humanity of all the respondents was more significant. On the other hand, the type of situation which was exemplified in the "internal-external" category was clearly related to differential intellectual ability. The interpretation given to this range of experience was more viable.

Reasons for Prayer

Introduction—The responses to this question were coded into ten classifications, although only four had sufficiently frequent responses to be treated statistically. The others were tabulated because of the significance of negative findings, even though it was not possible to treat them statistically to assay differential patterns.[23]

The classifications that were employed included: (1) petition, (2) intercession, (3) expressions of feeling of dependence, trust and/or relief with explicit theocentric reference, (4) thanksgiving, (5) forgiveness, (6) psychological comfort without explicit theocentric reference, (7) custom or habit, (8) need, (9) other, and (10) don't know. Each category will be discussed and described in turn.

Petition—This category was the one most frequently cited. A variety of responses was included in this classification, but all the responses contained the basic idea of petition, asking God's favor for a particular purpose. The most frequent kind of response was one which suggested that people ask for God's help in solving problems. This comment from a Lutheran man, a

---

23. For example, the percentage of persons citing a request for forgiveness as a reason for prayer was remarkably constant from area to area. About 10 percent of the interviewees cited this reason. The actual percentages were: Serviceville, 10 per cent; Maizeville, 9 per cent; Open Country, 9 per cent; and East Town, 9 per cent. Because of the inextricable relationship between the sense of sin and the prayer for forgiveness, it seems reasonable to infer that the self-conscious sense of sin among the interviewees was relatively low. Such an observation neither obviates nor sustains the doctrinal validity of the notion of original sin, since the doctrine does not rest upon the self-conscious awareness of the individual. The data did suggest, however, that there did not appear to be a vivid and meaningful self-consciousness of the doctrine among most of the people in Corn County. Some denominations were striking in their responses. Thus, no Presbyterians in Maizeville cited forgiveness as a reason for prayer, in spite of a strong doctrinal and liturgical motif which emphasizes the significance of sin in the Presbyterian tradition.

lower-middle class carpenter in Maizeville, represents the type: "I think that most people pray when they are really up agin'st it. At a time like that, they're apt to turn to the Almighty for help."

Prayers for guidance were another kind of response included in this general classification. Here is the response of a middle-aged, Methodist woman, the wife of a clerical worker in Service-ville: "Well, I'd say—gee, that's a tough one. I believe I'd say when a person doesn't know where to turn, he prays to God for guidance."

Yet another response in this classification specified that a person was apt to petition God in time of illness. Thus, a young Catholic woman, the wife of a factory worker in East Town, responded: "When you're sick. I know I had pneumonia when I was a kid and I prayed to the Lord to help me. I think He helped, too."

Two other types of responses, cited very infrequently, also were included in this classification. The first suggested that prayer was motivated by selfishness, a desire to get something, while the other stated that the persons prayed to get to heaven. The following quotation, from the response of a young mechanic in East Town, is representative of the first type: "I think most people are just plain selfish. They are prayin' to get something for themselves. That ain't right, but I think that's the way it is more times than not." An elderly Catholic woman, widow of an East Town miner, responded simply: "To get to heaven."

Intercession—A second general classification that was em-ployed in coding the responses to this question was intercession. The respondent asked God's intervention on behalf of someone else. Obviously, the request took a variety of forms. The follow-ing comment made by a Baptist man of lower-middle status in Maizeville depicts one type: "Well, I'll tell you. I remember when our girl was real sick. We prayed plenty then askin' the Lord to make her well again."

Expression of feeling of dependence, trust and/or relief—Another major classification was one in which the psychological expression of the feeling of dependence, trust, and/or relief was cited. A theocentric orientation was explicitly noted. Illustrative of the type was this response from a middle-aged Mission Covenant man, a proprietor in Maizeville: "That is difficult to answer, but I'd say one of the main reasons is the feeling of comfort you get when you commune with the Lord."

Thanksgiving—Thankfulness to God the Creator was a motive cited with considerable frequency. The following example of this type is drawn from the schedule of an upper-middle class Congregational woman, the wife of a merchant in Maizeville: "To thank God for all the blessings He has bestowed upon us."

Forgiveness—The last classification cited with considerable frequency was the category of forgiveness. This response of a middle-aged Mission Covenant woman illustrates the classification: "I think we pray for forgiveness. We all know that we have fallen short of God's standards and we pray to Him asking Him to forgive us for our sins."

Psychological comfort—Some responses suggested that psychological comfort was a reason for prayer. Responses that were coded in this category did not indicate a theocentric basis for the psychological comfort suggested. This response, drawn from the schedule of a Presbyterian lawyer in Maizeville, is illustrative of the type: "I'm not sure that it does any good, but I suspect a lot of people pray just for the psychological satisfaction that they get out of it."

Custom—A few respondents explained prayer by suggesting that it was a habit or a custom which the individual had learned. This response, drawn from an interview schedule of a young schoolteacher in Maizeville, a non-church member, is illustrative of the type: "To tell you the truth, I imagine that most people pray because they have always been taught to pray."

Instinct or need—The last substantive response to this question that was categorized was instinct or need. This category included responses which suggested that the desire for prayer was something innate within man, in contrast to the sociological interpretation given in the preceding category. A middle-aged Lutheran farmer gave this response: "I think it is something deep down in man that leads him to pray. He has the need to."

Other reasons—The final substantive group included all other responses except the "Don't Know" category. The responses were too·vague and diffuse to permit the presentation of an illustrative type.

The findings—The findings are summarized in Tables 77 and 78. The most significant single finding that emerged in the analysis was the constancy of the rank order of responses by geographical area and by denomination. In all cases where the number of responses was large enough to assure some statistical stability, the prayer of petition was cited most frequently. The actual percentage of the respondents citing this reason for prayer ranged from a high 63 per cent in Serviceville to a low of 52 per cent in East Town.

The second most frequently cited reason for prayer in all cases was an expression of the feeling of trust, dependence, and/or relief.

For all geographical areas, praise or thanksgiving was the third most frequently cited reason for prayer. The actual percentage of respondents citing this reason was quite low. The range was from a high of 21 per cent in Maizeville to a low of 10 per cent in East Town. It had been hypothesized that the Roman Catholic tradition, with its relatively greater emphasis on natural goodness, might have a higher frequency of respondents citing thanksgiving as a reason for prayer. However, this hypothesis must be rejected as revealed by Table 78 and by other data, not presented here, dealing with responses of nuclear and modal members of average and above average intellectual ability in Maizeville. There was no evidence that a higher proportion of Roman Catholic church members of comparable intellectual functioning and institutional involvement cited thanksgiving more frequently.

The fourth most frequently cited category was prayers of forgiveness, in all geographical areas and for almost all of the groupings employed in the analysis. The percentage of the respondents who gave this response was so low that interdenominational analysis was not possible. It may be observed, however, that the data did not suggest that any of the denominations had been markedly successful in communicating the classical Christian understanding of sin to its members insofar as the

Table 77. Reasons for Prayer by Broad Membership Groups and Residential Areas in Per Cent

Church Membership of Respondent	N =	Petition	Inter-cession[a]	Feeling of Dependence, etc.	Forgive-ness[a]	Thanks-giving	Psycho-logical Comfort[a]	Custom[a]	Instinct or Need[a]	Other[a]	Don't Know[a]
						REASONS CITED					
MAIZEVILLE											
Catholic	52	64	4	40	14	35	8	0	2	4	6
Protestant	490	59	6	41	9	19	9	7	3	6	5
None	111	56	3	26	8	14	6	7	1	3	5
EAST TOWN											
Catholic	102	62	3	20	5	13	5	8	2	5	6
Protestant	82	51	6	27	15	11	5	7	1	7	1
None	49	33	2	29	6	4	0	4	0	10	20
SERVICEVILLE											
Catholic[b]	23	83	4	13	4	4	9	9	0	4	4
Protestant	133	65	4	29	10	17	3	5	2	8	8
None[c]	31	42	6	36	16	16	0	7	0	3	10
OPEN COUNTRY											
Catholic[b]	14	79	0	7	14	14	0	14	0	0	0
Protestant	65	55	3	45	12	25	5	8	0	5	2
None[c]	31	55	3	39	0	16	7	13	0	16	0

$\chi^2 = 48.01$ $p < .01$ $C = .16$

a. Columns combined in chi square analysis.
b. Rows combined in chi square analysis.
c. Rows combined in chi square analysis.

Table 78. Reasons for Prayer for Selected Denominations, Maizeville, in Per Cent

Church Membership of Respondent	N =	Petition	Inter-cession[a]	Feeling of Dependence, etc.	Forgive-ness[a]	Thanks-giving	Psycho-logical Comfort[a]	Custom[a]	Instinct or Need[a]	Other[a]	Don't Know[a]
Baptist	44	61	5	43	9	18	16	2	9	9	5
Catholic	52	64	4	40	14	35	8	0	2	4	6
Christian[b]	20	40	15	70	10	20	10	5	0	0	0
Congregational	73	63	8	42	8	8	7	11	0	3	3
Lutheran, Augustana	42	50	5	45	14	14	7	12	10	14	7
Lutheran, United	81	51	6	37	6	19	7	10	1	5	7
Methodist	82	73	6	48	12	21	10	2	2	5	4
Mission Covenant	54	67	7	35	15	32	9	4	4	4	2
Presbyterian	44	68	5	34	0	32	5	14	2	5	5
None[b]	111	56	3	26	8	14	6	7	1	3	5

$\chi^2 = 27.90$ $.10 < p < .20$

a. Columns combined in chi square analysis.
b. Rows excluded in chi square analysis.

sense of sin and prayers of forgiveness are interrelated.[24] The data revealed that neither denominational affiliation, intellectual ability, social status, sex, or type of church membership affected the percentage of respondents who cited forgiveness as a reason for prayer. A confessional liturgical tradition did not seem to encourage higher responses in this category than did a free church non-liturgical tradition.[25]

Although they are not presented here, the data for Maizeville were examined by broad membership groups and sex, by intellectual ability for the 30-64 age group, by social status for the 30-64 age group, by selected membership groups of nuclear and modal members of above average intellectual ability, by selected membership groups of nuclear and modal members of average intellectual ability, and by type of church membership for persons of average intellectual ability. A statistical analysis of these data revealed that in no case were the differentials observed statistically significant. While the data do not demand such a conclusion, the writers' doctrinal presuppositions would suggest the interpretation that prayer is a universal response to the cognitive or emotive awareness of the divine and therefore that common patterns of response are to be expected.[26]

Summary of Theological Understanding and Religious Life Data— Generally, Protestants displayed a broader range of responses

24. This argument is particularly persuasive when it is considered in relation to the findings dealing with the character of God cited earlier, in which only a very small number of respondents characterized God as "Judge."

25. The present comments are designed to illumine the current discussions about the efficacy of traditional liturgical patterns. Whatever the theological rationale and whatever may be the feelings of the small literate groups of leaders concerned with this issue, the data did not support the contention that churches having a traditional liturgical pattern have more effectively communicated elements of the cognitive structure of the Christian faith or the feeling tones related to them to their adherents than have churches in non-liturgical traditions.

26. Works such as Friedrich Heiler's *Prayer* (Oxford University Press, 1932) and Rudolph Otto's *The Idea of the Holy* (Oxford University Press, 1923) suggest certain of the universal elements alluded to in this analysis. Because of the Kantian bias of these writers, there would be some differences in the interpretation between our analysis and theirs. Either approach would, however, affirm the status of certain universals which would be explanatory in interpreting the kind of findings reported here.

to questions exploring theological understanding than did Catholics.

Nuclear and modal church members manifested somewhat greater theological sensitivity, insofar as this dimension can be assessed by the types of question employed in this study. Persons who were not church members consistently gave the highest proportion of "don't know" responses to questions in this area. Persons of above average intellectual ability and of high social status responded most sensitively.

Those questions in the interview schedule that focused most directly upon fundamental religious experience, that is, those questions in which the respondents were asked to cite the circumstances under which a person is most religious and to give reasons for prayer, received a lower proportion of "don't know" responses than any other questions on Biblical or theological understanding. In most instances, the findings showed no significant relationship between the religious affiliation of the respondent and his theological sensitivity as assessed by these questions. From our interpretive perspective, which affirms the universal character of man's religious situation and which affirms the pervasiveness of religious experience—although not necessarily self-consciously—as God participates in all that is, these findings are not unexpected and are of major importance. At the same time, the vague and diffuse character of the responses highlights the limited success the various religious denominations have had in communicating the cognitive sides of their traditions to laymen.

There was some suggestion of greater female sensitivity to religious feelings as revealed by responses to certain questions reported in this section of the study. On the cognitive side, however, there was no evidence of differential appropriation.

The findings indicated that nuclear and modal members of above average intellectual ability seemed to appropriate some of the emphases of their tradition's understanding of the nature and character of God. At the same time, the findings for nuclear and modal members of average intellectual ability did not show such differential appropriation.

The Churches and the World:
Social, Political, and Economic Orientation
of Church Members[27]

Introduction—In some fashion or other, the church throughout its entire history has had to relate itself to the social, the political, the economic, and the cultural spheres.

While almost all facets of the Christian heritage have entertained a type of transcendental understanding of the nature of reality in which God's self-revelation in history of His ultimate character of redemptive love in Jesus as the Christ has been affirmed, the relation of the church to the world has been subject to diverse interpretation.[28]

Formally, three broad types of relationships between the church *qua* church and the world are possible. Whatever formulation is espoused serves to guide the direction of the Christian believer in relation to the world; and, at least implicitly, it serves to indicate how the relationship between love and justice is conceived.[29]

First, an unqualified distinction between the church and all other kinds of human association may be asserted. Two possibilities inhere within this first type of relationship. On the one

---

27. For a corollary treatment of these data, see Victor Obenhaus and W. Widick Schroeder, "Church Affiliation and Attitudes Toward Selected Public Questions in a Typical Midwest County," *Rural Sociology,* 28 (March, 1963), 35-47.

28. The employment of what may be characterized as a "theovolitional" principle is common to theologians who make this affirmation. In some fashion, the large majority of theologians have affirmed the peculiar character of this understanding of God's nature. Whether the affirmation of a principle of rationality, in which it is assumed that reason can penetrate the nature of things and that all revelation is general in the sense that the rigorous examination of any experience would lead to this understanding of God's character, is a viable epistemological option in Christendom, is subject to some discussion.

29. No effort has been made in this typological formulation to indicate the internal grounds on which the relationships noted here are made. Further, the internal complexity and divergences within each grouping have been ignored. Our interest here is to see if the major and salient emphases of a tradition have been appropriated by laymen, since only a very, very small segment of them are able to fathom fine distinctions and differentiations.

hand, although a radical distinction between the church and the world may be envisioned, the Christian is counseled to serve in the fallen and sinful world. Adherents of this Lutheran "two worlds" position have argued that all social institutional forms stand sharply under God's judgment, while the idea that the Christian faith might provide a guide to an appropriate form of social organization is categorically rejected. This tradition was sufficiently represented in Corn County for analysis of the contemporary descendants in this heritage. On the other hand, it may be held that the Christian not only should maintain the distinction between the church and the world but that he should also attempt to withdraw radically from the world and to refuse to participate in the principalities and powers. While a small number of Mennonites and Jehovah's Witnesses were present in Corn County and might be viewed as representatives of this option, there were too few to treat statistically.[30]

The second major option is to see an ambiguous relationship between the church and the world. The Christian believer is counseled to participate in the world and to be guided by Christian understanding while doing so. Of the six forms of political organization formally possible, only two have been affirmed on theological or quasitheological grounds by major adherents of this second broad option in Christendom.

In one wing of Calvinism, the Christian attempts to transform the world to attain a modicum of the harmony of life with life encompassed in the experiential confrontation of God as Redemptive Love. It is this tradition that has consistently and persistently claimed a relationship between theological understanding and a democratic social order. The Christian would view participation in the world as a manifestation of his Christian responsibility, although the distinction between the church and the world would remain. For adherents of this kind of Calvinism, the emergence of a democratic political order would represent the sort of basic transformation of the world that would enable them to participate positively in the political order. In Corn

---

30. There is an interesting relationship, both formally and subjectively, between radical withdrawal from the world and radical transformation of the world, which is considered here as the first subtype of a third major option.

County, what we have called the transforming wing of Calvinism (Congregational, Presbyterian, and Methodist) would represent this option.

In Roman Catholicism, because of a different formulation of "natural" and "supernatural" and because of a different interpretive framework, a different type of relationship to the state and a different theory of social organization have developed historically. The monarchical and hierarchical character of the church, the direction assigned to it in relation to the state, the reflective relationships envisioned between the church and other voluntary associations, and the integrative role assigned to a common Catholic belief system all point to a theory of social organization based on a more intimate relationship between the church and the world than that espoused in transforming Calvinism. The relatively greater clarity about the appropriate form of social organization and the development of an elaborate system of casuistry have led to more specific ethical formulations and to more specific suggestions regarding appropriate lay attitudes toward a variety of issues than exist in Calvinism. While this Catholic stance has been modified in the modern world, some elements or components of the tradition, symbolized by such phenomena as the parochial school system, the confession, and the attitude toward birth control, are still extant. The Catholic church was sufficiently represented in Corn County to permit extended analysis.

Finally, the distinction between the church and the world may be denied, either in principle or *de facto*. Again, two possibilities exist within this broad option. On the one hand, one may articipate a radical transformation and sanctification of the world. The church and the believer may become identified with particular programs or with particular forms that seem to them to permit the manifestation of the harmony of life with life in the world. While some of the extreme sectarians included in the sample may have adhered to this view, there were too few cases to treat statistically. In a much less extreme form, however, the groups we have characterized as the perfectionist wing of Calvinism may be seen as related to this option empirically. Their behavior seems to affirm belief in a type of sanctification that possesses some of the characteristics of the more extreme form.

Persistent efforts to commit persons unqualifiedly to certain political, economic, and social programs on the basis of Christian
understanding reflect this type of stance—and they are con-
tingently manifest in all of the historical traditions extant in the
United States. Empirically and formally, there is a relationship
between this type and the second subtype of the first broad
option enumerated earlier. On the other hand, one may begin
with the world, identifying a particular culture or form of social
organization with the experience of the ultimate harmony of
things seen in the Christ. Certain militant nationalists might
exemplify this type, although no facet of the Christian heritage
has explicitly affirmed it.[31] This type of "culture" religion may
be expected to manifest itself universally at some levels, although
the interpretation of this manifestation will depend upon which
of the outlined options the critic affirms.[32]

In this investigation, questions were designed to discern the
extent to which church members in the various traditions in
Corn County were informed by their theological heritages, either
cognitively or emotionally. In order to give a measure of concrete-
ness to issues, respondents were asked to respond to questions
dealing with the federal social security program, the United Nations, labor unions, federal health insurance, and farmers' organizations. They were asked to indicate whether they approved or
disapproved of each and why. Fewer than five persons in the
more than 1200 interviewed made any attempt to relate their
responses to these questions explicitly to the Christian faith.
Although he had not been asked to do so, it seems reasonable
to assume that, if the Christian faith played a considerable role

---

31. The possible exception may be certain kinds of so called "liberalism."
As is the case with all the other characterizations, the formal option does
not coincide precisely with the contingencies manifest in historical periods.
Further, as the presentation of the empirical data will show, church members representing each possibility were present in each of the manifest
churches of Corn County.

32. In the last chapter of this book, attention is directed briefly to the
problem of the alternative interpretation of the findings from stances that
are Lutheran or Calvinist. Social scientists who reject the basic type of
transcendental understanding that makes possible the distinctions developed
in this typology will resolve the matter differently at the root level. Most
commonly, the analyst will function operationally or will attempt to discern
more elemental factors or clusters of factors that have allegedly given rise
to these ideas.

in the individual's consideration of social issues, he would have introduced an informing structure from his faith into his responses to these questions. Because of the paucity of this kind of response, the reasons cited for the respondent's attitudes toward these various programs or organizations have not been analyzed here in detail, although the tables presented in this section give the responses by the categories "approval," "qualified approval," and "disapproval" for each question.

In addition to these findings, data on two other dimensions of the relationship of church and world were gathered. The first had to do with the respondent's understanding of the stand of his church on major social, political, and economic issues. The second explored his attitude toward his minister's understanding of social, political, and economic matters.

The best understanding of the interviewee's relation to the major options developed here emerged in response to this question. It is clear that the relationship was vague and ill-defined, for all the religious groups considered included members in each of the major options noted here.

As the detailed analysis of the data reveals, probably the most salient finding in this portion of the study was the lack of any informing cognitive structure to order the respondents' attitudes toward various political, social, and economic matters. The vast majority of the respondents were issue-oriented rather than principle-oriented. Although the judgments were related to the respondent's political party, the pragmatic response to issues was clear. Such a phenomenon is undoubtedly a boon to the democratic process, unless one is willing to affirm that there is an appropriate form or pattern of social organization valid for all time.[33]

The Findings—*Attitudes toward labor unions*—The findings by broad membership groups and residential areas are shown in Table 79, and the attitudes toward labor unions for selected denominations in Maizeville are shown in Table 80.

Although none of the denominational groups in any of the

---

33. If the alternative to the pragmatic approach to issues discerned in this study were a rigid doctrinaire position, characteristic of numerous political parties in Europe, one might not be so concerned about the lack of the respondent's relation of these issues to the Christian faith.

Table 79. Attitude Toward Labor Unions by Broad Membership Groups and Residential Areas in Per Cent

Church Membership of Respondent	N =	Approval	Disapproval	Qualified Approval	Don't Know
			ATTITUDE INDICATED		
			MAIZEVILLE		
Catholic	49	41	12	41	6
Protestant	475	22	14	47	17
None	105	41	15	30	14
			EAST TOWN		
Catholic	100	48	6	40	6
Protestant	80	43	10	43	5
None	47	49	6	40	4
			SERVICEVILLE		
Catholic[a]	22	46	5	14	36
Protestant	132	33	23	25	20
None[b]	31	48	19	16	16
			OPEN COUNTRY		
Catholic[a]	14	29	0	50	21
Protestant	64	19	16	47	19
None[b]	31	26	6	58	10

$$\chi^2 = 102.93 \qquad p < .01 \qquad C = .29$$

a. Rows combined in chi square analysis.
b. Rows combined in chi square analysis.

Table 80. Attitude Toward Labor Unions for Selected Denominations, Maizeville, in Per Cent

Church Membership of Respondent	N =	Approval	Disapproval	Qualified Approval	Don't Know
			ATTITUDE INDICATED		
Baptist	43	28	14	37	21
Catholic	49	41	12	41	6
Christian*	20	20	15	45	20
Congregational	70	24	7	53	16
Lutheran, Augustana	40	15	18	40	28
Lutheran, United	78	21	18	42	19
Methodist	79	24	14	53	9
Mission Covenant	53	28	9	40	23
Presbyterian	43	12	16	58	14
None*	105	41	15	30	14

$$\chi^2 = 31.90 \qquad .05 < p < .10$$

* Rows excluded in chi square analysis.

areas studied had a large proportion of people who opposed labor unions, Serviceville had significantly more respondents who indicated they were opposed to labor unions than was the case in any of the other areas. In many ways, Serviceville was a very isolated community and it probably reflected attitudes more widespread a generation or so ago. Although, with the exception of Maizeville, there was little difference between the three membership groups in responses indicating approval of labor unions, the evidence suggested somewhat greater support of unions among Catholics than among Protestants. In all cases, however, the percent of respondents indicating open disapproval of labor unions was very low.

Although there was only minimal variation in percentage of respondents indicating disapproval of labor unions in Maizeville, those churches in the transforming wing of the Calvinist tradition had a higher percentage of respondents indicating qualified approval. This phenomenon probably reflected differences in intellectual ability and social status rather than theological differences, since no theological rationale for such qualified approval was cited.

While they are not presented here, data showed that women were generally less informed about labor unions than were men and were somewhat less supportive. However, the large majority of respondents of both sexes affirmed that labor unions had been good for the American working man.

The percentage of respondents who expressed qualified approval of labor unions increased sharply in moving from the below average intellectual ability grouping of the respondents 30-64 years old in Maizeville to the above average intellectual ability grouping.[34]

Attitudes toward social security—As Tables 81 and 82 reveal, a consensus was achieved with respect to the social security program. While somewhat higher proportions of Maizeville residents indicated qualified approval of the program and a somewhat higher percentage of respondents living in the open

---

34. At the time this study was undertaken, investigations of graft and inordinate labor power were receiving national publicity. Apparently, the interviewees of superior intellectual ability were much more responsive to these revelations and were more critical of the operations of labor unions.

country indicated disapproval of the program, the overwhelming majority of the respondents in all areas and in all membership groups indicated approval of the program. As Table 82 shows, there was no variation in response by selected denominational membership in Maizeville.

From the point of view of this study, probably the most interesting fact to emerge was the very low percentage of respondents who cited a theological or quasi-theological reason for their support of the social security program. These data highlight the observation made earlier about the issue-centered rather than principle-centered basis for political judgments by the vast majority of respondents in this study. When the federal social security program was introduced a generation ago, considerable opposition to the program was evident in Corn County; however, opposition has changed to overwhelming support in the course of a generation.

While the variations by sex were negligible, the usual pattern of significantly higher percentages of qualified approvals among

Table 81. Attitude Toward Social Security Program by Broad Membership Groups and Residential Areas in Per Cent

Church Membership of Respondent	N =	ATTITUDE INDICATED			
		Approval	Disapproval[a]	Qualified Approval[a]	Don't Know[a]
			MAIZEVILLE		
Catholic	49	76	8	14	2
Protestant	475	70	6	18	6
None	105	74	5	14	7
			EAST TOWN		
Catholic	100	86	3	3	8
Protestant	80	86	3	5	6
None	47	83	6	6	5
			SERVICEVILLE		
Catholic[b]	22	82	9	0	9
Protestant	132	80	7	8	5
None[c]	31	86	7	7	0
			OPEN COUNTRY		
Catholic[b]	14	72	14	7	7
Protestant	64	68	19	13	0
None[c]	31	69	16	9	6

$\chi^2 = 23.46$ $p < .01$ $C = .14$

a. Columns combined in chi square analysis.
b. Rows combined in chi square analysis.
c. Rows combined in chi square analysis.

Table 82. *Attitude Toward Social Security for Selected Denominations, Maizeville, in Per Cent*

Church Membership of Respondent	N =	Approval	Disapproval[a]	Qualified Approval[a]	Don't Know[a]
			ATTITUDE INDICATED		
Baptist	43	72	7	16	5
Catholic	49	76	8	14	2
Christian[b]	20	85	5	5	5
Congregational	70	76	7	10	7
Lutheran, Augustana	40	68	3	30	0
Lutheran, United	78	73	5	16	6
Methodist	79	75	3	20	2
Mission Covenant	53	68	4	23	5
Presbyterian	43	63	9	23	5
None[b]	105	74	5	14	7

$$\chi^2 = 3.78 \qquad .80 < p < .90$$

a. Columns combined in chi square analysis.
b. Rows excluded in chi square analysis.

Table 83. *Attitude Toward Farmers' Organizations by Broad Membership Groups and Residential Areas in Per Cent*

Church Membership of Respondent	N =	Approval[a]	Disapproval[b]	Qualified Approval[a]	Don't Know[b]
			ATTITUDE INDICATED		
			MAIZEVILLE		
Catholic	49	61	2	12	25
Protestant	575	58	6	10	26
None	105	68	6	4	22
			EAST TOWN		
Catholic	100	49	2	2	47
Protestant	80	56	4	3	37
None	47	60	4	0	36
			SERVICEVILLE		
Catholic[c]	22	55	9	9	27
Protestant	132	54	11	8	27
None[d]	31	74	16	3	7
			OPEN COUNTRY		
Catholic[c]	14	50	14	7	29
Protestant	64	75	8	11	6
None[d]	31	55	26	10	9

$$\chi^2 = 30.13 \qquad p < .01 \qquad C = .16$$

a. Columns combined in chi square analysis.
b. Columns combined in chi square analysis.
c. Rows combined in chi square analysis.
d. Rows combined in chi square analysis.

respondents of above average intellectual ability emerged. Variation by social status was not statistically significant.

Attitudes toward farmers' organizations—In rather sharp contrast to the high percentage of qualified responses to the question
dealing with labor unions, the respondents overwhelmingly expressed the sentiment that farmers' organizations had been of
benefit to the American farmer, as Tables 83 and 84 reveal.
Urban-oriented East Town respondents had significantly more
people who did not know how to respond to this question. As
Table 84 indicates, Maizeville responses did not vary significantly
by church membership.

Somewhat more females had "Don't Know" responses to this
question than did males in Maizeville, but the percentage differentials in the "Disapproval" category were insignificant. No
difference in the percentage of "Disapproval" responses was noted
by intellectual ability or social status, although the usual pattern
of a higher percentage of "Qualified Approval" responses was
noted in moving from below average to above average intellectual ability groupings.

Attitudes toward U.S. membership in the United Nations—

Table 84. Attitude Toward Farmers' Organizations for Selected Denominations,
Maizeville, in Per Cent

Church Membership of Respondent	N =	ATTITUDE INDICATED			
		Approval[a]	Disapproval[b]	Qualified Approval[a]	Don't Know[b]
Baptist	43	51	2	7	40
Catholic	49	61	2	12	25
Christian[c]	20	60	15	5	20
Congregational	70	50	10	7	33
Lutheran, Augustana	40	60	13	13	14
Lutheran, United	78	62	1	14	23
Methodist	79	62	4	8	26
Mission Covenant	53	59	6	9	26
Presbyterian	43	61	0	14	25
None[c]	105	68	6	4	22

$$\chi^2 = 9.88 \qquad .10 < p < .20$$

a. Columns combined in chi square analysis.
b. Columns combined in chi square analysis.
c. Rows excluded in chi square analysis.

A consensus had been achieved on U.S. membership in the United Nations, as Tables 85 and 86 show; variation from group to group was negligible. The reason for approval cited with overwhelming frequency by respondents was that the United Nations contributed to world peace. While the respondents may indirectly have seen this desire in relationship to the Christian tradition, almost no one explicitly so stated.

An outstanding exception to the usual pattern of a higher percentage of qualified approval responses by people of above average intellectual ability and of white-collar social status was apparent in response to this question. The percentage of "Qualified Approval" responses to this question was very low among all intellectual ability groupings and among all social status groupings. In light of the serious operational difficulties which this organization has encountered and will undoubtedly continue to encounter, this lack of constructive critical thinking is understandable but of dubious merit. Apparently all people so ferv-

Table 85.   Attitude Toward United States Membership in United Nations by Broad Membership Groups and Residential Areas in Per Cent

Church Membership of Respondent	N =	Approval[a]	ATTITUDE INDICATED		
			Disapproval[b]	Qualified Approval[a]	Don't Know[b]
			MAIZEVILLE		
Catholic	49	78	8	8	6
Protestant	475	72	7	5	16
None	105	66	9	4	21
			EAST TOWN		
Catholic	100	63	7	6	24
Protestant	80	80	5	2	13
None	47	68	6	2	24
			SERVICEVILLE		
Catholic[c]	22	41	14	9	36
Protestant	132	59	16	8	17
None[d]	31	65	16	0	19
			OPEN COUNTRY		
Catholic[c]	14	79	0	14	7
Protestant	64	89	3	3	5
None[d]	31	74	13	3	10

$$\chi^2 = 27.37 \qquad p < .01 \qquad C = .15$$

a. Columns combined in chi square analysis.
b. Columns combined in chi square analysis.
c. Rows combined in chi square analysis.
d. Rows combined in chi square analysis.

ently desired peace that they were almost blind to some of the alleged inadequacies of one of the instruments designed to help maintain it.

Attitudes toward federal health insurance—Because a consensus had been achieved with reference to the social security program, a question involving the role of the federal government in welfare activities in an area in which disagreement was still sharp was included in the interview schedule to highlight differentials between the various groupings. The respondents were asked whether or not they would approve the idea of federal health insurance. The data are summarized in Tables 87-91. Rather sharp Catholic-Protestant differences emerged in most areas on this question (see Tables 87 and 88). Roman Catholics generally supported such a program, while Protestants were generally opposed.

However, as Tables 89 and 90 reveal, a most interesting differential emerged between Roman Catholics of above average intellectual ability and those of average intellectual ability. Because of the small number of Roman Catholics with above average intellectual ability in this study, the data must be treated with

Table 86. **Attitude Toward United States Membership in United Nations for Selected Denominations, Maizeville, in Per Cent**

Church Membership of Respondent	N =	ATTITUDE INDICATED			
		Approval[a]	Disapproval[b]	Qualified Approval[a]	Don't Know[b]
Baptist	43	77	2	2	19
Catholic	49	78	8	8	6
Christian[c]	20	65	15	10	10
Congregational	70	71	7	9	13
Lutheran, Augustana	40	60	8	2	30
Lutheran, United	78	67	5	5	23
Methodist	79	85	6	6	3
Mission Covenant	53	66	7	4	23
Presbyterian	43	84	0	5	11
None[c]	105	66	9	4	21

$$\chi^2 = 22.48 \qquad p < .01 \qquad C = .22$$

a. Columns combined in chi square analysis.
b. Columns combined in chi square analysis.
c. Rows excluded in chi square analysis.

Table 87.   Attitude Toward Federal Health Insurance by Broad Membership Groups and Residential Areas in Per Cent

Church Membership of Respondent	N =	Approval	Disapproval	Don't Know
		ATTITUDE INDICATED		
		MAIZEVILLE		
Catholic	51	51	35	14
Protestant	463	30	43	27
None	59	31	34	35
		EAST TOWN		
Catholic	100	42	22	36
Protestant	82	45	38	17
None	46	50	15	35
		SERVICEVILLE		
Catholic[a]	22	59	23	18
Protestant	132	39	39	22
None[b]	31	39	35	26
		OPEN COUNTRY		
Catholic[a]	14	36	43	21
Protestant	63	25	56	19
None[b]	31	48	32	20

$$\chi^2 = 57.54 \qquad p < .01 \qquad C = .22$$

a. Rows combined in chi square analysis.
b. Rows combined in chi square analysis.

Table 88.   Attitude Toward Federal Health Insurance for Selected Denominations, Maizeville, in Per Cent

Church Membership of Respondent	N =	Approval	Disapproval	Don't Know
		ATTITUDE INDICATED		
Baptist	43	26	44	30
Catholic	51	51	35	14
Christian*	19	32	53	15
Congregational	65	35	49	16
Lutheran, Augustana	41	29	42	29
Lutheran, United	77	31	42	27
Methodist	74	30	43	27
Mission Covenant	54	20	33	47
Presbyterian	41	22	58	20
None*	59	31	34	35

$$\chi^2 = 23.15 \qquad .05 < p < .10$$

* Rows excluded in chi square analysis.

some reserve. Nevertheless, the data strongly suggested that Roman Catholics of above average intellectual ability had adopted the dominant community attitude on this issue, while Roman Catholics of average intellectual ability had a much smaller proportion of respondents who indicated disapproval of such a projected program. These data suggested that other than religious factors were dominant in affecting attitudes toward this program.

Members of the middle and upper status Presbyterian church

Table 89.   Attitude Toward Federal Health Insurance for Selected Membership Groups of Nuclear and Modal Members of Above Average Intellectual Ability, Maizeville, in Per Cent

Church Membership of Respondent	N =	ATTITUDE INDICATED	
		Disapproval	Approval or Don't Know
Perfectionist Wing Calvinist Tradition	24	75	25
Transforming Wing Calvinst Tradition	36	53	47
Lutheran*	16	50	50
Catholic*	13	69	31
Total	89	61	39

$$\chi^2 = 3.47 \qquad .05 < p < .10$$

* Rows excluded in chi square analysis.

Table 90.   Attitude Toward Federal Health Insurance for Selected Membership Groups of Nuclear and Modal Members of Average Intellectual Ability, Maizeville, in Per Cent

Church Membership of Respondent	N =	ATTITUDE INDICATED	
		Disapproval	Approval or Don't Know
Perfectionist Wing Calvinist Tradition	35	46	54
Transforming Wing Calvinist Tradition	41	68	32
Lutheran	29	52	48
Catholic	34	26	74
Total	139	49	51

$$\chi^2 = 13.25 \qquad p < .01 \qquad C = .29$$

in Maizeville were strongest in their disapproval of such a program, although the plurality of respondents for all Protestant denominations in Maizeville except for Pentecostal-type church members disapproved such a program. As Table 90 reveals, nuclear and modal members in churches of the transforming wing of the Calvinist tradition of average intellectual ability were the strongest in their opposition to such a program, while the comparable Roman Catholic group was the most supportive. Protestant males in Maizeville were the group most frequently indicating opposition to federal health insurance, while many more females gave a "Don't Know" response.

As Table 91 indicates, there was no evidence to indicate that the type of church membership affected the respondents' attitude on this question.

Table 91. Attitude Toward Federal Health Insurance by Type of Church Membership for Persons of Average Intellectual Ability, Maizeville, in Per Cent

Type of Church Membership of Respondent	N =	ATTITUDE INDICATED		
		Disapproval	Approval	Don't Know
Nuclear	86	52	24	23
Modal	53	43	32	25
Marginal*	54	54	31	15
Dormant*	24	38	37	25
Total	217	49	29	22

$$\chi^2 = 2.60 \qquad .50 < p < .70$$

* Rows combined in chi square analysis.

Not surprisingly, social status was the most significant variable in affecting attitudes toward federal health insurance. For the 30-64 age group in Maizeville, the percentage of respondents indicating disapproval of federal health insurance ranged from a low of 33 per cent among blue-collar social status respondents to a high of 60 per cent among white-collar social status respondents.

Knowledge of denominational social issue statements—Most of the denominations included in this study have social action groups, general assemblies, or both, which make policy state-

ments on various social issues in the United States. To learn to
what extent these denominational formulations have penetrated
to the local level, a question was included in the interview schedule that asked whether the interviewee was acquainted with any
social or ethical policy formulations that his denomination had
made. The results are summarized in Tables 92-96.

As Table 92 shows, the overwhelming majority of the inter-

Table 92. Knowledge of Denominational Social Issue Statements by Broad
Membership Groups and Residential Areas in Per Cent

Church Membership of Respondent	N =	RESPONSE	
		No Knowledge	Knowledge of at Least One Issue
		MAIZEVILLE	
Catholic	50	60	40
Protestant	479	83	17
None	73	88	12
		EAST TOWN	
Catholic	100	86	14
Protestant	82	88	12
None	48	96	4
		SERVICEVILLE	
Catholic[a]	21	86	14
Protestant	129	75	25
None[b]	30	100	0
		OPEN COUNTRY	
Catholic[a]	14	86	14
Protestant	64	77	23
None[b]	31	90	10

$$\chi^2 = 48.20 \qquad p < .01 \qquad C = .20$$

a. Rows combined in chi square analysis.
b. Rows combined in chi square analysis.

viewees in all the churches in all the areas studied were not
acquainted with any social policy of the denomination of which
they were members or which they preferred. Of the small percentage indicating that they were informed, only a very few
knew of more than one issue on which the denomination had
taken a stand. The two issues cited most frequently were opposition to liquor and opposition to racial segregation. One of the
interesting things that emerged in these responses was the negative manner in which they were couched; rarely were the
responses conveyed as positive affirmations that the church was

for wholesome community life. Instead, respondents would in-variably say that the church was against divorce, against racial segregation, etc. It seems likely that the negative character of these responses is related to the lack of cognitive structure, a finding which has emerged again and again in the course of this study.[35]

Roman Catholic respondents had the highest proportion of members in Maizeville who were aware of their church's position on at least one social issue. Even in this group, however, the respondents possessing knowledge of at least one social issue were in a minority (see Table 93). The disparity between the Lutheran tradition, which has historically entertained the "two worlds" doctrine discussed earlier, and the other major traditions was most striking. For example, no member of the United Lutheran Church indicated that he possessed knowledge of a social issue statement or policy on a social issue by his church.

An analysis of the responses of the knowledge of denomina-tional social issue statements by intellectual ability for the 30-64 age group in Maizeville revealed no statistical difference by intellectual ability of the respondent, although the differentials approached the 5 per cent level of statistical significance; these data are not presented here. They suggested that among the 30-64 age group in Maizeville there was a somewhat greater knowledge by persons of white-collar social status than among any of the other groupings. For example, only 14 per cent of the blue-collar respondents indicated that they had knowledge of any denominational social issue statement, while 27 per cent of the white-collar group responded positively.

As Table 96 reveals, modal and nuclear church members were somewhat more knowledgeable than were marginal and dormant church members. Once again, the evidence suggested greater cognitive involvement for modal and nuclear members.

Reasons cited for minister's knowledge about social issues— In an effort to assess what informing structure ordered the respondent's understanding of the relationship between the

---

35. Of course, the high proportion of negative responses to this ques-tion does not indicate that social issue statements are of little or no value. Their impact on key opinion leaders, within and without the Congress and in administrative branches of the government, may be considerable.

Christian faith and the world, the respondents were asked the question, "Do you think your minister should be informed about such present day problems as politics, race, the schools, U.S. foreign policy? Why or why not?"

The substantive responses were classified in five major groups.

Table 93. Knowledge of Denominational Social Issue Statements for Selected Denominations, Maizeville, in Per Cent

| | | RESPONSE | |
Church Membership of Respondent	N =	No Knowledge	Knowledge of at Least One Issue
Baptist	43	81	19
Catholic	50	60	40
Christian*	19	79	21
Congregational	71	85	15
Lutheran, Augustana	42	88	12
Lutheran, United	77	100	0
Methodist	80	67	33
Mission Covenant	54	78	22
Presbyterian	44	86	14
None*	73	88	12

$$\chi^2 = 43.56 \qquad p < .01 \qquad C = .29$$

* Rows excluded in chi square analysis.

Table 94. Knowledge of Denominational Social Issue Statements for Selected Membership Groups of Nuclear and Modal Members of Above Average Intellectual Ability, Maizeville, in Per Cent

| | | RESPONSE | |
Church Membership of Respondent	N =	No Knowledge	Knowledge of at Least One Issue
Perfectionist Wing Calvinist Tradition	24	58	42
Transforming Wing Calvinist Tradition	42	74	26
Lutheran*	16	93	7
Catholic*	13	38	62
Total	95	68	32

$$\chi^2 = 1.69 \qquad .10 < p < .20$$

* Rows excluded in chi square analysis.

The first group, doctrinal responses, was further subdivided into three subgroups, while the other groupings were not subdivided. Although it was difficult to categorize doctrinal responses because of the looseness of the responses, the data did permit some rough categorization. The first subgroup referred to a "two worlds" doctrine in which the respondent affirmed that the sphere of religion and the sphere of government were not related. The second doctrinal response affirmed that the moral principles of Jesus could be applied to society, while the third subgroup included responses explicitly stating that the church had to be

Table 95. Knowledge of Denominational Social Issue Statements for Selected Membership Groups of Nuclear and Modal Members of Average Intellectual Ability, Maizeville, in Per Cent

Church Membership of Respondent	N =	RESPONSE	
		No Knowledge	Knowledge of at Least One Issue
Perfectionist Wing Calvinist Tradition	36	83	17
Transforming Wing Calvinist Tradition	48	60	40
Lutheran	31	94	6
Catholic	37	65	35
Total	152	74	26

$$\chi^2 = 13.89 \qquad p < .01 \qquad C = .29$$

Table 96. Knowledge of Denominational Social Issue Statements by Type of Church Membership for Persons of Average Intellectual Ability, Maizeville, in Per Cent

Church Membership of Respondent	N =	RESPONSE	
		No Knowledge	Knowledge of at Least One Issue
Nuclear	93	70	30
Modal	59	80	20
Marginal*	64	94	6
Dormant*	26	92	8
Total	242	81	19

$$\chi^2 = 16.41 \qquad p < .01 \qquad C = .25$$

* Rows combined in chi square analysis.

concerned with the community. Because of the vagueness of most responses, the categorization into the groupings discussed earlier in this chapter was not feasible. Thus, the persons arguing for a radical separation of the church and the world and those persons arguing for each sphere having its appropriate place would both espouse what was called in the coding a "two worlds" doctrine. Hence, the perfectionist wing of the Calvinist tradition and the Lutheran tradition would both be expected to give this type of substantive response. Similarly, persons standing in what we have termed the transforming wing of the Calvinist tradition and in the Roman Catholic tradition might be expected to give comparable responses, namely, responses explicitly stating that the church had to be concerned with the community.

The use of the term "two worlds" doctrine does not mean either that the respondents were aware of the roots of such a doctrine or that they were explicitly conscious of the theological rationale for such a doctrine. This response from a Baptist crafts-man in Serviceville is typical of the type that was coded in this subgroup: "Yeah, well, let me see. I'll tell you this. The way I see it religion and politics don't mix. I seen too many preachers gettin' tangled up in things that wasn't none of their affairs."

This response from a Methodist farmer's wife illustrates the second subgroup in the first major classification: "I've always said that the teaching of the Lord ought to be applied to everyday life. 'Course, they sometimes aren't and I think that's why there's so much grief in the world. Besides, a minister just ought to know what's goin' on in the world."

The last sentence of the above response illustrates the second major category used, i.e., the office of the minister requires knowledge about social issues.

The final subgroup in the doctrinal response classification was the most sophisticated of all. A response was coded in this group if it affirmed that part of the Christian's mandate was to be concerned with his community. Only a very small number of respondents suggested that social and economic structures affected the life of the individual, although some of the responses hinted at it.

This response drawn from the schedule of a Lutheran house-wife in Maizeville, the wife of a retired farmer, illustrates the type: "I think—ah—that the Christian ought to pay attention and know what goes on in his community—to help make it better."

The second major category included responses, like the one cited above, in which some reference to the office of the minister was made. The type of comments coded here included those suggesting that such knowledge would help the people who sought counsel from him, that such knowledge was expected of a leader of a congregation, and that such knowledge would make sermons more interesting.

The last substantive category was one in which no specific reference to doctrine or office was made; rather, it was affirmed that all people should be informed about such issues as a matter of good citizenship. No reference to the source or to the rationale for such a doctrine was offered. This response of a Christian operative in Maizeville was common: "Everybody ought to be informed about those things if he is a good citizen."

The "other" classification included many of the responses which did not apply directly to the question, while the "Don't Know" group simply failed to respond. Only a minimal understanding of the rationale either for or against the concern of the church with social, political, and economic issues was revealed by analysis of responses to this query as presented in Tables 97-99.

Only a small segment of the sample gave a positive doctrinal reason for ministers' knowledge about social issues. Although there was relatively wide variation between church members and non-church members responding that the office of the ministry required knowledge about social issues (see Tables 97 and 98), there was no evidence of systematic variation between Protestant and Catholic responses to this question. It had been hypothesized that those traditions in which the office of the ministry was invested with strong institutional sanctions (in this sample, the Roman Catholic tradition) would have higher proportions of their respondents referring to some facet of the office as a reason for knowledge on social issues. No clear patterns of relationship by church membership emerged.

As Table 98 also shows, the percentage of Lutherans citing a form of the "two worlds" doctrine as a reason for a minister's lack of knowledge on social issues was not higher than the percentages of several other groups so responding. The data sup-

Table 97. Reasons Cited for Ministers' Knowledge About Social Issues by Broad Membership Groups and Residential Areas in Per Cent

REASONS CITED

Church Membership of Respondent	N =	DOCTRINAL			Office of Minister Requires Knowledge	All Should Be Informed	All Other	Don't Know
		Two Worlds[a]	Moral Principles Applicable to Society[a]	Church Concerned with Society[a]				
				MAIZEVILLE				
Catholic	52	8	2	6	54	25	29	4
Protestant	429	16	7	5	42	20	27	8
None	111	19	3	6	26	22	22	15
				EAST TOWN				
Catholic	102	18	1	1	37	12	30	14
Protestant	82	24	2	1	39	15	32	6
None	49	18	0	4	20	8	37	29
				SERVICEVILLE				
Catholic[b]	23	26	4	0	0	9	48	22
Protestant	135	7	4	1	32	11	44	7
None[c]	31	6	0	0	26	16	42	13
				OPEN COUNTRY				
Catholic[b]	14	0	0	0	22	57	14	7
Protestant	65	14	8	0	49	28	23	3
None[c]	31	26	3	0	35	39	23	3

$\chi^2 = 106.62$ $p < .01$ $C = .28$

a. Columns combined in chi square analysis.
b. Rows combined in chi square analysis.
c. Rows combined in chi square analysis.

Table 98. Reasons Cited for Ministers' Knowledge About Social Issues for Selected Denominations, Maizeville, in Per Cent

REASONS CITED

Church Membership of Respondent	N =	DOCTRINAL			Office of Minister Requires Knowledge	All Should Be Informed	All Other[b]	Don't Know[b]
		Two Worlds[a]	Moral Principles Applicable to Society[a]	Church Concerned with Society[a]				
Baptist	44	18	2	5	64	27	16	7
Catholic	52	8	2	6	54	25	29	4
Christian[c]	20	5	10	5	45	20	25	5
Congregational	41	10	20	2	22	15	32	15
Lutheran, Augustana	42	12	2	2	45	21	29	5
Lutheran, United	81	19	6	5	40	25	23	11
Methodist	53	17	11	2	32	15	32	11
Mission Covenant	54	15	11	9	41	17	24	2
Presbyterian	44	20	5	9	57	20	32	7
None[c]	68	19	3	6	26	22	22	15

$\chi^2 = 27.25$ $.10 < p < .20$

a. Columns combined in chi square analysis.
b. Columns combined in chi square analysis.
c. Rows excluded in chi square analysis.

ported the observation made earlier that no clear denominational patterns emerged.[36] Table 99 further highlights the impotence of the churches to transmit a rationale for relating the church to social issues. For persons of average intellectual ability in Maizeville there was no variation between dormant, marginal, modal, and nuclear church members citing a positive doctrinal reason for ministers' knowledge about social issues. As a matter of fact, with the possible exception of a relatively high percentage of dormant church members who cited a "two worlds" doctrine, variations by type of church membership in response to this question were negligible.

Data not examined here indicated that there was no evidence of statistically significant variations in response by broad membership groups and sex in Maizeville or by social status for the 30-64 age group in Maizeville.

More than twice as many respondents of above average intellectual ability than respondents of below average intellectual ability for the 30-64 age group in Maizeville suggested that the office of the minister required knowledge about social issues (58 per cent as compared with 21 per cent). Significantly, however, of those respondents of above average intellectual ability citing a doctrinal reason for ministers' knowledge about social issues, more persons cited a variant of the "two worlds" doctrine, suggesting that religion and politics don't mix, than cited the idea that the church should be concerned with society, or noted that moral principles of Christianity were applicable to society. These data highlight the fact that even among the intellectually superior group the churches have been unable to implant cognitive structures in the minds of their laymen which would encourage the heritage of the transforming wing of the Calvanist tradition or the Catholic tradition.

Summary of the Findings on the Church's Relation to the World— To the extent that the issue-oriented responses in this section can be generalized, Catholic preference for government involvement in the economic order seemed greater than Protestant

---

36. The point made earlier about the types of responses given to this question should be underscored. Almost no one possessed the theological understanding necessary to give a response which was theologically acute. These categories represent a higher level of abstraction from what were, in the original interview schedules, quite simple and direct responses.

Table 99. Reasons Cited for Ministers' Knowledge About Social Issues by Type of Church Membership for Persons of Average Intellectual Ability, Maizeville, in Per Cent

REASONS CITED

Church Membership of Respondent	N =	DOCTRINAL						
		Two Worlds	Moral Principles Applicable to Society[a]	Church Concerned with Society[a]	Office of Minister Requires Knowledge	All Should Be Informed	All Other[a]	Don't Know[b]
Dormant[c]	21	38	5	0	24	24	19	14
Marginal[c]	52	13	4	6	40	29	21	10
Modal	50	20	2	8	40	20	24	14
Nuclear	82	9	9	6	46	23	23	6
Total	205	17	5	6	41	24	22	10

$\chi^2 = 13.26$ $p < .05$ $C = .23$

a. Columns combined in chi square analysis.
b. Column excluded in chi square analysis.
c. Rows combined in chi square analysis.

preference. It is clear, however, that no clear theoretical understanding related to theological tradition was manifest for either
group. Persons in the transforming wing of Calvinism were most
opposed to the idea of federal health insurance, for example.
Among modal and nuclear members of average intellectual ability
in Maizeville, Protestant-Catholic differences on this issue were
extremely sharp.

In each tradition examined, persons who represented the
various possible options of relating the Christian faith to the
world were found, but there was no clear configuration in any
of the traditions. Only in a very few cases did respondents in
any of the traditions extant in Corn County reveal any self-
conscious reflection on the issue of the relationship between the
church and the world.

On some of the questions considered in this portion of the
study, significant variations by sex and by social status were
observed. Usually, these variations were as significant as the
variations by intellectual ability. Generally, females and persons
of white-collar social status were less supportive of labor unions
and of federal health insurance than were males and persons
of blue-collar social status.

The overwhelming majority of the interviewees had no
knowledge of any social policies or pronouncements of denominations of which they were members or that they preferred.

The facts that the interviewees who were not church members
had consistently the lowest proportion of responses to substantive
questions and that nuclear and modal church members had
consistently the highest substantive responses suggest some differential appropriation of religious motifs.

4. ROLE EXPECTATION OF THE MINISTER BY LAYMEN[1]

Lay expectations of the ministerial role in the churches of Corn County centered on affective or emotive elements. Part of the reason for the relative ineffectiveness of the teaching and the prophetic functions of the minister as revealed in this study may be attributed to the difference between role expectation by laymen and a normative theological understanding of that role. Because of our intention to present the data at a low level of abstraction, it is beyond the scope of our study to consider normative definitions of the ministry. These attempts are almost always undertaken by theologians of the church and, in our judgment, are an essential part of any total consideration of the minister's role. However, for our purposes it is sufficient to note that these normative efforts are one further element contributing to the definition of the role.

In order to assess the role expectation of the minister that was entertained by various types of laymen in the several denominations, two questions in the interview schedule focused on this issue.

First, interviewees in denominations in which polity permitted it were asked to imagine that they were members of a pulpit committee assigned the task of selecting a new minister. They were then asked to enumerate the qualities or characteristics they felt were most important for a minister to possess. In churches where polity arrangements did not permit such a pulpit

1. For another treatment of this topic in which the data reported in this chapter have been re-ordered and presented at a somewhat higher level of abstraction, see W. Widick Schroeder, "Lay Expectations of the Ministerial Role: An Exploration of Protestant-Catholic Differentials," *Journal for the Scientific Study of Religion*, II (Spring, 1963), 217-227. The data are not directly comparable, but the conclusions are the same.

committee, the interviewees were asked simply what qualities or characteristics they would look for most in a new minister or a new priest.

Second, respondents were asked "Do you think a minister should conduct himself differently than other people in town?"

Qualities Expected in a Minister

The responses to these questions were divided into two major substantive groups. Included in the first group were responses which referred to professional qualities of the minister. The second group contained responses that referred to personal qualities of the minister.[2]

Each of these major groups was further divided into subgroups. Four subgroups were analyzed under the major heading "professional qualities." They were: quality of sermons, theological orientation, quality of education, and the other professional qualities. The last was employed to categorize a variety of responses referring to professional qualities. Each of these was mentioned so infrequently as to prevent statistical comparisons, although collectively they constituted a relatively large percentage of responses. While such a variety of responses prevents interdenominational comparison, the fact of variety was in itself a very significant finding. Included in this subgroup was a variety

---

2. The same intrinsic problem presents itself here as in the problem of internal-external relations discussed earlier. Strictly speaking, one must note that the classification used here really distinguishes in degree and not in kind. This problem makes the categories employed somewhat arbitrary. This situation is particularly acute in the inclusive subgroups, "other professional qualities" and "other personal qualities." As they stand, these classes are of very limited analytic value and only passing reference is made to them in the text. In the context of all of the findings, almost all the qualities cited as "other professional qualities" contribute to the harmonizing, integrating functions of ministerial leadership which is clearly the dominant expectation of Corn Countians.

From our point of view, in spite of their great usefulness and analytic power, this difficulty is inherent in the "pattern variables," developed by Parsons and his colleagues and so fashionable in contemporary sociology. They are abstractions from a reality which is inextricably contextual in which distinctions are a matter of degree rather than of kind, except for part of the distinction between God and the world. It is beyond the scope of this book to explore this problem in detail.

of responses such as: experience, parish and community visita-
tion, ability to work with young people, ability to work with old
people, dependability, and general activity in the church.

Two subgroups were considered under the heading "personal
qualities." The first included responses that referred to the
warmth in interpersonal relations which the minister expressed.
The second group of responses referred to the exemplary conduct
which a minister was expected to display. The third subgroup
of this major grouping included all other personal qualities referred to by the interviewees, such as sincerity, humanness,
type of family, friendships, age, personal habits, and leadership
qualities.

This response, drawn from the schedule of a middle-aged,
Lutheran carpenter in Maizeville, illustrates "quality of sermons,"
"quality of education," and "other" subgroups of the professional
qualities grouping: "Good sermons. Sermons that you can understand. 'Course, he ought to have a good education and be a good
talker."

The following response from a Baptist woman in Serviceville
emphasized the theological orientation of the minister and the
quality of his sermons: "He's got to be a Bible preacher. Got to
—ah—have a Scriptural outlook, I guess you'd say."

And this response, drawn from the schedule of an elderly,
middle-status Episcopalian woman in Serviceville, cited several
qualities: "Kindness—and—ah—well, that takes in a lot. Well, of
course, if he's a good speaker, but not necessary. Of course, we
just have a wonderful priest. He is kind and a good preacher and
takes so much interest in everything."

Next, this response, drawn from the schedule of a middle-
aged Catholic man, a clerk, was typical of many that emphasized
the quality of interpersonal relations: "Well, one is personality.
One that gets along with his congregation."

Finally, this response, taken from the schedule of a 35-year-
old wife of a truck driver in East Town, represents the exemplary
category: "Live up to what he's preachin'—if he lived right. Set
a good example."

Two other major groups were used. The first was an "other"
group to include any other positive responses. Most of these
responses were vague references to the kind of man one expected

a minister to be. It may be looked upon as a professional-personal quality joint grouping. Most of the persons who were coded in this group possessed low verbal facility. And a "Don't Know" class was used for the nonrespondents.

From an analysis of some of the findings in Tables 100 and 101, three things are seen.

The first outstanding fact was the very high proportion of people who responded that their minister must possess a "good personality." When used, this term implied that the person was to be a warm, friendly, outgoing person, "able to get along with people." Clearly, the significance of this factor cannot be minimized. The possession of these personal qualities is of extreme importance in parish ministry. Insofar as the possession of these qualities is incompatible with the notion of "the learned ministry"—a condition about which little is known—persons possessing a different orientation will probably encounter some difficulty in the parish ministry.[3]

The second salient fact that is noted in the tables was the relatively high frequency with which the respondents cited the professional criterion of sermon quality as a significant item in the evaluation of a minister. While this area was not explored further in the questioning, it is clear that this kind of response indicated that some professional competence was expected of the minister. It is not clear, however, precisely what criteria the interviewee used to determine what constituted a "good sermon." Probably the criteria were twofold: (1) the personal subjective response of the individual church member,[4] and (2) the type of preaching

---

3. It is not suggested that it is impossible to combine the qualities of scholarship and friendliness. It is true, however, that because of the very great importance placed upon these personal qualities by parishioners, a person who possesses the requisite professional qualities but who lacks the personal qualities embodied in the idea of a good personality would be handicapped in the parish ministry. Although empirical data are lacking, it would seem that there would be some difficulty in one person completely internalizing both elements. The difference is probably one of emphasis. In part, institutional structures sustain alternative vocational roles, each with a dominant set of values. Probably many persons in the ministry who place a premium on the importance of cognitive structures and scholarship go into teaching or other related forms of the ministry, while those persons who place a premium on interpersonal relations go into the parish ministry.

4. In other sections of this study, the relative absence of informing cognitive structures by which laymen could evaluate sermons has been demonstrated.

Table 100. Qualities or Characteristics Expected of Minister by Broad Membership Groups and Residential Areas in Per Cent

QUALITIES EXPECTED

Church Membership of Respondent	N =	PROFESSIONAL QUALITIES				PERSONAL QUALITIES			
		Good Sermons	Good Education[a]	Theological Ideas[a]	Other[a]	Good Personality	Exemplary Conduct[b]	Other[b]	Other
MAIZEVILLE									
Catholic	50	24	6	6	28	32	12	34	30
Protestant	479	46	11	11	41	55	12	50	19
None	105	31	1	5	19	49	15	37	8
EAST TOWN									
Catholic	102	10	2	0	24	41	13	27	16
Protestant	82	24	9	12	20	39	12	34	16
None	49	16	2	2	18	20	10	14	16
SERVICEVILLE									
Catholic[c]	23	9	4	0	22	43	13	9	26
Protestant	133	26	6	8	20	44	8	30	8
None[d]	31	29	3	0	26	26	7	26	16
OPEN COUNTRY									
Catholic[c]	14	29	7	14	14	50	14	43	7
Protestant	63	29	14	24	44	49	22	49	11
None[d]	31	10	6	19	19	68	16	39	13

$\chi^2 = 98.87$ $p < .01$ $C = .20$

a. Columns combined in chi square analysis.
b. Columns combined in chi square analysis.
c. Rows combined in chi square analysis.
d. Rows combined in chi square analysis.

Table 101. Qualities or Characteristics Expected of Minister for Selected Denominations, Maizeville, in Per Cent

Church Membership of Respondent	N =	PROFESSIONAL QUALITIES				PERSONAL QUALITIES			Other
		Good Sermons	Good Education[a]	Theological Ideas[a]	Other[a]	Good Personality	Exemplary Conduct[b]	Other[b]	
Baptist	43	35	19	9	63	54	12	42	30
Catholic	50	24	6	6	28	32	12	34	30
Christian[c]	20	50	20	5	20	75	15	49	10
Congregational	71	54	16	6	47	51	13	58	13
Lutheran, Augustana	42	38	5	7	36	26	10	60	26
Lutheran, United	77	47	7	14	29	64	7	52	23
Methodist	80	56	5	15	39	71	26	46	15
Mission Covenant	54	46	9	17	63	46	2	41	24
Presbyterian	44	43	21	9	27	52	7	61	14
None[c]	105	31	1	5	19	49	15	37	8

$\chi^2 = 50.02$ $p < .01$ $C = .27$

a. Columns combined in chi square analysis.
b. Columns combined in chi square analysis.
c. Rows excluded in chi square analysis.

expected in the tradition of which the respondent was a member. The latter element introduced a quasi-objective criterion into the evaluation. However, the relationship between these two elements was ambiguous. It was this structural ambiguity which permitted rather wide ranges in types and varieties of sermons, even though the various traditions might be relatively distinct as far as style of preaching was concerned. For example, the Baptists, on the one hand, had a rather clear idea of what constituted "Biblical" preaching. Their minister was expected to adhere to a form of Scriptural exegesis. However, rather wide latitude in the interpretation was tolerated. The Congregationalists, on the other hand, expected a form of preaching which was not so closely tied to Scriptural exegesis. Again, given the prescribed form, rather wide latitude in content was permitted.[5]

The third factor that stands out in the data was the relatively diffuse character of the responses. In addition to the two criteria noted above, the only other mentioned with considerable frequency was that of exemplary conduct. However, the combination of a wide range of other qualities that were cited amounts to a large cumulative total for both the grouping of professional qualities and the grouping of personal qualities.

These data suggest that the role definition of the minister was quite vague and diffuse from the viewpoint of laymen. While he was not expected to be all things to all men, there was a broad range of qualities and attitudes which he was expected to possess and a broad range of skills which he was expected to master. An adequate performance in all the professional areas enumerated and possession of all the personal attributes cited as desirable by laymen was clearly beyond the competence of any man, particularly since some of the cited attributes were mutually exclusive.[6]

---

5. It seems highly likely that in most congregations the sermon has become a part of an indigenous liturgical pattern. The very limited cognitive structure possessed by most parishioners would support this interpretation of the data found here.

Normatively, the style and type of sermon depends upon one's sustaining theological tradition. The process of communication and the appropriation that is made by laymen of sermons is an area in which further research is most emphatically needed. In the light of the emphasis upon the spoken word in Protestantism, it is curious that so little empirical investigation dealing with the cognitive facet of the "Word" has been undertaken.

6. For example, some people preferred a young minister. Others pre-

This situation suggests that, aside from the presence of persons in a congregation habitually critical of any minister, there were some elements of disequilibrium inherent in the minister's role. The minister may placate and minimize but not eliminate them.

In connection with this consideration of attributes, one further observation should be made here. Only five respondents were unable to respond to this question, and the number of multiple responses was higher than for any other question in the schedule. Everyone had a judgment about the qualities he expected in a minister. The fact that some of them were vague, some were specific, some were ambiguous, and some were mutually exclusive illustrates the lack of clear role definition which characterized the laymen's understanding of the ministry. At the same time, there was a consensus among members of all denominations that a certain pattern or style of life was expected of a minister. Detailed findings on this subject will be presented below.

The evidence suggested that the members of the Roman Catholic church, which has the most rigorously institutionalized role definition of its religious leader, were best able to accept their religious leadership. Even here, however, the qualities embodied in the expression "A good personality" were very important for Roman Catholic laymen. Nevertheless, there was not such a spread of desirable attributes cited for the Roman Catholic priest as for the Protestant minister.

When one turned to a consideration of Protestant churches in the traditional liturgical pattern, the evidence was ambiguous. The Augustana Lutheran church members included in the sample cited a relatively low number of qualities or characteristics while the United Lutheran church members cited somewhat more than an average number of qualities. In any case, the data were not as decisive as for the Roman Catholic priest, whose sacerdotal role in the economy of salvation is more clearly defined for the believers.

One of the most significant negative findings was the low proportion of laymen who cited educational background as a significant consideration in the selection of a minister. The Congregationalists and Presbyterians in Maizeville had the highest

---

ferred a middle-aged man. This problem is discussed at further length in connection with the analysis of the behavior expected of ministers.

proportion of members who cited this criterion. The Baptists in Maizeville also cited this criterion relatively frequently (19 per cent of the respondents). Although it was hypothesized that many of the Presbyterians and Congregationalists would desire a well-educated ministry, it was surprising to find such a high proportion of Baptists citing this criterion. This phenomenon may be related to the fact that the Baptist church had recently called a young minister with a B.D. education. Probably, this factor had been the subject of some discussion among the congregation. This finding may also be related to the mobility in status that was in some evidence in the Baptist church in Maizeville. By contrast, no Baptists in the service town of Serviceville mentioned this criterion. In general, only very few people in any of the other denominations mentioned that a minister should possess a good education. The data suggested that a sufficient number of people manifested an interest in the education of the minister that some consideration would be given to this factor, although there seemed to be almost no laymen in any of the denominations competent to evaluate the quality of the education obtained.

Among Maizeville Protestants, there was no difference of opinion between men and women regarding the two most frequently cited qualities that should be sought in a minister—good sermons and a good personality. The significance played by personality was further highlighted by consideration of the Maizeville responses for the 30-64 age group by intellectual ability. There was no statistical difference in the percentage of the three groups that cited a good personality as a quality expected in a minister. Similarly, variations by social status were not significant. Although the data are not presented here, an examination of the responses of persons from Maizeville of above average intellectual ability who were nuclear and modal members in the four broad traditions, of persons of average intellectual ability who were nuclear and modal members in the four broad traditions, and of dormant, marginal, modal, and nuclear members of average intellectual ability revealed patterns of responses comparable to the ones presented in the tables shown here. For every grouping, a good personality was the most frequently cited quality or characteristic, while the quality of the sermons was the second most frequently cited characteristic in almost all of the groupings.

Conduct Expected of a Minister

In order to assess the uniformity of understanding about the role of the minister, respondents were asked "Do you think a minister should conduct himself differently than other people in town?" Three basic types of responses were coded.

The first type affirmed the basic exemplary role that the respondent expected the minister to perform. By far the most common type of response affirmed the idea that the minister was expected to set an example of personal conduct for people in the community. This response from a lower-middle or upper-lower status Methodist woman in Maizeville is illustrative of the type: "Yes, live better than the people to show an example. You look up to the preacher."

Two kinds of responses were included in the first type affirming the basic exemplary role of the minister. One of these contended that the minister should act like anyone else who was a Christian. The other affirmed the idea that the minister should behave somewhat differently from the people, but that his behavior should not deviate too markedly from the rest of the population. This mediate position was probably a relatively important one and was implicit in some of the responses that suggested an exemplary role for the minister.

This response, drawn from the schedule of a Lutheran man, a mechanic in Maizeville, is illustrative of the Christian exemplary type: "Well, put it this way. He should act like anybody else who claims to be a Christian."

This response from a middle-aged, Methodist woman, the wife of a postal clerk, illustrates the qualified example type: "I think he [the minister] should act somewhat different from the people. 'Course, he shouldn't be stand-offish or anything like that, but he should be a little different from the ordinary people."

The second basic category of response was termed "neutral." The responses coded in this category suggested that the behavior pattern of ministers should be similar to anyone else in the community. Although this response was not probed, it most assuredly did not mean that the person intended to sanction the type of behavior engaged in by some persons in the community. It probably meant that these respondents wanted to soften the rigid moralism that might be implicit in the first type of response, but they recognized that some reasonable behavior pattern sanctioned by the community was expected of ministers.

The following response by a Presbyterian man in Maizeville, a member of one of the professions, illustrates this type of response.[7] "I'd say a minister today can pretty much act like anyone else in the community. Of course, if he were to behave like some of the lower element, there would be plenty of action, all right. But he can do pretty much what your average business or professional person can do."

The last type was explicitly negative. It was somewhat difficult to interpret this category, but it suggested a rather antagonistic feeling on the part of the respondent toward the moral self-righteousness he felt that he experienced in the behavior of ministers. This comment from a non-church male machinist illustrates the type: "Ministers are no damn better than anyone else. I get tired of seein' them go around actin' so high and mighty."

Two other classes were employed. An "other" category was used to code responses not fitting the above schema and a "Don't Know" category was used for those failing to respond to the question.[8] The findings are summarized in Tables 102 and 103. Table 102 shows the distribution of responses by church membership and geographical area. The data revealed that the dominant expectation in all the areas was that the minister should be a model of personal conduct. The most significant difference that emerged was the lower proportion of non-church members who suggested that the minister should be an example of personal conduct. This phenomenon is to be explained by the fact that the non-church group was drawn dominantly from the lower-status groups and that their patterns of behavior were most deviant from the dominant community norms.

While the differences are not statistically significant, the

---

7. It happens that this particular response did explicitly qualify the people to whose behavior pattern he is appealing.

8. Many of the responses totaled more than 100 per cent because of multiple responses. All of these multiple responses occurred in the "exemplary" classification.

direction suggested some differences between church membership on this question in Maizeville, as Table 103 reveals. Those
groups in the perfectionist wing of the Calvinist tradition tended
to have a higher proportion of respondents indicating that ministers should play an exemplary role in the community. When
data, not presented here, focusing on modal and nuclear members of the four broad traditions of above average and of average
intellectual ability were examined, some qualifications of these
patterns emerged. The only group having a markedly abnormal
response to this question were persons of above average intellectual ability in the perfectionist wing of the Calvinist tradition
who expected their minister to set an example of personal
conduct.

Only an extremely small segment of the respondents in any
of the groups considered cited a negative response to this question. This finding, as have some others in this study, clearly
documents the fact that the vast majority of the citizens affirmed
both the church and its ministers.

Table 102.   Conduct Expected of Minister by Broad Membership Groups and
             Residential Areas in Per Cent

Church Membership of Respondent	N =	CONDUCT EXPECTED				
		Exemplary	Neutral	Negative[a]	Other[a]	Don't Know[a]
				MAIZEVILLE		
Catholic	52	76	35	0	8	2
Protestant	490	77	34	1	2	3
None	111	53	36	4	1	11
				EAST TOWN		
Catholic	102	71	16	3	7	8
Protestant	82	63	23	7	10	1
None	49	49	25	0	4	22
				SERVICEVILLE		
Catholic[b]	23	57	17	0	17	17
Protestant	133	44	35	1	14	8
None[c]	31	26	48	0	10	16
				OPEN COUNTRY		
Catholic[b]	14	100	21	0	14	7
Protestant	65	91	14	2	5	5
None[c]	31	58	19	13	10	10

$$\chi^2 = 49.46 \qquad p < .01 \qquad C = .19$$

a. Columns combined in chi square analysis.
b. Rows combined in chi square analysis.
c. Rows combined in chi square analysis.

The significance of common elements, in contrast to differentiating dimensions between the various traditions, was highlighted by the fact that most of the findings in this area were not statistically significant. There was no statistical evidence of variation in response by type of membership, by broad membership groups and sex, by intellectual ability for the 30-64 age group in Maizeville, or by social status for the 30-64 age group in Maizeville. There was evidence that dormant church members less frequently cited an exemplary response, a finding consistent with the lower percentage of responses among non-church members in all of the areas examined. Thus, it is apparent that a special status was ascribed to the minister by all of the social groupings considered in this study.

Summary of Role Expectation Findings

The adjusive and integrative expectations which laymen in Corn County entertained with respect to the ministerial role was due in part to the diffuseness involved in any leadership role. It was accentuated by a lacuna of theological understanding which did not foster the prophetic or critical function that normatively many would set in juxtaposition to the priestly function, a con-

Table 103. Conduct Expected of Minister for Selected Denominations, Maizeville, in Per Cent

Church Membership of Respondent	N =	CONDUCT EXPECTED				
		Exemplary	Neutral	Negative[a]	Other[a]	Don't Know[a]
Baptist	44	89	34	0	2	2
Catholic	52	77	35	0	8	2
Christian[b]	20	85	25	0	5	0
Congregational	73	60	41	0	0	4
Lutheran, Augustana	42	95	26	0	0	2
Lutheran, United	79	73	38	3	1	3
Methodist	82	78	29	1	4	2
Mission Covenant	54	96	26	0	2	6
Presbyterian	44	68	46	2	7	2
None[b]	111	53	36	4	1	11

$$\chi^2 = 11.27 \qquad .10 < p < .20$$

a. Columns excluded in chi square analysis.
b. Rows excluded in chi square analysis.

serving sustaining function which was so strongly evident in the expectations of laymen in Corn County.

Lay expectations of professional religious leadership focused most strongly on personal adjustive and integrative qualities, manifest in their expressed desire that the minister have a good personality and "be able to get along with people." Technical, professional, rational competence, either cognitive or administrative, was not highly valued by laymen.

The diffuse orientation and the affective qualities cited by Corn County laymen when they indicated the qualities expected in a religious professional stand in contrast to the particularistic orientation and the instrumental qualities dominant in other institutions of American society, particularly the economic order. These expectations highlight the difficulties a religious professional in a local church could expect if he attempted to exercise a prophetic function. The premium placed on personal qualities, however, would suggest that such prophetic efforts might be tolerated if the local religious leader had endeared himself to his congregation. The consequences of such behavior on the social order are, however, another matter.

The comparable rank order of responses for qualities expected in professional religious leadership for Protestants and Catholics indicated a tendency on the part of laymen toward a common understanding of the role of the professional religious leader. Further, the persistence of lay-professional distinctions is documented by the lay-professional differences in conduct expected by the persons interviewed in Corn County.

The premium which laymen placed on the sermon, when it is placed in the context of adjustive integrative role expectation and of the paucity of cognitive appropriations reported in other chapters of this book, suggests that its function is primarily emotive rather than cognitive. Although this emotive component is clearly a segment of any sermonic discourse, most theological understanding would place it in relation to *logos* or cognitive elements.[9]

---

9. The authors have deliberately refrained from exploring the normative character of evocation, form, and unification in sermonic discourse. Theologians may want to reformulate the type of interpretation suggested here in light of their own internal understanding of the nature and character of sermonic discourse.

5. SOME PSYCHOLOGICAL CORRELATES OF RELIGIOUS AFFILIATION

NOT only do religions possess doctrines that are objective or quasi-objective; but these doctrines are also inextricably related to the psychic life and personality of the believer. It was hypothesized that the four broad traditions extant in Corn County would tend to produce different personality types, if the doctrinal emphasis which might be characteristic of each of the traditions were communicated to the adherents of that tradition in an emotive, feeling-tone manner.[1] If such were the case, it was felt that the use of some type of psychological instrument to assess basic personality patterns would indicate the effects of the various traditions on the personality of their adherents. Negative findings would suggest that the general cultural milieu would be more significant in contributing to the basic personality pattern of the interviewees than the religious traditions to which they belonged.[2]

---

1. As has been shown in earlier chapters of this book, none of the traditions has been able to transmit the cognitive structure which informs its particular heritage, although some general notions may be communicated. For example, fewer Congregationalists than Baptists seemed to be Biblical literalists. However, no coherent doctrinal position emerged among laymen of either church.

2. The fact that "creative minorities" or "elites" in the various traditions have helped shape the general cultural milieu is acknowledged. One of the serious limitations intrinsic to the survey method employed in this study is that equal weights are given to all respondents. Although this approach is useful in assessing the "average" sentiments and feeling tones of a group and in discerning differential influences among selected variables, it is less than adequate in assessing the influence of the elite, who are frequently initiators of social action and who may incorporate in their being the feeling tones and the cognitive structures of their traditions.

As we have noted earlier, four broad facets of the Christian heritage were represented in Corn County.[3] In the analysis presented here they have been characterized as the Catholic tradition, the Lutheran tradition, the perfectionist wing of the Calvinist tradition, and the transforming wing of the Calvinist tradition.

The first major tradition present in Corn County was the Catholic heritage, the oldest and most rationally ordered. Because God's grace is looked upon as an addition to an already existent natural virtue, the Catholic doctrine of man is more optimistic than many doctrines supported in the Protestant heritage. The means of grace and the method of salvation through the sacerdotal system are well defined and relatively unambiguous. The objectivity of the worship pattern, coupled with rather clear doctrinal support for specified modes of conduct, suggest powerful psychological support for the adherents of this tradition. The relatively optimistic doctrine of man and the encouragement of Christian virtue which the tradition fosters should help in the sustenance of relatively warm relationships. Further, the authority claimed by the church might be expected to contribute to the development of personality types tending to be submissive to authority.

The dominance of form in the theological structure and the encouragement of contemplation might well be expected to produce passive basic personality types, while the well developed system of casuistry ought to foster rigid systems of inner control. The affirmation of created goodness and of the world ought to encourage acceptance of one's inner life and foster a positive sexual adjustment. No relationship between intellectual function-

Some critics of the survey method have been most vitriolic in their criticism of this approach. For example, see Lindsay Rogers, *The Pollsters* (Alfred A. Knopf, 1949). Although the authors would agree with much of the criticism given by Rogers and others, they would argue that properly developed depth interviews provide an indispensable base for much social research. It is the use to which such analysis is put and to the understanding of the nature of democracy which informs that usage toward which criticism may most legitimately be directed.

Our analysis of the intellectually superior in Maizeville is an effort to consider one type of elite differentially.

3. See also pp. 58ff.

ing or imaginative functioning and any of the traditions was hypothesized.

The second major tradition extant in Corn County was the Lutheran tradition. Broadly speaking, this tradition stands in a line historically running back through Augustine to Paul. In its formulation by Luther, and as implanted in the Lutheran tradition, the notion of original sin precludes any original virtue in man. Only through the redeeming act of God through Jesus Christ is the reality of God's ultimate redemptive love available to man. Man's redemption, however, is ambiguous. Although he has experienced God's redeeming love, the vision of the harmony of life with life involved in that revelation is not realizable in the world. Principalities and powers exist because of man's sinfulness. A radical dualism between the church and the world remains. In the political realm, man is to be obedient to the prevailing powers. It was hypothesized that the type of dialectical somersaulting characteristic of this position is not conducive to psychological certitude. On the contrary, it encourages doubt and ambiguity in the religious realm, in spite of the redemption that is offered the adherent ultimately. At the same time, a submissiveness toward authority or a rebellion against it seems implicit in this perspective. The emphasis on man's sinfulness and the impossibility of sanctification, it was hypothesized, would result in less open and friendly interpersonal relationships. The ambiguity emphasized, it was further hypothesized, would encourage either weak or flexible systems of inner psychological control on the part of communicants and an ambivalent attitude toward one's inner life. Next, the system might be expected to result in ambiguous sexual adjustment. Finally, it would be difficult to predict the type of basic personality pattern that might emerge in this tradition.

The third major tradition widespread in Corn County was conceived broadly as the Calvinistic tradition. Although the notion of original sin is taken as seriously as in the Lutheran heritage, the doctrine of sanctification provides the possibility for the transformation of the world into a place in which greater harmony of life with life is achieved.

Two alternative notions of sanctification are possible. One

variant affirms that, although transformation of the world is desired, human sinfulness prevents the ultimate accomplishment of that objective. At the same time, partial achievements are possible in history; hence, an activism directed toward a certain transformation of the world is espoused. In our analysis, we have characterized this tradition as the transforming wing of the Calvinist heritage.

There is a transition from this notion to one of Christian perfectionism that entertains a vision of the Kingdom of God on earth. Closely related to the latter variant is a type of ethical legalism which outlines rather specific behavior patterns its adherents are expected to observe. The emphasis on humility and on Christ-like perfection on the part of these groups ought to foster rather warm family and peer relationships; however, it is possible that the legalism implicit in the structure may foster group closure.[4] Thus, it seemed that either of these two patterns might emerge.

In practice, the Methodists seem to institutionalize the more benign version. The emphasis upon fellowship, friendliness, and a limited moralism point in this direction.

On the other hand, Baptist, Christian, and Mission Covenant church members would seem to represent groups emphasizing inclusiveness within the group but a relative exclusiveness so far as other groups are concerned.[5]

Psychologically, one would expect the former to encourage positive interaction among family and peer groups, to encourage a more positive attitude toward the individual's inner life, and to encourage a flexible system of inner control, while the latter is apt to be intrinsically more ambiguous. This ambiguity, it was hypothesized, would manifest itself in lower proportions of persons with good peer and family relations in the perfectionist

---

4. This alternative is manifest sociologically among such groups as the Amish, the Hutterites, and some segments of the Mennonite groups. The effects on the internal personality structure of the members of these groups, however, is not clear. The sample drawn in this study contained a small number of Mennonite respondents, but the number was too few to treat statistically.

5. One of the powerful latent functions of doctrinal emphasis is the solidification of the group and the exclusion of non-members.

wing of the Calvinist tradition. Similarly, this group would be expected to manifest more rigid systems of inner control and to display greater ambiguity toward one's inner life.

Because of liberal versions of sanctification which many persons in the Congregational and Presbyterian churches have entertained in recent decades, it was hypothesized that these groups would rank high, relatively, on good peer and family relationships and on acceptance of inner feelings, and might display more flexibility in inner control than the average. Thus, a convergence was hypothesized in which Methodists, Presbyterians, and Congregationalists would theoretically manifest comparable personality traits. This grouping has been characterized as the transforming wing of the Calvinist tradition in this analysis.

Both wings of the Calvinist tradition would be expected to encourage assertive basic personality patterns. Because of the contrast between the ideal and the actual, it was felt that members in the perfectionist wing would display ambivalent attitudes toward sex, while the transforming wing would encourage acceptance of sex. It was further hypothesized that both wings of the tradition would encourage the acceptance of legitimate authority, although a case could be made for hypothesizing that the prophetic dimensions of the tradition might lead to rebellion against authority.

It should be emphasized that this typology does not purport to provide an adequate theological definition of the various traditions. The typology is intended only to provide very brief characterizations of the various traditions and to hypothesize the kinds of personality types that each tradition might encourage if the sustaining theological perspective of the tradition were incorporated into the being of the adherent. The reader may quarrel with the characterization undertaken by the authors and may want to reformulate some of the qualities expected in the various traditions. He may then refer to the presentation below of the empirical findings to assess how his hypothesized personality characteristics would relate to those manifest in church members in Corn County.

In addition to the use of a projective psychological instrument to be discussed shortly, the verbal questions that dominated the interview schedule used in this study were also supplemented by a picture about which the respondent was asked to give the religious significance to aid the researchers in illuminating the subjects' religious feeling tones.

The Thematic Apperception Test

After a review of alternative psychological tests available to assess personality structure, it was decided to employ the Murray Thematic Apperception Test in this study.[6] Three pictures in the series were administered. They were numbers 1, 2, and 4 of the series.[7] Although it would have been desirable to have obtained a larger number of records, the overall length of the interview made it necessary to confine the number to three. The three pictures that were selected for use provided stimuli to obtain

---

6. For those who are unacquainted with the Thematic Apperception Test, the following brief description is provided.

The interviewee is presented a sequence of pictures in turn and is asked to tell a story that the picture suggests to him. He is asked to tell a story that has a beginning, a middle, and an end. The interviewer then transcribes *verbatim* the story that is told by the interviewee. The pictures are designed to provide stimulus dealing with various types of human situations.

It is presupposed that the type of story that is told is a reflection of the basic personality type of the teller. The emotive tones, the structure of of the story, the degree of closure, the ideational content, and similar qualities are noted by the trained analyst who then assesses the qualities that are being examined. Because of our desire for statistical analysis, nine areas were delineated, and the analyst was asked to ascribe the appropriate quality for each area.

We are indebted to Mrs. Gisele Mendel, a graduate student in the Department of Psychology of the University of Chicago, for her work in scoring the records of the interviewees.

7. The description given by Murray of these three pictures is as follows: (1) A young boy is contemplating a violin which rests on a table in front of him (drawing by Christiana D. Morgan). (2) Country scene: in the foreground is a young woman with books in her hand; in the background a man is working in the fields and an older woman is looking on (mural by Leon Kroll, reproduced by special permission of the U. S. Department of Justice). (4) A woman is clutching the shoulders of a man whose face and body are averted as if he were trying to pull away from her (illustration by C. C. Beall, reproduced by special permission of *Collier's* copyright 1940, by the Crowell-Collier Publishing Co.).

Henry A. Murray, M. D., *Thematic Apperception Test* (Harvard University Press, 1943).

certain data dealing with a variety of components of personality.

The reasons for the selection of the Thematic Apperception Test were four:

1. Ease of administration
2. Relative speed of administration
3. Richness of material gathered
4. Relative ease of interpretation

The first and second considerations were important because of the cross-section character of our interview sample. The test was simple and quick to administer. The directions were easy to understand and did not require paper and pencil manipulation on the part of the interviewee.

Of the psychological tests commonly employed, only the Rorschach permits the analyst to assess both the emotive and intellectual life of the interviewee as rapidly and as easily as the Thematic Apperception Test. The latter test's relative simplicity of administration and analysis made it preferable to the Rorschach for our purposes.

Nine areas relating to the psychic life of the interviewees were examined. In order to facilitate statistical analysis, responses for each group were categorized in one of the three substantive responses or in a "no information" classification. The following dimensions of the psychic life were considered:

1. Family emotional attitudes
2. Peer identification
3. Relationship to authority
4. Sexual adjustment
5. Basic personality pattern
6. Attitude toward inner life
7. System of inner control
8. Intellectual functioning
9. Imaginative ability

Table 104 summarizes the dominant characteristics that have been hypothesized as a consequence of the internalization of inner theological understanding of the tradition by its adherents.[8]

---

8. It is beyond the scope of this book to deal critically with the validity of the Thematic Apperception Test or to discuss the method extensively.

Family Emotional Attitudes

The following categories were employed for the classification of family emotional attitudes:

1. Positive
2. Neutral
3. Negative
4. No information

The meaning of these categories is reasonably self-evident. Respondents whose records contained warm overt or covert family references were characterized by positive family emotional attitudes. A placid motif suggested a neutral attitude, while negative expression in the records indicated negative family emotional attitudes.

It had been hypothesized that the interpretation of the Christian faith in the Catholic tradition would produce positive family emotional attitudes. It was felt that the Lutheran tradition was apt to be ambiguous on this issue, as on most others, because of its intrinsic dialectical character. Because of its relatively greater emphasis on the doctrine of sanctification, it was hypothesized that the transforming wing of the Calvinist tradition would also foster positive family emotional attitudes. It was felt that the thin line between the law and grace characteristic of the perfectionist wing of the Calvinist tradition would result in an ambiguous situation among respondents in that tradition. As Tables 105 and 106 reveal, and as other data not presented here indicate, the hypotheses must be rejected, although differentials related to type of community and non-church members did

Because the records were not used clinically, a margin of error in the analysis was permissible. Since this study is interested primarily in differentials and not so much in absolute percentages, interpreter bias is not too serious a problem if it is systematic. Since all of the records were interpreted by the same person, the likelihood of different interpretation is minimized. The age and sex of the interviewee were known to the analyst who made the interpretation, but no other data were known to her. In this study, it is assumed that the kind of analysis undertaken in the interpretation of Thematic Apperception Test is a useful instrument to aid in the assessment of basic personality characteristics. The burden of proof is on the critic who denies its efficacy in obtaining valuable personality data.

emerge. The data did not reveal any close relationship between family emotional attitudes and church membership. The group with lowest percentage of persons having negative family relationships in Maizeville, for example, was the United Lutheran group, while the second lowest was the Congregational (see Table 106). The group with the largest per cent of its members revealing negative family emotional attitudes in Maizeville was the Christian, while the Catholics were second highest in that community. Clearly, religious factors were not crucial in affecting family emotional attitudes of the respondents. in the manner hypothesized.

In a further effort to substantiate this conclusion, an analysis of the characteristics of nuclear and modal church members of above average and average intellectual ability in Maizeville for

Table 104. *Hypothesized Psychological Correlates of Dominant Theological Traditions in Corn County*

| | | THEOLOGICAL TRADITION | | |
| | CATHOLIC | LUTHERAN | CALVINIST | |
Psychological Attitude		Augustana and United Lutheran	Perfectionist (Baptist, Christian, Mission Covenant)	Transforming (Congregational, Presbyterian, Methodist)
Family emotional attitudes	Positive	Ambiguous	Ambiguous	Positive
Peer identification	Positive	Ambiguous	Ambiguous	Positive
Relationship to authority	Submission or acceptance	Submission or rebellion	Acceptance	Acceptance
Basic personality pattern	Passive	Ambiguous	Assertive	Assertive
Sexual adjustment	Acceptance	Ambiguous	Acceptance	Acceptance
Attitude toward inner life	Acceptance	Ambivalence	Ambivalence	Acceptance
System of inner control	Rigid	Flexible or weak	Rigid	Flexible
Intellectual functioning	No relationship	No relationship	No relationship	No relationship
Imaginative functioning	No relationship	No relationship	No relationship	No relationship

Table 105.   Family Emotional Attitudes by Broad Membership Groups and Residential Areas in Per Cent

Church Membership of Respondent	N =	Positive	Neutral	Negative	No Information[a]
			FAMILY EMOTIONAL ATTITUDES		
			MAIZEVILLE		
Catholic	49	43	24	33	0
Protestant	450	40	35	20	5
None	100	38	38	22	2
			EAST TOWN		
Catholic	95	50	37	12	0
Protestant	79	52	42	5	1
None	40	30	53	17	0
			SERVICEVILLE		
Catholic[b]	18	22	56	22	0
Protestant	121	30	50	1?	1
None[c]	30	20	53	27	0
			OPEN COUNTRY		
Catholic[b]	13	54	46	0	0
Protestant	63	52	35	13	0
None[c]	28	36	53	11	0

$$\chi^2 = 45.90 \qquad p < .01 \qquad C = .20$$

a. Column excluded in chi square analysis.
b. Rows combined in chi square analysis.
c. Rows combined in chi square analysis.

Table 106.   Family Emotional Attitudes for Selected Denominations, Maizeville, in Per Cent

Church Membership of Respondent	N =	Positive	Neutral	Negative	No Information[a]
			FAMILY EMOTIONAL ATTITUDES		
Baptist	38	37	34	24	5
Catholic	49	43	24	33	0
Christian[b]	20	30	15	45	2
Congregational	73	45	40	¡4	1
Lutheran, Augustana	39	31	46	18	5
Lutheran, United	71	39	42	13	6
Methodist	79	42	34	19	5
Mission Covenant	49	37	33	24	6
Presbyterian	41	44	22	29	5
None[b]	100	38	38	22	2

$$\chi^2 = 17.72 \qquad .20 < p < .30$$

a. Column excluded in chi square analysis.
b. Rows excluded in chi square analysis.

the four broad traditions were further examined. The findings were negative. Similarly, an examination of the data of persons of average intellectual ability in Maizeville by type of church membership was undertaken. There was no evidence of any relationship between dormant, marginal, modal, and nuclear church membership and family emotional attitudes. In addition, variation by broad membership groups and sex in Maizeville and variation by social status for the 30-64 age group in Maizeville were not statistically significant.

More significant was the factor of intellectual ability. There was an increase in both positive and negative family emotional attitudes as one moved from the below average to the above average intellectual ability grouping. The below average group was most neutral in its responses. For those analysts who see an inextricable relationship between thought and feeling, this finding is not surprising.

Peer Identification

In a manner comparable to the method employed in the analysis of family emotional attitudes, the peer identification of the respondents was assessed. The same categories, positive, neutral, negative, and no information were employed.

Hypotheses based on the same reasoning outlined in the preceding discussion on family emotional attitudes had been entertained with reference to peer identification. Again, however, the hypotheses were not sustained by the data. No evident relationships between denominational affiliation, broad membership groupings, and peer identification emerged; rather, the data suggested no clear pattern of relationships between the dominant theological tradition of which a person was a member and the peer identification of the respondent. (See Tables 107 and 108.)

An examination of the data for East Town (see Table 107) suggested that ethnic and status factors were probably more significant in relation to peer identification than was religious tradition. In dominantly Catholic East Town, characterized by a network of family relationships, Catholics had a significantly higher proportion of respondents indicating positive peer identi-

Table 107.   Peer Identification by Broad Membership Groups and Residential Areas
in Per Cent

Church Membership of Respondent	N =	PEER IDENTIFICATION			
		Positive	Neutral	Negative[a]	No Information[a]
		MAIZEVILLE			
Catholic	49	76	16	2	6
Protestant	450	71	13	4	13
None	100	73	14	2	11
		EAST TOWN			
Catholic	95	72	21	1	6
Protestant	79	54	42	3	1
None	40	53	32	0	15
		SERVICEVILLE			
Catholic[b]	18	67	28	5	0
Protestant	121	64	30	4	2
None[c]	30	67	23	3	7
		OPEN COUNTRY			
Catholic[b]	13	69	31	0	0
Protestant	63	78	20	0	2
None[c]	28	60	32	4	4

$$\chi^2 = 46.13 \qquad p < .01 \qquad C = .21$$

a. Columns excluded in chi squar analysis.
b. Rows combined in chi square analysis.
c. Rows combined in chi square analysis.

Table 108.   Peer Identification for Selected Denominations, Maizeville, in Per Cent

Church Membership of Respondent	N =	PEER IDENTIFICATION			
		Positive	Neutral[a]	Negative[a]	No Information[a]
Baptist	38	82	8	2	8
Catholic	49	76	16	2	6
Christian[b]	20	75	10	0	15
Congregational	73	79	11	1	8
Lutheran, Augustana	39	54	18	3	25
Lutheran, United	71	73	7	4	16
Methodist	79	72	14	5	9
Mission Covenant	49	66	18	4	12
Presbyterian	41	69	12	7	12
None[b]	100	73	14	2	11

$$\chi^2 = 11.85 \qquad .10 < p < .20$$

a. Columns combined in chi square analysis.
b. Rows excluded in chi square analysis.

fication. The confinement of this differential to one of the communities strongly suggests that this difference was not due to religious factors.

Although the data are not presented here, an examination of the responses of persons of above average and of average intellectual ability in Maizeville who were nuclear and modal church members in the four broad traditions revealed negligible differences between the groups. Similarly, there was no evidence of any relationship between peer identification and type of church membership.

The data revealed no significant variation in peer identification by sex and by broad membership groups or by social status for the 30-64 age group in Maizeville. Although the percentage of respondents showing positive peer identification increased very sharply with an increase in intellectual ability, there was no change in the percentage of respondents with negative peer identification as intellectual ability increased.

Relationship to Authority

One of the crucial areas of interest was the way in which the various religious traditions affected the respondent's relationship to authority. From an analysis of the structure and content of the TAT records, the respondent was categorized in one of the following four groups:

> 1. Acceptance
> 2. Rebellion
> 3. Submission
> 4. No information

If the respondent indicated a willingness to accept authority in an adult manner, recognizing the legitimate claims of people in authority over him, he was placed in the first group. If he gave evidence of rejecting or denying the authority of others, he was categorized in the group indicating rebellion against authority. If he gave evidence of submitting to authority, but displayed a sulking or negative feeling-tone in relation to this submission, he was placed in the submission group.

One of the most interesting and controversial theses developed in recent years has suggested that the structure of Lutheran theology encourages the development of a personality type which vacillates between submission to authority and rebellion against authority. It had been argued that this type of vacillation encouraged the emergence of strong dictatorial leaders such as Hitler. While the Corn County data did not directly cast light on this thesis, they did enable us to assess whether the Lutheran tradition in this country tends to produce this personality characteristic.

It had been further hypothesized that the Roman sacerdotal system would encourage either patterns of submission to authority or of acceptance of authority, while both Calvinist traditions, because of their doctrine of sanctification, would encourage the acceptance of authority. Again, the data did not sustain any of these hypotheses, as Tables 109 and 110 show. No sharp patterns emerged by church membership.

Table 109. **Relationship to Authority by Broad Membership Groups and Residential Areas in Per Cent**

Church Membership of Respondent	N =	RELATIONSHIP TO AUTHORITY			
		Acceptance	Rebellion	Submission	No Information[a]
		MAIZEVILLE			
Catholic[b]	49	65	10	19	6
Protestant	451	61	11	17	11
None	100	60	10	21	9
		EAST TOWN			
Catholic	95	64	14	22	0
Protestant[c]	79	82	6	12	0
None[d]	40	78	5	17	0
		SERVICEVILLE			
Catholic[b]	18	61	17	22	0
Protestant	121	69	12	17	2
None[d]	30	70	3	16	3
		OPEN COUNTRY			
Catholic[b]	13	77	8	15	0
Protestant[c]	63	75	0	25	0
None[d]	28	75	4	21	0

$$\chi^2 = 16.93 \qquad .10 < p < .20$$

a. Column excluded in chi square analysis.
b. Rows combined in chi square analysis.
c. Rows combined in chi square analysis.
d. Rows combined in chi square analysis.

When the data were examined by broad membership groupings for nuclear and modal members of average intellectual ability in Maizeville, Catholic respondents had the lowest percentage of persons indicating acceptance of authority. The actual data ranged from 56 per cent for nuclear and modal Catholics to 81 per cent for nuclear and modal members in the transforming wing of the Calvinist tradition. Although the number of responses was too small to treat rebellion and submission categories separately, most of the other responses for Roman Catholics of average intellectual ability fell into the submission group.

Although the number of Catholics of above average intelligence was too small to treat statistically, this pattern was not observed. Of the thirteen nuclear or modal Catholics of above average intellectual functioning in Maizeville in the sample, ten, or 77 per cent, were categorized as accepting authority. Thus, there was some evidence to suggest that Roman Catholics of above average intellectual functioning accepted authority in disproportionate numbers.

Although the data are not presented here, there was no evidence of statistically significant variation when the responses were examined by broad membership groups and sex, by intel-

Table 110.   *Relationship to Authority for Selected Denominations, Maizeville, in Per Cent*

Church Membership of Respondent	N =	RELATIONSHIP TO AUTHORITY			
		Acceptance	Rebellion[a]	Submission[a]	No Information[a]
Baptist	38	48	26	21	5
Catholic	49	65	10	19	6
Christian[b]	20	50	5	15	30
Congregational	73	69	8	16	7
Lutheran, Augustana	39	64	13	10	13
Lutheran, United	71	59	7	16	18
Methodist	79	75	6	17	2
Mission Covenant	49	59	14	14	12
Presbyterian	41	56	12	22	10
None[b]	100	60	10	21	9

$$\chi^2 = 11.28 \qquad .10 < p < .20$$

a. Columns combined in chi square analysis.
b. Rows excluded in chi square analysis.

lectual ability for the 30-64 age group and by social status for the 30-64 age group in Maizeville. There was no evidence to suggest that those persons in blue-collar occupations were resentful of authority. Sixty-three per cent of the blue-collar respondents indicated acceptance to authority while 62 per cent of the white-collar respondents were so categorized.

Basic Personality Pattern

From an examination of the basic themes of the stories, of the kinds of verbs employed, of the approach to the stories, and of similar factors, the basic personality patterns of the respondents were assessed. The main categories employed were:

1. Assertive
2. Passive
3. Hostile
4. No information

The kind of person who was basically dominant and out-going, and who tended to express himself emphatically and to act vigorously, was typed "assertive." One who was quiet and withdrawn was categorized as passive, while those persons whose records suggested aggressiveness coupled with negative feelings were categorized as hostile.

It had been hypothesized that the various religious traditions would tend to produce differing basic personality types. It was suggested that the Catholic tradition, with its objective structures, its clear doctrinal position, its hierarchical structure, and its encouragement of contemplation would tend to produce passive basic personality types. Because of its essentially dialectical and polar character, coupled with its doctrine of calling expressed in the individual's vocation, it was hypothesized that in the Lutheran tradition no clear-cut patterns would emerge, while both segments of the Calvinist tradition would tend to produce assertive personality types. What has been called the perfectionist wing would encourage, it was hypothesized, a kind of dynamics aimed at changing the world into the kind of world envisioned by the perfectionist group, while the transforming wing would be motivated either to alter the existing structures or to accomplish some goals within the existing structures.[9]

As Tables 111-115 reveal, none of these hypotheses could be sustained. As has been the case repeatedly in examining the findings, no clear patterns by denomination affiliation emerged. The evidence did suggest that higher proportions of non-church members possessed passive basic personality patterns, but this phenomenon was more closely related to the intellectual ability and social status than it was to religious affiliation. There was no evidence to suggest basic and significant differences between Catholics and Protestants in any of the areas examined.[10]

An examination of the Maizeville data by type of church membership revealed no difference in the percentage of dormant, marginal, modal, and nuclear church members who possessed assertive basic personality patterns. Similarly, the differences between the four broad traditions for nuclear and modal members of above average intelligence and of average intellectual ability were comparable, as Tables 113-115 reveal.

Data not presented here indicated that intellectual ability was a much more important variable than church membership, sex, or social status in effecting basic personality patterns. There was a very sharp decrease in passive basic personality patterns with an increase in intellectual ability. Conversely, there was a very sharp increase in the percentage of respondents with assertive basic personality patterns with an increase in intellectual ability. The percentage of respondents with hostile basic person-

9. In the latter case, the type of motivation explored by Max Weber in his *The Protestant Ethic and the Spirit of Capitalism* (George Allen and Unwin, Ltd., 1930) is illustrative. Broadly speaking, the Catholic heritage has a greater emphasis upon the life of contemplation, while the Calvinist heritage has a greater emphasis upon the life of action. The Lutheran position is seen here as intermediate between the other two. There were too few cases of the withdrawing sects to treat them statistically.

In other terms, we conceive that in the Catholic heritage there is a dominance of form over dynamics, while the converse is true in the Calvinist tradition.

10. Interestingly, the percentage of respondents with passive basic personality patterns was somewhat higher among males than among females. These data indicated that many suggestions made about the increased assertiveness of males in a competitive society are subject to serious question.

Table 111.   *Basic Personality Pattern by Broad Membership Groups and Residential Areas in Per Cent*

Church Membership of Respondent	N =	BASIC PERSONALITY PATTERN			
		Assertive	Passive	Hostile	No Information[a]
		MAIZEVILLE			
Catholic[b]	49	53	27	18	2
Protestant	450	64	21	11	4
None	100	49	36	13	2
		EAST TOWN			
Catholic	95	74	21	5	0
Protestant	79	77	18	5	0
None[c]	40	70	23	5	2
		SERVICEVILLE			
Catholic[b]	18	78	17	6	0
Protestant[d]	124	66	18	14	0
None[c]	30	57	33	10	0
		OPEN COUNTRY			
Catholic[b]	13	69	31	0	0
Protestant[d]	63	81	17	2	0
None[c]	28	60	32	4	4

$$\chi^2 = 28.20 \qquad p < .01 \qquad C = .16$$

a. Column excluded in chi square analysis.
b. Rows combined in chi square analysis.
c. Rows combined in chi square analysis.
d. Rows combined in chi square analysis.

Table 112.   *Basic Personality Pattern for Selected Denominations, Maizeville, in Per Cent*

Church Membership of Respondent	N =	BASIC PERSONALITY PATTERN			
		Assertive	Passive	Hostile[a]	No Information[a]
Baptist	38	61	18	18	3
Catholic	49	53	27	18	2
Christian[b]	20	55	40	5	0
Congregational	73	71	17	8	4
Lutheran, Augustana	39	59	23	13	5
Lutheran, United	71	61	27	7	5
Methodist	79	68	20	9	3
Mission Covenant	49	59	20	18	2
Presbyterian	41	64	24	2	10
None[b]	100	49	36	13	2

$$\chi^2 = 4.13 \qquad .70 < p < .80$$

a. Columns excluded in chi square analysis.
b. Rows excluded in chi square analysis.

Table 113. Basic Personality Pattern for Selected Membership Groups of Nuclear and Modal Members of Above Average Intellectual Ability, Maizeville, in Per Cent

Church Membership of Respondent	N =	BASIC PERSONALITY PATTERN	
		Assertive	Passive or Hostile
Perfectionist Wing Calvinist Tradition	24	87	13
Transforming Wing Calvinist Tradition	42	86	14
Lutheran*	16	87	13
Catholic*	13	100	0
Total	95	88	12

$$\chi^2 = 0.94 \qquad .50 < p < .70$$

* Rows combined in chi square analysis.

Table 114. Basic Personality Pattern for Selected Membership Groups of Nuclear and Modal Members of Average Intellectual Ability, Maizeville, in Per Cent

Church Membership of Respondent	N =	BASIC PERSONALITY PATTERN	
		Assertive	Passive or Hostile
Perfectionist Wing Calvinist Tradition	34	56	44
Transforming Wing Calvinist Tradition	45	71	29
Lutheran	28	57	43
Catholic	32	63	37
Total	139	63	37

$$\chi^2 = 2.46 \qquad .50 < p < .30$$

Table 115. Basic Personality by Type of Church Membership for Persons of Average Intellectual Ability, Maizeville, in Per Cent

Type of Church Membership of Respondent	N =	BASIC PERSONALITY PATTERN	
		Assertive	Passive or Hostile
Nuclear	83	59	41
Modal	56	68	32
Marginal	58	55	45
Dormant	23	61	39
Total	220	60	40

$$\chi^2 = 2.02 \qquad .50 < p < .70$$

ality patterns remained constant in the three intellectual ability groupings.

Although the data were not statistically significant, the direction of variations suggested that white-collar social status respondents had a higher proportion of assertive basic personality patterns than did blue-collar workers (66 per cent versus 53 per cent).[11]

Sexual Adjustment

The following classifications were employed in the portion of the analysis focusing upon the sexual adjustment:

1. Mature
2. Inhibited
3. Immature, conflictful
4. No information

If the respondent dealt relatively openly with the stimulus which suggested this area to the interviewee, giving evidence of the acceptance of sex as a part of the world, the respondent's sexual adjustment was categorized as mature.

If the phenomenon were skirted or suppressed when the picture suggesting some type of heterosexual relationship was presented, the respondent's sexual adjustment was categorized as inhibited. Although some persons would be inclined to so argue, the authors do not imply that this type of response necessarily represents a less mature sexual adjustment than the first type of response. The immature or conflictful category was used if the response gave evidence of handling the issue in an irresolute manner.

While all of the theological traditions extant in Corn County would ultimately foster the acceptance of sex as a part of the goodness of creation, it had been hypothesized that adherents of

---

11. Perhaps none of the psychological correlates considered is more significant than this one in assessing the relative influence of the four traditions. At this level, we do not find the difference between Catholics and Protestants that Lenski, not using projective techniques, discovered in Detroit. (See Lenski, *The Religious Factor, op. cit.*)

the Lutheran tradition would be more likely to display ambiguity toward sexual adjustment than would be the members of the other religious traditions. The hypothesis was based on the type of reasoning employed earlier. If this hypothesis were to be validated, one would expect a higher percentage of members of Lutheran churches to exhibit immature and conflictful sexual adjustment.

As Tables 116 and 117 reveal, this situation did not, in fact, exist. The percentage of Lutherans who were categorized as having immature or conflicting sexual adjustment was about the same as the average for the Maizeville population.

Data not presented here dealing with the responses for nuclear and modal church members of above average intelligence in Maizeville for the four broad traditions indicated the same type of pattern. There was no evidence to suggest that there was a relationship between sexual adjustment and church membership.

Table 116. **Sexual Adjustment by Broad Membership Groups and Residential Areas in Per Cent**

Church Membership of Respondent	N =	SEXUAL ADJUSTMENT			
		Mature	Inhibited	Immature, Conflictful	No Information[a]
		MAIZEVILLE			
Catholic	49	33	43	22	2
Protestant	450	39	40	14	7
None	100	25	52	17	6
		EAST TOWN			
Catholic	95	39	37	24	0
Protestant	79	44	33	23	0
None	40	27	43	27	3
		SERVICEVILLE			
Catholic[b]	18	33	33	34	0
Protestant	121	32	45	22	1
None[c]	30	33	50	17	0
		OPEN COUNTRY			
Catholic[b]	13	46	31	23	0
Protestant	63	40	33	27	0
None[c]	28	32	47	21	0

$$\chi^2 = 22.72 \qquad .20 < p < .30$$

a. Column excluded in chi square analysis.
b. Rows combined in chi square analysis.
c. Rows combined in chi square analysis.

The data did suggest that females who were non-church members indicated the lowest per cent of mature sexual adjustment and the highest per cent of inhibited sexual adjustment, while persons of below average intellectual ability had the lowest percentage of mature sexual adjustment and the highest percentage of immature or conflictful sexual adjustment. Although the data were not statistically significant, the direction of response by social status suggested a higher percentage of mature sexual adjustment among white-collar respondents than among blue-collar respondents. Similarly, persons of above average intellectual ability indicated by far the highest proportion of mature sexual adjustment.

Attitude Toward Inner Life

A *sine qua non* of the religious life is the richness and complexity of one's inner feelings and life—the kind of dialogue a person carries on with himself. Most religious and theological writings deal, in part, with the inner feelings and experiences of the writer. Data drawn from introspection are often of great importance.

Table 117.   Sexual Adjustment for Selected Denominations, Maizeville, in Per Cent

Church Membership of Respondent	N =	SEXUAL ADJUSTMENT Mature	Inhibited	Immature, Conflictful	No Information[a]
Baptist	38	34	50	13	3
Catholic	49	33	43	22	2
Christian[b]	20	30	50	15	5
Congregational	73	37	45	14	4
Lutheran, Augustana	39	28	49	13	10
Lutheran, United	71	41	34	11	14
Methodist	79	42	37	20	1
Mission Covenant	49	49	25	18	8
Presbyterian	41	54	32	10	4
None[b]	100	25	52	17	6

$$\chi^2 = 17.60 \qquad .20 < p < .30$$

a. Column excluded in chi square analysis.
b. Rows excluded in chi square analysis.

From an analysis of the type of approach the interviewee took toward the stories, from the manner of personal identification with figures in the stories, from the feelings expressed toward persons, things and ideas, from the complexity of ideas and feelings expressed in the stories, from his attitudes toward those feelings and ideas, and from similar factors, the interviewee's attitude toward his own inner life was categorized. The four categories employed here were:

1. Acceptance
2. Ambivalence
3. Rejection
4. No information

Ultimately, the Christian faith in each of the four traditions extant in Corn County would suggest the acceptance of one's inner life. However, the more Pelagian doctrine of man extant in the Catholic tradition and the doctrine of sanctification extant in the perfectionist wing of the Calvinist tradition, it was hypothesized, would lead adherents in these two traditions to an acceptance of their inner thoughts and emotions. On the other hand, it was hypothesized that the transforming wing of the Calvinist tradition and the Lutheran tradition ought to foster somewhat more ambiguity in the attitude of their adherents toward their inner life.

As the data reported in Tables 118 and 119 reveal, all of these hypotheses must be rejected. There was no evidence of any relationship between attitude toward one's inner life and religious affiliation. Further, there was no evidence of any difference between church members of any of the traditions and non-church members.

Although they are not presented here, the customary analysis of nuclear and modal members of above average intellectual ability and of average intellectual ability in Maizeville was made by broad membership groupings, as was the analysis of church members of average intellectual ability in Maizeville by type of church membership—dormant, marginal, modal, and nuclear. With the possible exception of nuclear and modal members of the Lutheran tradition of above average intellectual ability, who had a lower proportion of respondents indicating acceptance of their

Table 118.   Attitude Toward Inner Life by Broad Membership Groups and
             Residential Areas in Per Cent

Church Membership of Respondent	N =	ATTITUDE TOWARD INNER LIFE			
		Acceptance	Ambivalence	Rejection	No Information[a]
		MAIZEVILLE			
Catholic	49	55	29	16	0
Protestant	450	59	25	14	2
None	100	54	21	21	4
		EAST TOWN			
Catholic	95	65	21	14	0
Protestant	79	60	19	21	0
None	40	60	20	20	0
		SERVICEVILLE			
Catholic[b]	18	61	22	17	0
Protestant	121	63	22	14	1
None[c]	30	67	20	13	0
		OPEN COUNTRY			
Catholic[b]	13	61	31	8	0
Protestant	63	62	24	14	0
None[c]	28	46	18	36	0

$$\chi^2 = 12.23 \qquad .80 < p < .90$$

a. Column excluded in chi square analysis.
b. Rows combined in chi square analysis.
c. Rows combined in chi square analysis.

Table 119.   Attitude Toward Inner Life for Selected Denominations, Maizeville,
             in Per Cent

Church Membership of Respondent	N =	ATTITUDE TOWARD INNER LIFE			
		Acceptance	Ambivalence	Rejection[a]	No Information[a]
Baptist	38	58	26	16	0
Catholic	49	55	29	16	0
Christian[b]	20	60	10	25	5
Congregational	73	67	16	15	2
Lutheran, Augustana	39	49	36	13	2
Lutheran, United	71	55	28	16	1
Methodist	79	58	23	18	1
Mission Covenant	49	68	22	6	4
Presbyterian	41	68	17	12	3
None[b]	100	54	21	21	4

$$\chi^2 = 8.52 \qquad .20 < p < .30$$

a. Columns excluded in chi square analysis.
b. Rows excluded in chi square analysis.

inner life, the findings were all negative. Unfortunately, the number of cases in the cell (16) rendered the validity of this finding questionable. Similarly, 11 of the 13 Roman Catholic nuclear and modal members of above average intellectual ability in Maizeville indicated acceptance of their inner life. This wide variation did suggest some possible influence in the superior intellectual group; however, the data for persons of average intellectual ability strongly suggested no variation by church membership. There was no evidence of variation in attitude toward one's inner life by broad membership groups and sex in Maizeville or by social status for the 30-64 age group in Maizeville.

There were slightly higher proportions of persons of above average intellectual ability in Maizeville who indicated acceptance of their inner life. The range, however, was not great. (Forty-six per cent acceptance for the below average group, 57 per cent acceptance for the average group, and 61 per cent acceptance for the above average group.)

System of Inner Control

Every individual has a basic system of inner control by which he directs his thought and activity. Some people are rather flexible in their approach to situations, willing to adjust their behavior and attitude depending upon the circumstances extant. Others are quite rigid in their approach to situations, tending to maintain their stance regardless of the setting. Still others are not well controlled, tending to lack any sort of basic pattern. They appear to be deficient in any sort of integrating or guiding element.[12]

Thus, the four classifications employed to describe the respondent's system of inner control were:

---

12. The "flexible" and "rigid" classes are analogous to Riesman's "other-directed" and "inner-directed" types. The primary difficulty with either typology is that the pure type is impossible. Even people with the most rigid systems of inner control must take some account of the situation, while those with the weakest systems make a decision as to what they will become in a particular setting.

1. Flexible
2. Rigid
3. Weak
4. No information

Although a case might be made for hypothesizing that all religious traditions might be expected to sustain a rigid system of inner control, it was decided on the basis of doctrinal and ecclesiastical structures to suggest differences that might emerge between the various traditions. It was hypothesized that the Catholic and the perfectionist wing of the Calvinist tradition would tend to encourage rigid systems of inner control. The former, with its liturgical and doctrinal emphasis, the dominance of form over dynamics and its elaborate system of casuistry, it was hypothesized, would tend to encourage such a rigid system, while the latter type would tend to produce ethical legalism. With its rigorous insistence upon justification by faith and its denial of the efficacy of salvation by works, coupled with the ambiguity of dynamics and form, it was felt that the Lutheran tradition might tend to produce either a flexible or a weak system of inner control. Because of its effort to relate the vision of the ultimate harmony of things to the actual world, it was hypothesized that the transforming wing of the Calvinist tradition would tend to encourage a flexible system of inner control.

The findings shown in Tables 120 and 121 did not support any of these hypotheses. There was no evidence of any relationship between the individual's system of inner control and his religious affiliation.

However, when the data were refined, one suggestive differential emerged. Table 122 presents the responses of nuclear and modal members of the four traditions of average intellectual ability in Maizeville. While there was no difference between members of the Calvinist tradition and the Roman Catholic tradition, fewer modal and nuclear church members of the Lutheran tradition had flexible systems of inner control. While not statistically significant, the direction of the finding was opposite to that hypothesized. Thus, instead of encouraging flexible or weak systems of inner control as was hypothesized, the data suggest that persons in the Lutheran tradition may have had more mem-

Table 120. System of Inner Control by Broad Membership Groups and Residential Areas in Per Cent

Church Membership of Respondent	N =	Flexible	Rigid	Weak	No Information[a]
			SYSTEM OF INNER CONTROL		
			MAIZEVILLE		
Catholic[b]	49	45	33	20	2
Protestant	449	45	31	15	9
None	100	39	29	22	10
			EAST TOWN		
Catholic	95	51	38	10	1
Protestant	79	56	37	7	0
None[c]	40	55	28	17	0
			SERVICEVILLE		
Catholic[b]	18	42	29	29	0
Protestant	121	53	31	15	1
None[c]	30	80	7	13	0
			OPEN COUNTRY		
Catholic[b]	13	54	23	23	0
Protestant	63	53	33	14	0
None[c]	28	61	32	7	0

$$\chi^2 = 20.56 \qquad .10 < p < .20$$

a. Column excluded in chi square analysis.
b. Rows combined in chi square analysis.
c. Rows combined in chi square analysis.

Table 121. System of Inner Control for Selected Denominations, Maizeville, in Per Cent

Church Membership of Respondent	N =	Flexible	Rigid	Weak	No Information[a]
			SYSTEM OF INNER CONTROL		
Baptist	38	42	34	24	0
Catholic	49	45	33	20	2
Christian[b]	20	50	25	10	15
Congregational	73	52	27	14	7
Lutheran, Augustana	39	33	36	18	13
Lutheran, United	70	36	38	13	13
Methodist	79	51	29	13	7
Mission Covenant	49	45	18	25	12
Presbyterian	41	53	37	5	5
None[b]	100	39	29	22	10

$$\chi^2 = 17.49 \qquad .20 < p < .30$$

a. Column excluded in chi square analysis.
b. Rows excluded in chi square analysis.

bers possessing rigid systems of inner control. The overwhelming proportion of dormant and marginal church members of average intellectual ability who were Lutheran also exhibited rigid systems of inner control.

This combination of findings suggested that the dominant cultural heritage in which most Lutherans find themselves was probably more important in fostering a rigid system of inner control than was their theological heritage.

Table 122.   System of Inner Control for Selected Membership Groups of Nuclear and Modal Members of Average Intellectual Ability, Maizeville, in Per Cent

Church Membership of Respondent	N =	SYSTEM OF INNER CONTROL Flexible	Weak or Rigid
Perfectionist Wing Calvinist Tradition	33	45	55
Transforming Wing Calvinist Tradition	48	56	44
Lutheran	29	28	72
Catholic	33	52	48
Total	143	47	53

$$\chi^2 = 5.35 \qquad .10 < p < .20$$

Although the data are not presented here, there was evidence of a strong relationship between intellectual ability and a system of inner control. The percentage of persons with weak systems of inner control dropped markedly in moving from the below average intellectual ability group to the above average one. Persons of above average intelligence had a higher percentage of flexible systems of inner control. Thus, 34 per cent of the below average intellectual ability group, 18 per cent of the average intellectual ability group, and 7 per cent of the above average intellectual ability group evidenced weak systems of inner control. Conversely, 26 per cent of the below average intellectual ability grouping evidenced flexible systems of inner control, 44 per cent of the average intellectual ability grouping, and 58 per cent of the above average intellectual ability groupings indicated flexible systems of inner control.[13]

Intellectual Functioning

Based on such considerations as the time sequence exhibited in the stories, whole-part configurations, and richness and complexity of the stories, the respondents were ranked into four broad groups according to intellectual functioning:

1. Above average
2. Average
3. Below average
4. No information

A high level of intellectual functioning and of imaginative ability seemed to be a necessary (but not a sufficient) condition for the possession of a penetrating cognitive structure which informs the Christian faith. In light of the very small segment of the population that possessed a relatively developed theological understanding, it seemed desirable to assess the potential population that had the intellectual capacity to comprehend and to assimilate such a system of theological understanding and to determine the denominational distribution of such a population.[14]

Because there seemed to be no intrinsic relationship between either intellectual functioning or imaginative ability and any of the theological traditions delineated here, it was hypothesized that there would be no difference in either function by church membership.

The data on intellectual functioning are summarized in Tables 123 and 124. Two things stand out in these tables. The first salient finding was the relatively even distribution of membership by intellectual functioning. Although a refinement of the

---

13. Variation by social status for the 30-64 age group in Maizeville was not statistically significant.

14. The authors do not mean to suggest that only persons of high intellectual ability can be positively related to the Christian faith. They do mean to suggest, however, that cognitive structures which inform the faith seem to be largely limited to this group.

Table 123. Intellectual Functioning by Broad Membership Groups and Residential Areas in Per Cent

Church Membership of Respondent	N =	Above Average	Average	Below Average[a]	No Information[a]
			INTELLECTUAL FUNCTIONING		
			MAIZEVILLE		
Catholic[b]	49	12	80	8	0
Protestant	450	16	74	8	2
None	101	11	81	4	4
			EAST TOWN		
Catholic	95	10	85	4	0
Protestant	79	20	79	1	0
None[c]	40	5	95	0	0
			SERVICEVILLE		
Catholic[b]	18	6	88	6	0
Protestant	121	8	92	0	0
None[c]	30	10	90	0	0
			OPEN COUNTRY		
Catholic[b]	13	8	92	0	0
Protestant	63	24	76	0	0
None[c]	28	21	79	0	0

$$\chi^2 = 16.08 \qquad p < .05 \qquad C = .12$$

a. Columns excluded in chi square analysis.
b. Rows combined in chi square analysis.
c. Rows combined in chi square analysis.

Table 124. Intellectual Functioning for Selected Denominations, Maizeville, in Per Cent

Church Membership of Respondent	N =	Above Average[a]	Average	Below Average[a]	No Information[a]
			INTELLECTUAL FUNCTIONING		
Baptist	38	13	84	3	0
Catholic	49	12	80	8	0
Christian[b]	20	10	75	10	5
Congregational	73	25	63	11	1
Lutheran, Augustana	39	10	77	10	3
Lutheran, United	71	16	75	8	1
Methodist	79	15	77	8	0
Mission Covenant	49	12	72	14	2
Presbyterian	41	24	66	5	5
None[b]	101	11	81	4	4

$$\chi^2 = 9.53 \qquad .20 < p < .30$$

a. Columns combined in chi square analysis.
b. Rows excluded in chi square analysis.

data not shown here indicated slightly more persons in the transforming wing of the Calvinist tradition exhibited above average intellectual functioning, the differences were not great. It was not clear that in town and country settings certain churches attract greater proportions of the intellectually superior.

Data not presented here did, however, suggest greater differentials of involvement of members by intellectual ability in the Protestant churches than in the Catholic church.[15] For example, 28 per cent of the members of churches in the perfectionist wing of the Calvinist tradition were of above average intellectual ability, while 42 per cent of the nuclear members in that tradition were above average in intellectual ability. Comparable figures for members in the transforming wing of the Calvinist tradition were 33 per cent and 42 per cent, while they were 21 per cent and 30 per cent in the Lutheran tradition. In the Roman Catholic church, the percentages were 20 and 21 per cent, respectively.

At the same time, the churches in the perfectionist wing of the Calvinist tradition, the Roman Catholic church, and the Lutheran tradition had significantly higher proportions of their members of above average intellectual ability in the nuclear groups than had the churches in the transforming wing of the Calvinist tradition. For example, out of 27 persons of above average intellectual ability in the churches in the perfectionist wing of the Calvinist tradition, 22 were nuclear members. Comparable groups in the transforming wing of the Calvinist tradition were 17 members out of a total of 54.

The second salient fact was that the proportion of rural people of above average intellectual functioning in this rich agricultural area was the highest of any of the areas studied. These data did not support the thesis that the best of the rural people were being drained into cities in disproportionate numbers.[16] The town with the lowest proportion of able people was

---

15. As here used, "intellectual ability" means that the respondent ranked above average in intellectual functioning or imaginative ability or both.

16. The problem of the low density of population in such areas does, however, constitute a problem of first magnitude for institutional church life. In areas like Corn County, the data suggested that a major institutional

Serviceville. It was this service-center village of about 1,000, most·of whose functions had been assumed by the county seat town of Maizeville, that had suffered the most from differential migration.

Table 125.   Imaginative Ability by Broad Membership Groups and Residential Areas in Per Cent

Church Membership of Respondent	N =	IMAGINATIVE ABILITY			
		Above Average	Average	Below Average	No Information[a]
MAIZEVILLE					
Catholic[b]	49	16	68	16	0
Protestant	451	17	62	20	1
None	100	9	61	28	2
EAST TOWN					
Catholic	95	15	70	15	0
Protestant	79	20	74	6	0
None[c]	40	10	78	12	0
SERVICEVILLE					
Catholic[b]	18	6	83	11	0
Protestant	121	8	89	3	0
None[c]	30	7	93	0	0
OPEN COUNTRY					
Catholic[b]	13	15	70	15	0
Protestant	63	27	70	3	0
None[c]	28	11	78	11	0

$$\chi^2 = 71.82 \qquad p < .01 \qquad C = .25$$

a. Column excluded in chi square analysis.
b. Rows combined in chi square analysis.
c. Rows combined in chi square analysis.

Imaginative Ability

The last psychological factor on which analysis was undertaken was the imaginative ability of the respondent. While it is closely related to intellectual functioning, imaginative ability is, in part, distinguishable from it. By considerations such as the depth and the contrast of the stories and the uniqueness of the plot, a fourfold grouping identical with the previous one was made:

problem is to get a large enough membership base to have a reasonable number of persons of high intellectual ability in one congregation.

1. Above average
2. Average
3. Below average
4. No information

The findings are shown in Tables 125 and 126. While the distribution between the three groups was broader, patterns similar to those noted in the analysis of the responses by intellectual functioning emerged.

Every church had a considerable proportion of people with below average imaginative ability. The problems encountered by a church are great when more than one-third of the congregation is of below average imaginative ability, as was the case of some of the churches in Maizeville.[17] The data did not suggest, however, differential distributions by denominations. (See Table 126.)

Religious Stimulus

The verbal questions that dominated the interview schedule used in this study were supplemented not only by the Thematic Apperception Test but also by a picture to which the respondent was asked to give religious significance. The picture that was selected for use was drawn from the Edward Steichen "The Family of Man" group, first exhibited in the Museum of Modern Art and subsequently published.[18]

The picture employed was one of a woman and a baby lying on a bed, with the woman looking at the infant. A cat was lying on the bed near the child. The interviewee was instructed to give the religious significance of the picture as he saw it. No cues were given as to what meaning the interviewee was to attach to the term "religious." The respondent interpreted the term as he understood it.

A fourfold grouping was employed to order the responses to this question. Three of the classifications were related to the

17. These data do demonstrate that a liturgical pattern does not insure the development of rich imaginative life on the part of its adherents.

18. Edward Steichen, *The Family of Man* (Maco Magazine Corporation, 1955).

level of abstraction evident in the response to the question, while the fourth classification was a "no religious significance" grouping.

The term "level of abstraction" as employed here does not mean to suggest a dialectical reading of the responses. In this particular context, only the richness and complexity of the response was evaluated. The form of the response was not considered.

A response that described the picture without elaboration was classed as a "low level abstraction." Here, for example, is the response of a Maizeville housewife, a Methodist and the wife of a clerical employee, which was classed as low level abstraction: "Well, gee, I don't know. Ah—it is a picture of a mother—a-lookin' at her baby. Don't know why the cat is there. That's all."

A moderate level abstraction was a response which interpreted the relationship that was conceived to exist between the woman and the child, although the religious meaning was implied rather than explicit. This response, drawn from the schedule of a middle-aged, Serviceville mechanic, a Baptist, is illustrative of the type: "That's mother love. The mother is lyin' there lookin' at that baby and wonderin' how it all happened—the wonder of birth and all."

Table 126. Imaginative Ability for Selected Denominations, Maizeville, in Per Cent

Church Membership of Respondent	N =	IMAGINATIVE ABILITY			
		Above Average	Average	Below Average	No Information[a]
Baptist	38	21	61	18	0
Catholic	49	16	68	16	0
Christian[b]	20	10	60	30	0
Congregational	73	21	63	15	1
Lutheran, Augustana	39	20	49	31	0
Lutheran, United	72	6	68	25	1
Methodist	79	19	65	16	0
Mission Covenant	49	19	63	16	2
Presbyterian	41	15	68	12	5
None[b]	100	9	61	28	2

$$\chi^2 = 15.53 \qquad .30 < p < .50$$

a. Column excluded in chi square analysis.
b. Rows excluded in chi square analysis.

The latter part of this response moved in the direction of a high level abstraction, although, because no explicit religious categories were employed, the response was put in the "moderate level abstraction" classification.

This response from a farmer's wife in the open country is unqualifiedly a "moderate level abstraction" type: "Well, seeing the baby and all there, I'd say that the picture represents mother love, the love of that woman for her baby. It's a nice picture, isn't it?"

This response, one of the most complex received in Corn County, came from a Presbyterian proprietor in Maizeville: "Religious meaning, eh? Well, of course, I'd have to treat that picture symbolically to get a religious meaning out of it, although, of course, you could look at it from several different levels. I'd say three things stand out here. First, the miracle of creation and birth, symbolizing that God is the Creator of us all. Second, mother love, showing the higher love of God for man. Third, the innocence of childhood."

While the respondent did not elaborate on the third point, the difference between the quality and depth of this response and the others quoted was remarkable. The appropriation of the picture was markedly different. The ability of this respondent to deal with ideas was far superior to that of the other respondents quoted.

The last classification employed included responses affirming that the picture had no religious significance. This type of response was related to the idea that only those activities related to the church in a formal way are "religious." The findings are summarized in Tables 127 and 128.

The most salient single finding was the relatively low percentage of the respondents in all the communities and in most of the churches who gave high level responses to this question. The responses pointed to the same kind of problem raised by the analysis of the intellectual level of the interviewees, i.e., the relatively small number of high level intellects found in any of the churches. There were a few churches which were fortunate enough to possess a relatively high percentage of keen minds, but the evidence presented earlier suggested that the churches have not devised the means to utilize them and to develop a

Table 127. *Interpretation of Religious Stimulus by Broad Membership Groups and Residential Areas in Per Cent*

Church Membership of Respondent	R =	LEVEL OF ABSTRACTION			No Religious Significance
		Low	Average	High	
		MAIZEVILLE			
Catholic[a]	50	6	66	12	16
Protestant	419	13	61	15	11
None	80	19	65	5	11
		EAST TOWN			
Catholic	97	11	60	7	22
Protestant	82	5	65	17	13
None[b]	42	14	60	2	24
		SERVICEVILLE			
Catholic[a]	23	13	70	4	13
Protestant[c]	126	9	81	4	6
None[b]	31	29	61	3	7
		OPEN COUNTRY			
Catholic[a]	11	0	91	0	9
Protestant[c]	62	2	71	19	8
None[b]	31	0	68	6	26

$$\chi^2 = 56.07 \qquad p < .01 \qquad C = .22$$

a. Rows combined in chi square analysis.
b. Rows combined in chi square analysis.
c. Rows combined in chi square analysis.

Table 128. *Interpretation of Religious Stimulus for Selected Denominations, Maizeville, in Per Cent*

Church Membership of Respondent	N =	LEVEL OF ABSTRACTION			No Religious Significance[a]
		Low[a]	Average	High[a]	
Baptist	37	5	73	16	6
Catholic	50	6	66	12	16
Christian[b]	15	13	67	7	13
Congregational	65	23	52	16	9
Lutheran, Augustana	39	15	67	8	10
Lutheran, United	64	13	59	14	14
Methodist	74	12	57	15	16
Mission Covenant	43	14	67	16	16
Presbyterian	42	5	55	26	14
None[b]	80	19	65	5	11

$$\chi^2 = 7.33 \qquad .30 < p < .50$$

a. Columns combined in chi square analysis.
b. Rows excluded in chi square analysis.

core of lay leadership which is informed by a cognitive structure that can guide action. It is the 10 or 15 per cent of the people who gave high level abstractions to this question—no church is without its core of this group—that would be most able to appropriate an informing intellectual structure if such were offered by the churches.

Variation by sex and broad membership groupings to this question was negligible, although about twice as many white-collar respondents gave high level abstraction responses as did blue-collar social status respondents.

The data are not presented here in tabular form, but an analysis of the responses of nuclear and modal members of above average intellectual ability for the four broad traditions indicated no differences in responses by church tradition. Similarly, a consideration of the responses of dormant, marginal, modal, and nuclear church members of average intellectual ability revealed no differential by these categories. The data did reveal a somewhat higher proportion of high level abstraction responses for nuclear and modal members of average intellectual ability in the transforming wing of the Calvinist tradition. Unfortunately, the number of cases was so small as to be only suggestive and cannot be treated without qualification. In any event, the differences were modest.

Summary of Psychological Findings

The data that have been examined in this chapter indicate that generally the relationship between the several theological traditions and the personality characteristics of their members was not great. When the data have been examined by type of church membership and by intellectual ability, the same patterns persisted.

Protestant-Catholic differentials were less frequent and of less magnitude on the psychological characteristics considered in this chapter than on the cognitive structures. Of particular interest, we think, was the finding that there was no difference in basic personality patterns between Protestants and Catholics.

Thus, the data suggested that the press of the general cultural milieu has been more pervasive at the feeling-tone level than at the cognitive level, even if one grants the impossibility in principle of differentiating between the two areas.

The major positive findings may be summarized as follows:

1. There was a much stronger relationship between personality characteristics and intellectual ability than between any of the other variables considered in this study.
2. There was some clustering of persons of superior intellectual ability in the county-seat town of Maizeville and in the open country. The small service-center community examined in this study had the lowest proportion of people of superior intellectual ability.
3. Persons who were not church members had somewhat lower imaginative ability and were more apt to be passive in basic personality structure. These factors were related to status and intellectual ability, as the data in this chapter indicate.
4. All of the churches possessed a basic core of persons of superior intellectual ability. There was no evidence of marked selectivity by theological traditions.

The essentially negative character of the findings in this portion of the study is, of course, open to diverse interpretation. It might be argued, for example, that these data demonstrate the relatively small influence played by religion in the life of people in Corn County. So far as self-conscious religious understanding and sharp denominational differences are concerned, the authors are inclined to make such an interpretation; they would also suggest that the present situation probably represents the amalgamation of the various traditions in the American ethos.

As has been noted before, it is this process which probably is fostering grass roots sentiment for the ecumenical movement. The lack of distinctive denominational cognitive structures, revealed in earlier portions of this book, is supported by the generally nonintellectual American ethos and undoubtedly contributes to lay support of ecumenicity. Both through the process of inter-denominational membership mobility and through the press of the general culture, distinctions among denominations, which may have been more significant in an earlier period, are becoming very blurred.[19]

At the same time, the various heritages may have contributed in both positive and negative fashion to the total ethos that characterizes contemporary America. The research design employed in this study does not permit an adequate consideration of these possibilities.

---

19. In a general way, these findings would support Will Herberg's thesis in *Protestant, Catholic, Jew* that Americans' operative religion is the "American way of life." The problem of the adequacy of historical records as criteria for the assessment of mass attitudes and of participation patterns for earlier periods constitutes a major methodological problem when comparisons between various time periods are attempted.

6. SUMMARY AND CONCLUSIONS

THE multiplicity of specific findings that have been presented in this book might tend to obscure some of the more salient findings if they were not brought up for special comment. It is the authors' hope, as suggested earlier, that the empirical findings which have been presented here will be helpful to workers who are informed by alternative cognitive structures. The relatively low level of abstraction at which most of the findings have been presented is a consequence of this hope and of our belief that the considerable importance of idiosyncratic factors in human existence rather severely limits the level of generality to be achieved in the social studies.[1] Further, our refusal to attempt to isolate a large number of variables was determined by the fact that the statistical abstraction which results from such an analysis is rather far removed from the complex and interrelated entity that is human society. This point of view further means that only patterns or configurations will be looked for in social studies.[2]

Before a summary of the findings is presented, three observations should be made. First, the primary focus of attention in this study was what has traditionally been called the manifest Church, the empirical and concrete manifestation of the Church in Corn County. No systematic attempt was made to consider the latent or universal Church. While the authors' constructive

---

1. For similar reasons, we prefer the term "social studies" to the term "behavioral sciences" to describe the type of work undertaken by people interested in studying the behavior of human beings.

2. Although their overall theoretical structure would differ, the authors would concur with Max Weber's notion that the social studies lack intrinsically the kind of precision that characterizes some sciences. Whether the difference in lack of precision is a matter of degree or a matter of kind is an issue which need not concern us here. The point to be argued here is that a convergence exists between the understanding of human freedom which informs our ordering of this issue and the Weberian notion of *verstehen* sociology, so far as its application to the study of society is concerned.

position does not permit distinction in principle between a consideration of the manifest Church and of the latent Church, the primary emphasis in this analysis was upon the former.

Second, the findings in this study were much more definitive in areas exploring cognitive structures, interactive patterns, and basic feeling tones than they were in the areas attempting to probe those feelings which people affirm as "religious." From our point of view, it could not be otherwise, since the latter dimensions involve the way in which the individual responds to and integrates his feelings, both physical and conceptual. From a consideration of the psychological data, some measure of the degree of internal harmony attained by the respondent can be assessed, but there is an intrinsic limitation to what can be achieved in this area through research efforts. Since cognitive structures, interactive patterns, and basic feeling tones are more public, the research efforts which are designed to explore these areas are more definitive than research efforts designed to explore the individual's religious feelings. The inadequacy and elliptical character of language are especially evident in this latter area, although the level of abstraction represented by language constitutes a basic problem and a limitation in almost all social scientific research.

Third, this analysis has relied primarily upon the method of difference. The difference between selected variables (for different segments of the sample) has been considered. No attempt has been made to deal adequately with those general or universal aspects of Christianity which would manifest themselves in the several traditions. The overarching and pervasive effects of the Christian tradition in Western civilization are very important. Any general cultural analysis would note some of the root notions which seem to be presupposed by most of the people in that culture. Similarly, pervasive feeling tones may inform an entire people or culture. These commonly shared elements may be more important in many ways than the differences that emerge between subgroups in the culture.[3] The authors acknowledge

---

3. For extended treatments assessing these dimensions, see works like Bernard Meland's *Faith and Culture* (Oxford University Press, 1953), or F. S. C. Northrop's *The Meeting of East and West* (The Macmillan Company, 1953).

the importance of this general kind of analysis and of the critique of studies like the current one which might be informed from such a perspective. They would see the two types of studies as complementary. Our primary intent was to examine the differences existent among the various facets of the Christian tradition and to assess some of the significant factors contributing to differential responses by church members. At the same time, the kinds of categorizations employed have frequently seen these distinctions in relation to universal overarching commonalities. How the Christian faith in its unity has promoted pervasive feeling tones is very difficult to assess, for to answer this question, the method of difference fails; the appropriate method for analysis would be different from the one employed here.[4] It is apparent from the findings of this study that such influences are residual in their cognitive dimensions, although there is some evidence to suggest that the churches foster a rather considerable pervasive emotive feeling tone which affects a community which in some measure justifies a positive interpretation of the role of the churches in contemporary midwestern towns and country.

This pervasive general influence is particularly significant for those theological traditions which see a positive relationship between theology and forms of social organization. The manifest and latent effects of Calvinism in relation to a democratic social order are well known. In spite of the negative findings reported in this study the fact remains that the impact of religion on the political and economic order in this broad manner has been most important. For part of the Calvinist tradition, a basic transformation of the world has been effected with the emergence of a democratic social order and the widespread support of welfare agencies by the state. A dominantly harmonizing, integrating function may well be the appropriate function for religious institutions to exercise in such a society from some theological perspectives.[5]

---

4. This basic methodological difference is the primary reason for the different interpretations of religion in American culture offered by Herberg in *Protestant, Catholic, Jew* and by Lenski in *The Religious Factor*.

5. It is revealing that interpretive and basically critical studies of the role of religion in American culture like Marty's *The New Shape of American Religion* (Harper, 1959) and Berger's *The Noise of Solemn Assemblies* (Doubleday, 1961) are informed by a Lutheran theological perspective.

The data presented in this study have focused upon four general areas of interest. The first area dealt with participation and associational patterns of residents in the geographical areas selected for analysis. The second area examined the dimensions of the informing cognitive structure of the respondents with reference to ecclesiastical, theological, social, political, and economic matters. The third area dealt with some segments of the problem of the role of the minister. The last area considered the relationship between church membership and selected psychological characteristics of the respondents.

Somewhere between 30 and 40 per cent of the population were considered nuclear church members.[6] Although these data suggested a relatively high participation in an institution which, because of the character of the nation in which it was set, partook of some of the characteristics of a voluntary association, nevertheless, the data strongly suggested that the institution had communicated portions of its cognitive structure to its members only in most minimal fashion. The data did not suggest that the forms of worship service, the content of belief or doctrine, or the form of ecclesiastical structure contributed significantly to the communication of cognitive structures, although at one level of understanding Protestants exhibited greater substantive appropriations than did Catholics. Further, the data indicated that the type of worship service had little effect on the motivations cited for church attendance.

Exceptions to these generalizations were found among some groups in which social interaction, belief structures, and participation patterns functioned to maintain strong group cohesiveness. Even among these groups, however, the level of theological penetration was low.

With the exception of these groups, friendship patterns tended to cut across religious lines. These data and the data dealing with attitudes toward other religious institutions strongly

---

6. In our analysis, nuclear church members were defined as persons who attend church 41 times per year and over. Modal church members attend church 12-40 times a year. Marginal church members attend 1-11 times a year, while dormant church members do not attend. About 20 per cent of the adult population fell into each of the other three categories considered, i.e., modal, marginal, and dormant.

suggested that religion emerged rather infrequently as a point of discussion in friendship circles.

The large proportion of the findings were negative when the other variables were correlated with sex. The data did indicate higher participation patterns for females and possibly somewhat richer religious feelings, as far as our questions could probe this area. There was no evidence, however, to suggest significantly higher cognitive appropriation by females.

The data indicated two antithetical factors in Catholic-Protestant relations. On the one hand, there was a relatively high proportion of Protestant-Catholic friendships in all the areas studied. On the other hand, there was clear-cut feeling of differences between Protestant and Catholic churches. In general, the people of Corn County had almost no information about religious institutions other than their own. Such ignorance could fan the fires of bigotry if religion were taken more seriously than it apparently is in the present epoch.

The findings revealed that only an extremely small segment of the population of Corn County had appropriated any *logos* dimensions of faith. Over 99 per cent of the sample possessed no coherent informing structures from which they might interpret political, social, and economic issues. Less than 10 people in the sample employed in this study attempted to relate the Christian faith to political and economic life.

The data suggested that although there was a consensus about some facets of the ministerial role, people also entertained mutually exclusive notions about some of the qualities and attributes which the minister was expected to possess. The professional qualities of scholarship and theological understanding were held in minimal regard by the general population. Congeniality and a good personality were the prime requisites cited by the respondents in this study. The authors do not interpret this finding to mean that the formal requirements were completely ignored by laymen, but it is clear that they occupied a secondary position. The data suggested that Roman Catholic priests, representing the tradition with the most clearly institutionalized ministerial role, were not as frequently evaluated by the personal qualities of congeniality and a good personality as were his Protestant colleagues. Even among Roman Catholics, how-

ever, relatively high proportions of respondents cited these qualities. Lay expectations of the ministerial role clearly suggest that
a basic integrative and adjustive role was expected of professional
religious leadership. An expectation that it be critical, rational,
and innovating was conspicuous only by its absence.

Even though the findings dealing with cognitive structures
indicated that the degree of communication at this level was
minimal for all denominations, it was hypothesized that the
internalization of the motifs of the various traditions might result
in differing psychological characteristics for persons in different
traditions. Almost all of the findings were negative. The most
significant positive finding in this area indicated that Lutherans
had a higher proportion of church members possessing rigid
systems of inner control. Such a finding, however, did not support
the hypothesized influence that the Lutheran theological tradition ought to foster. No other significant findings between church
membership and salient personality characteristics emerged.

The data did reveal much higher correlations between theological understanding and participation patterns and the variables
of intellectual ability and of social status. Clearly, intellectual
ability and social status were far more influential in affecting
participation and associational patterns, cognitive structures, and
psychological characteristics than the variable of church membership or the variable of sex.[7]

The distribution of persons of high intellectual ability by
church membership and by residential area poses serious institutional difficulties for the churches. There was some tendency for
persons of superior intellectual ability to cluster around some

---

7. The consistently negative findings with reference to psychological characteristics and cognitive structures leads us to somewhat different conclusions
about the influence of religion than Gerhard Lenski draws from the Detroit
area study. (See Gerhard Lenski's *The Religious Factor, op. cit.*) It is our
feeling that ethnic factors, related to an entire cultural complex, are dominant factors in explaining variations in response. Because we are informed
by a perspective that is partially interactional (due to the affirmation of
the principle of relativity), we are not inclined to look for determining
variables as do some social scientists in the Pareto tradition. All we can
say is that a cluster of variables seems to be of considerable significance in
conditioning a person's responses. It is not possible to demonstrate con-
clusively which variables are most influential and on what grounds some
may be eliminated. Hence, we have refrained from the use of factor analysis and related statistical manipulations.

of the churches, but in none of them did they constitute more than one-quarter of the total church membership. Similarly, there was no church which did not possess at least a small nucleus of persons of superior intellectual ability. Because the data strongly suggested that it was this group which was able to deal with cognitive structures most adequately, it is to these persons that the churches must turn if there is to be a more widespread appropriation of cognitive structures by Christian laymen and by ministers.

There was no evidence to suggest that any of the churches in Corn County was consciously making an attempt to cultivate these elite groups. The number of persons involved is not large, but because of their actual and potential leadership qualities, this group is significant far out of proportion to the size of its membership. They constitute a potential "creative minority" which could provide strong Christian lay leadership.[8]

We do not intend to suggest that church life should be focused around the interests of this intellectually superior group. Such a practice would be neither practicable nor desirable. However, what is needed, in our judgment, is the deliberate effort to cultivate special interest groups within local churches and some groups that transcend denominational and/or geographical lines. Religious professionals need to be encouraged to direct some effort toward this numerically small but potentially influential group in their churches. Further, they need to be encouraged to utilize persons with special competences in various areas. Denominational and interdenominational specialists should be trained and used to deal with these groups. A variety of approaches for the use and cultivation of elites ought to be encouraged.[9]

---

8. It is outside the scope of our study to consider the problem of the ways in which various types of elite groups are treated in a variety of philosophical and theological traditions. In the Christian heritage elite groups have usually been possessed of "wisdom" or an experiential confrontation of God as will and personality. In either case some affirmation of the ultimate harmony of things is made. The groups may further differ on the relationship between this vision or experience and its actualization in the world. It is these latter efforts which are subject to the kind of analysis common in the social studies in which the focus of attention is on causal efficacy.

9. These comments are not meant to disparage the novel efforts in this

For many of the churches and, in part, for the entire town and country area, the paucity of able leadership—both professional and lay—constitutes an institutional problem of the first magnitude. A case could be made for the thesis that the way in which various levels of quality of ministerial leadership distribute themselves involves a process of cultural and of intellectual selectivity. It is difficult to see how the cultural and intellectual climate in several of the areas studied (explicitly, Serviceville, the open country, and East Town) would sustain superior ministerial leadership for an extended period of time. While the percentage of rural people of superior intellectual ability in this rich farming area was relatively high, they were dispersed over a very wide area. Not only intellectual capacity but also the availability of the requisite resources for its employment are necessary for this potential to be actualized. As we have noted earlier, institutional structures to foster this potential are not extant in Corn County at the present time.

The implications of these findings for communication in churches are suggestive. A perusal of literature directed toward church members indicates the relatively high level of competence which writers usually presuppose. Further, denominational strategies to communicate theological and ethical understanding seem frequently to minimize the limited potential of most of the members of the churches in such areas.

Two related phenomena are involved. On the one hand, the level at which material is focused is too high for much of the church membership. On the other hand, minimal attention has been directed to the small group possessing the potential to appropriate cognitive dimensions of the faith for whom the current programs are not particularly illuminating or helpful. Denominational planning needs to consider both these factors in planning strategy for the churches. While the focus of our study has been the town and country churches, this problem is clearly one which confronts churches in urban areas as well.

Earlier it was stated that very limited attention had been

---

area now being undertaken by some groups. It is argued, however, that the number of groups and of people working in this area is extremely small. The rationale for and the implementation of this type of enterprise needs to be fostered.

directed to the latent Church in this study and that primary
attention had been focused on the manifest Church. The latter
focus of attention derives from no disregard for the former. On
the contrary, it is recognized that the manifest Church owes its
very existence to the latent Church. However, the data suggest
at least two reasons why the very fundamental conceptions of
the Church arĕ absent. First, the ministerial leadership has apparently neither provided nor been urged to provide such comprehension. Second, the basic concept of the Church requires
capacity for somewhat higher levels of abstraction than many
possess, judging by the total responses from the sample interviewed. Occasionally, throughout this analysis it has been inferred that the findings, though attained in a town and country
setting, are probably not different from what would be found in
urban areas. This inference is, of course, subject to question. The
reason for our daring to suggest this similarity is that so great a
measure of cultural solidarity has been achieved in this country
through a multitude of common media. The differences are significantly fewer with each generation—or even decade. This
observation is not intended to minimize regional attitudes such
as might distinguish residents of the deep South from residents
of the Great Plains. But in each instance, where those "typical"
residents have attended common schools, viewed the same TV
programs and used motor vehicles or a motor drawn machine, the
same fundamental forces have been at work. The newcomers
into Corn County represent experiences not greatly differing
from the experiences of less mechanized, urbanized, industrialized
people in other areas. In the span of one—or at the most two—
generations, they came to exhibit the pattern portrayed in the
data. Thus it is our conviction that the results portrayed are not
due primarily to a soil or climate favorable to corn but to influences at least nationwide and perhaps universal in industrialized areas.

It is usually easier to point to a dilemma than to provide a
remedy. Yet the first step in therapy is to diagnose accurately
the situation which prevails. Religious institutions in their very
nature are conservative in both faith and practice. But in the
Hebrew-Christian tradition they are required to be prophetic
too. Those who read history dialectically are apt to see the de-

velopment of the religious life of individuals and of whole
peoples moving in intermittent stages, jerkily, ebbing and flow-
ing. Forward moves result from dissatisfaction with the old order
and the discovery of new goals.

The purpose of the study—as has been said in many different
ways—was to examine some phases of religious belief and practice
in an area which would not present wide variation from the
standards, practices and beliefs extant in much of the rest of
America. A realistic view of the responses from people making
up a "typical" area might clarify the present situation and help
give direction to constructive efforts. Or to quote a famous son
of the Corn Belt, speaking of several major regions of the United
States, "If we but knew where we are, we might the better discern
which way we should go."

APPENDIX

THE UNIVERSITY OF CHICAGO
FEDERATED THEOLOGICAL FACULTY

A Study of the Factors Influencing Religious Life
in Town and Country in a Typical Mid-West Area

INTERVIEW SCHEDULE

1. Church Attendance:

	None	Very Rarely	1	2	3	4
Childhood						
High School						
Early Adulthood						
Early Married						
Middle-age						
Past middle-age						

2. Sunday School Attendance:

	None	Very Rarely	1	2	3	4
Childhood						
High School						
Early Adulthood						
Early Married						
Middle-age						
Past middle-age						

3. When you attend church, what are the main reasons that prompt you to go?

4. When you do not attend church, what are the main reasons for not going?

5. To what church organizations do you belong at the present time?
   (1) Organization   Main reasons for belonging?
   (2) Organization   Main reasons for belonging?
   (3) Organization   Main reasons for belonging?

6. To what organizations in _____ do you belong at the present time?

(1) Organization   Main reasons for belonging?
(2) Organization   Main reasons for belonging?
(3) Organization   Main reasons for belonging?
(4) Organization   Main reasons for belonging?
(5) Organization   Main reasons for belonging?

7. Church membership, method of meeting, and occupation of three closest friends:

Church Membership   Method of Meeting   Occupation
1.
2.
3.

8. What church in _____ is most like your own?
   Why?

9. What things do you like best about your church?
   What things do you like least about your church?

10. What church in _____ is least like your own?
    Why?
    (If Catholic) Which Protestant church is least like your own?

11. Do you think the Bible influences people today as much as it did a generation ago?
    Yes   No   Don't know   Why?

12. What do you think are some of the main differences between the Old and New Testaments?

13. What do you think was the importance of the message of the Old Testament Hebrew Prophets?

14. Are you acquainted with the New Testament parable of the Good Samaritan?
    Yes   No   Don't know
    If yes, what does the story mean to you?

15. What do you think is the importance of Easter?

16. If you were talking with some one of the Jewish faith, what would you say was special or distinctive about Jesus and Christianity?

17. If a child asks you what God is like, what would you say? (Probe for own understanding.)

18. Under what circumstances do you think a person is most religious?

19. Why do you think people pray?

20. If you were a member of a committee looking for a new minister, what would you think were the most important qualities he should have?

21. Have you ever consulted a minister about personal problems that were troubling you?
    Yes   No   Don't know

22. Do you think a minister should conduct himself differently than other people in town?

               Yes   No   Don't know

How?
Why?

23. Do you think your minister should be informed about such present-day problems as politics, race, the schools, U.S. foreign policy?

               Yes   No   Don't know

Why?

24. Do you think churches should work together to bring the influence of religion to bear on government in such matters as public welfare, civil rights, or agricultural policy?

               Yes   No   Don't know

Why?

25. Do you know of any social issues on which your denomination has taken a stand?

               Yes   No   Don't know

If yes, which ones and what is stand?

26. Do you think that unions have been a good thing for the American working man?

               Yes   No   Don't know

27. Do you think that farmers' organizations have been a good thing for the American farmer?

               Yes   No   Don't know

Why?

28. Do you approve of United States participation in the United Nations?

               Yes   No   Don't know

Why?

29. Do you approve of Federal Social Security programs?

               Yes   No   Don't know

Why?

30. Are there any activities or programs in which our government is engaging of which you disapprove?

               Yes   No   Don't know

If yes, which one(s)?
Why?

31. Are there any activities or programs or services in which you would not like to have the federal government engage which are not now being performed?

               Yes   No   Don't know

If yes, which one(s)?
Why?

32. Are you in favor of:
   a) Agricultural Price Supports?
      Yes   No   Don't know   More   Less
   b) Federal development of power (atomic, electric, water)?
      Yes   No   Don't know
   c) Federal aid to education?
      Yes   No   Don't know
   d) Federal Health Insurance?
      Yes   No   Don't know

In addition to these substantive questions, standard questions to obtain the customary background data were employed. Data on age, sex, years of school completed, house type, occupation, marital status, and church membership history were gathered.

INDEX